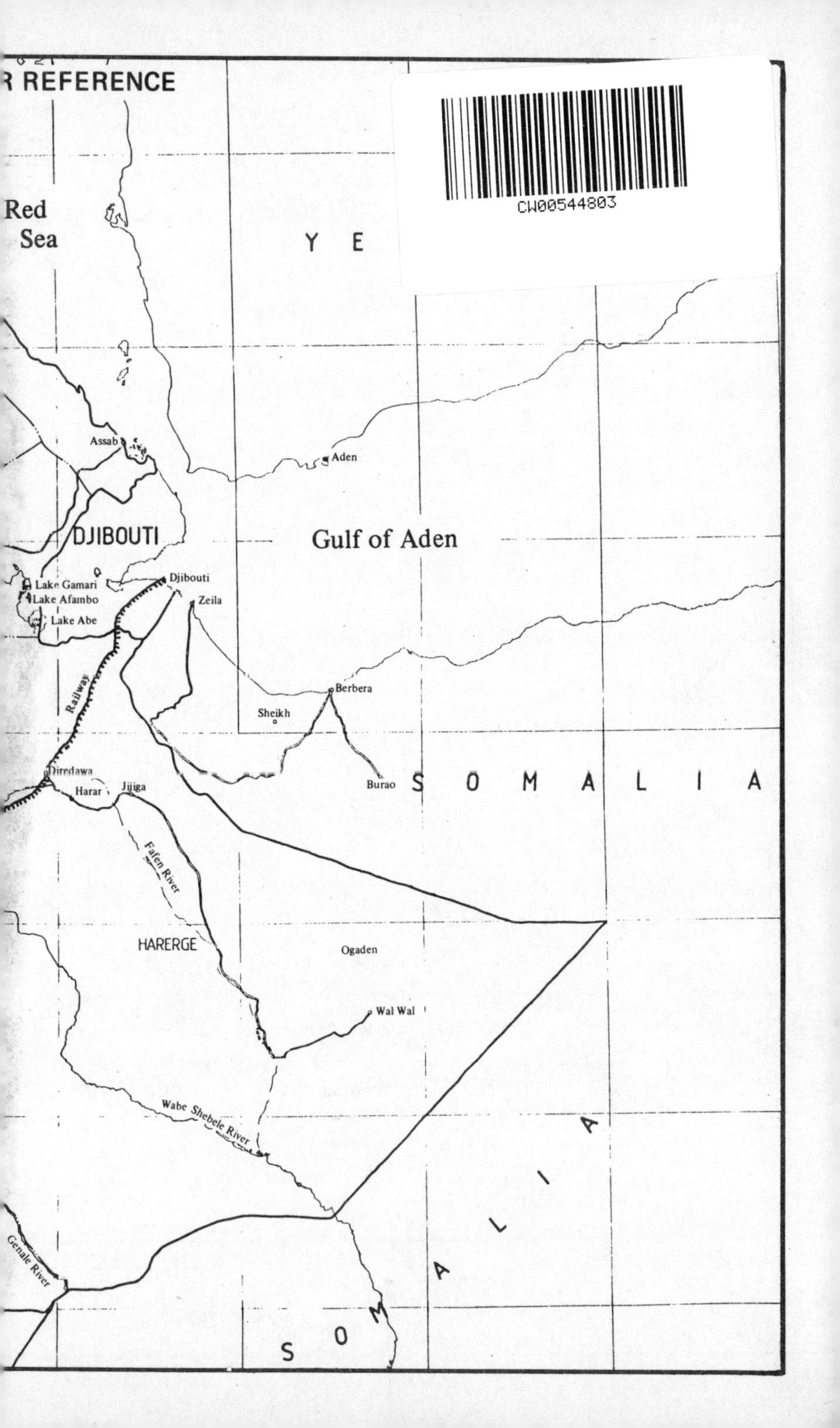
R REFERENCE
Red Sea
Y E
Assab
Aden
DJIBOUTI
Gulf of Aden
Lake Gamari
Lake Afambo
Lake Abe
Djibouti
Zeila
Railway
Berbera
Sheikh
Diredawa
Harar
Jijiga
Burao
S O M A L I A
Fafen River
HARERGE
Ogaden
Wal Wal
Wabe Shebele River
Genale River
S O M A L I A

THE INCURABLE OPTIMISTS

Chris and Dan Sandford of Ethiopia

THE INCURABLE OPTIMISTS

Chris and Dan Sandford of Ethiopia

Eleanor Casbon

UNITED WRITERS
Cornwall

UNITED WRITERS PUBLICATIONS LTD
Ailsa, Castle Gate, Penzance, Cornwall.

British Library Cataloguing in Publication Data

A catalogue record for this book is available from the British Library.

ISBN 1 85200 050 3

Printed in Great Britain by
United Writers Publications Ltd
Cornwall

This book is dedicated to
the people of Ethiopia
and to my family.

ACKNOWLEDGEMENTS

In writing this book, I have used, as my main source of information, the notes and letters collected by my mother, Chris Sandford, when she attempted to have a book written about her husband. Much of the groundwork was covered by James Grant and my uncle, the late Maurice Lush. To them I owe a deep debt of gratitude, as it made my research so much easier. I must also thank my daughter, Fiona Dixon, for her help in the research and later for assistance with the typing and setting out of the manuscript.

My thanks are also due to my family, aunts and uncles, brothers and sisters, who have helped and encouraged me in so many ways. Diana Oldridge has let me read through letters written by her mother, Emma Awdry and by Chris and Dan Sandford. My brother-in-law, Barty Knight, needs my special thanks for his advice and co-operation in correcting and improving the syntax of my book. I also wish to thank Julian Lush, my cousin, for his help in organising and reproducing the photographs for the book. Lastly I would like to thank my friend, Innes Marshall for all her encouragement and advice.

My thanks and acknowledgements are also due to the following authors and publishers for their permission to use quotations and information.

Wilfred Thesiger and Times Newspapers Ltd., for passages from the obituary of Mrs Christine Sandford on 12 May 1975.

Edward Ullendorff and Oxford University Press for the use of the glossary in *The Ethiopians, An Introduction to Country and People*, Third Edition paperback, 1973.

Christine Sandford and George Weidenfeld & Nicholson for quotations from speeches made by Emperor Haile Selassie, from *The Lion of Judah Hath Prevailed*, published by J.M. Dent & Sons Ltd.

Sir Denis Wright for quotations from the address he gave at Dan Sandford's Memorial Service on 5 May 1972.

My thanks and acknowledgements are also due to The Central Office of Information, London, for two photographs from *The Abyssinian Campaigns* 1942, entitled 'Mission 101, Colonel Sandford' and 'No Roads, No Bridges'.

Eleanor Casbon
Exeter 1992

CONTENTS

PREFACE

Why do so many of us think that an attempt should be made to write a book about the lives of these two people? What is it that they were and did that made their lives have such an impact, not only on their family and their nearest friends, but on a very wide circle of acquaintances from literally all over the world? They were man and wife for fifty-four years and they spent forty-six of those years in Ethiopia together. In essence, that answers the question, and when all the other ingredients of time, character, personalities, events and chance are added, the final result shows two lives and two characters, closely twined together and supportive of one another, courageous and ever optimistic, living in a country they both appreciated and loved. One other special ingredient must have its place here on the record; the man for whom both Chris and Dan felt such affection, respect and loyalty was Ras Tafari, Regent, King and finally Emperor of Ethiopia, Haile Selassie the First. His qualities, his character, his vision and his hopes for his country were a spur to the imagination, and for half a century, that mutual understanding and respect stood firm. There must be few people of whom it can be written that an Emperor requested his funeral to be delayed, so that he could return from a state visit abroad to be there at the grave side.

What was it that made Dan as he was? His background was solid Victorian gold, in its best aspects. He came from a large family where moral values were very strictly adhered to, but not in a meaningless way. The love, unity and support within the family were an accepted and welcome code of life and this played a very important part in Dan's future. The traditional choice in careers was there, the church, the army or navy, the colonial service or teaching. To start with, Dan followed the correct code and joined the army, but there came the break. During wartime Dan gave his all to being a good soldier and employing his military skill in the best possible way, but being a soldier in peacetime did not give him the necessary challenge, in either thought or action. He was not content to stay confined to one road through life but was always seeking new experiences and new outlets for his mental and physical energy. He read widely and had a clear vision of world issues over which he had very intense feelings. This, in its turn, made him impatient and intolerant with those he thought were slipshod, time-wasting and underhand. He was intensely loyal to his own country, to Ethiopia, its Emperor and his family, but at heart he was a rebel and a happy adventurer who wanted to try things for himself, not as directed by anyone else. Wealth in terms of money was not important to him, but wealth of experience and affection meant all.

Chris was eleven years younger than Dan and that gap of eleven years was to make her Edwardian rather than Victorian. Her family was smaller and typified a steady English urban life, dominated, in the best sense, by a wise and ambitious mother. Instead of the Public School, followed by the Oxford or Cambridge routine of the Sandfords, Christine Lush went to a reputable girls' day school, and what she made of her future was entirely up to her. This is where the Edwardian era, with the real beginnings of women's liberation came at the right time for a clever, gifted and ambitious young lady. With her brains she got to Cambridge and with her artistry she made music a real joy to herself and others, and with a loosening of the ties of convention, she was able to develop her own strong personality. It is one of the ironic quirks of fate that she, a woman, read classics at Cambridge, and Dan, who might have been expected to have gone to Oxford if he hadn't chosen the army, did a course of Economics at The London School of Economics.

So, when Chris and Dan were united in a love marriage

that was to last for more than half a century, they had the world before them and they made the most of what they had been given. They supported each other whole-heartedly, they recognised and acknowledged each other's special gifts, they met the challenges of living with optimism and laughter, and they trusted God, their family and mankind. Add to all this the faults and frailties of two lively human beings during a fascinating period of world history and it would be odd if the story that unfolded from all these conditions failed to make engrossing reading.

1

DAN SANDFORD'S EARLY LIFE

Dan Sandford was the fourth son of Ernest and Ethel Sandford. He was born on 18 June 1882 at Landkey in North Devon. His father was vicar of the parish and later moved to Exeter to become Archdeacon of Exeter Cathedral and Chaplain to the Bishop Frederick Temple. In a family of seven boys and two girls, life must always have been busy and varied in an atmosphere of constant movement, for both parents were bound up in parochial and diocesan affairs. The Archdeacon was very interested in the educational activities of the church, and during his administration, St. Luke's College for the Training of Teachers was founded in Exeter. Towards the end of his career he became a strict teetotaller. It is said that he had expounded the theory for several years, until one day a parishioner had rebuked him for not practising what he preached.

The family had a good athletic record. The father himself captained Oxford at cricket and later the Gentlemen v. Players at Lords. The brother in the Sudan Political Service was a rugby international, and Dan himself, no mean athlete, became later a hockey player in the army in India.

Dan was an ordinary little boy and, as many lads are, not over-keen on academic skills when physical prowess was so much more exciting. At the age of eleven he was sent to be a boarder at Pencarrick School in Honiton to be taught the desire to learn. After a preliminary escapade as a ghost in the small boys' dormitory, which met its inevitable retribution, he seems to have turned his attention more seriously to his work. He won the essay prize at his school and was finally elected a scholar of St. Paul's. He had the great good fortune to be asked to live in the household of Bishop Frederick Temple, who had been Bishop of Exeter, had then moved to Fulham Palace as Bishop of London and later still became Archbishop of Canterbury. So Dan was able to attend St. Paul's as a day boy from 1889 to 1895, first from Fulham and then from Lambeth Palace. He was treated as a member of the family and kept up his friendship with William Temple who also later became Archbishop. Years spent in the intimacy of the Archbishop's household and home had a profound and lasting effect on the schoolboy. To have been part of the family, except for the most formal occasions, through the years that covered the Diamond Jubilee of Queen Victoria, the First Lambeth Conference and the varying fortunes of the Boer War must have been an unforgettable experience. Certainly it gave Dan the ease of approach and manner of conversation that were to stand him in good stead all his life. He benefited especially from the warm-hearted and fun-loving care of Mrs Temple, and it was with her that he went to see and hear one of the first performances of *The Mikado*; it was also Mrs Temple who delighted the young with the witty nicknames she devised for the bishops of all colours and continents who came to take part in the first Lambeth Conference.

Dan's mother was tireless in writing to him while he was away in London, and one of her letters in particular shows the same anxiety a mother of the present day would feel if her son was living with a family in the public eye. She warned him against unscrupulous people who might try to get him to reveal items of interest about the private lives of the Temples. She said that this would be a breaking of the ties of friendship and trust conferred on him.

Dan's scholarship to St. Paul's was a great satisfaction to the rest of his family and certainly helped with the financial position at home. It was achieved by unremitting hard work and long hours of study, rather than by flights of genius. The High Master of St. Paul's once said to him, "My boy, I quite despair of you." Without any strong inclination for a particular career he was asked to consider entering for a clerkship in the House of Commons. It was then that he wrote home and begged to be allowed to put himself down for the army class. Permission was granted for this, and in 1899 he passed into Woolwich as a cadet in the Royal Garrison Artillery. With the Boer War in progress, Dan volunteered to go to South Africa once he had gained his commission in 1900, but instead he was sent to India to guard prisoners of war. The story goes that Dan lost one prisoner in his charge, but was relieved to find him in quarantine with measles.

Dan spent six years in India with the Royal Garrison Artillery in Bombay and Karachi. It was during this time that his gift for learning languages became apparent. The allowance of £60 from the army for learning a language for the first grade examination was a most satisfactory way for an impecunious young officer to afford travelling on local leave and indulging in some hunting trips. He passed the tests in Urdu and Hindi, and while on leave in England he also managed to do courses in French and Italian. Dan enjoyed his life in India and took full part in all its aspects. Ponies were fairly easily available and he learned to ride and play polo. He took part in some shooting trips, and on local leave he visited the hill stations in Kashmir. He was greatly excited by a tiger hunt and once went to the coast of Baluchistan to shoot ibex. His brief entries in some diaries speak of the sports in which he shared. Hockey was his favourite and he was a fairly consistent scorer. He played tennis, golf and cricket and even took part in a boat race. There were the usual military exercises and the examinations in tactics, strategy and so on. He acquired a bicycle which did not seem to work very well as his diary includes frequent references to taking it to bits.

Dan used to tell the story of the culinary rivalry between garrisons. His was renowned for its coffee. Their arch rivals were due to dine with them. Dan, as mess officer, went to check behind scenes and discovered to his horror that the coffee was being strained through an old sock. Disgusted, he threw it away. The great day came and the meal was superb, but the after dinner coffee was not up to usual standards. "What happened to the coffee?" was the inevitable query next day. "Well, Sahib, you threw away the sock!"

On Easter Monday, 24 April 1905, Dan left Karachi for three months leave up in Kashmir. He and his friend Major planned this, and it was a wonderful trip. They used all sorts of locomotion; trains, tongas, ponies, houseboats, and their own feet. They had two servants with them, and along the way they had coolies and ponies to carry their gear. Dan describes how, after arriving at Rawalpindi, or Islamabad, they had relays of ponies waiting for them every five miles and they accomplished the next fifteen miles at the gallop. Their journey took them from Karachi to Lahore and then north to Sopur and Srinagar. The culmination of the trip was the glaciers of Mt. Kolahoi which is 17,839 feet high. The opposite extremes of so many facets of the trip were a great experience. They crossed dry, dusty and very icy conditions. They encountered torrential rain which caused landslides, blocked roads and made the rivers rise so high that their boat could not pass under a bridge across one of them. Dan describes the busy bustling bazaars of some of the larger cities and also the vast, silent expanse of the glaciers on the mountains. He swam in the rivers and lakes, he fell in while poling the boat along, and he saw birds and flowers that he had never seen before. In the diary that he wrote, two things stand out and make an oddly startling comment on the life of the British in India in the early part of the century. First, right through the three month's leave wherever he was, Dan received letters from his mother and family very regularly. Not only did they reach him but it is obvious that he was not astonished at this military efficiency. The other aspect was that there were very few Sundays when he was unable to attend a service in church at some recognised place of worship.

In 1907 Dan left India for good and was stationed at Aden. The voyage from India took eight days, and his remarks about his first few days in Aden were not very complimentary. Once again he turned his mind to mastering another language, this time Arabic. He often used to say that he owed his pass in this language to the gharry driver who took him from his quarters to the examination centre. During the drive he asked the man several questions and learnt what the correct answers to them would be. On arriving at the examination, he finished the written paper and was ready for the oral section. As he looked out of the window, the examiner saw the gharry driver and called to him to come up and have a conversation with Dan. This gave Dan the heaven-sent opportunity to engage the gharry driver in a repetition of the conversation they had already shared, and the examiner was suitably impressed.

In the more restricted life in Aden, Dan began to ponder over his future and decided that a wider field than the peace-time routine of a military career would better suit him. An opportunity soon presented itself. Dan had snapped an Achilles' tendon while hurdling and was in a hospital tent alongside the ADG to Sir Reginald Wingate, Sirdar in the Sudan, who at that time was paying a visit to the Commander in Chief in Aden. When Sir Reginald came to visit his junior officer, Dan wrapped a towel round himself and stood to attention. As the General left, he stepped forward and asked whether an application for secondment to the Egyptian Army for service in the Sudan would be considered. Twenty years previously, Sir Reginald, then a young officer in Aden, had made the same request to Kitchener, and it had been granted. He promised to regard Dan's application kindly and permission was granted later in the year. Dan's interest in service in the Sudan was not a sudden shot in the dark. His elder brother, Ruscombe, was already working in the Sudan Political Service, and a secondment to the Egyptian Army with work as an administrator in the Sudan would be a very different and more interesting life than garrison work in Aden.

A few months later Dan was due for home leave as was his brother, Ruscombe, and as a result Dan reconnoitred the possibility of travelling to the Sudan and going home with him. Looking at a map, he saw that he could travel towards the Sudan via Ethiopia, and there was a railway from Djibouti part of the way towards the capital city. There was also a British Legation in Ethiopia and he hoped he might find ways and means to do an exciting trek into the Sudan. He went to his CO and asked for permission to do the trip but was refused. Nothing daunted, he applied to the British Resident Officer, this time as a civilian and dressed in suitable civvies.

The fact that his CO and the Governor were one and the same person did not worry him, and he was successful in gaining permission to travel. As Governor, the safety of a civilian in search of adventure was a minor consideration, and at the same time he would be able to give his Commanding Officer some useful information about the country and its geography.

He took a boat from Aden to Djibouti and then went by a short railway trip to Diredawa. The Franco-Ethiopian train was wood-burning, narrow gauge and single-line, and it wound its way through a hundred miles of stony, waterless desert. The guards' van was equipped with weapons to beat off any attack and a phoning equipment that could be run up any of the telegraph poles along the track in case of need. Diredawa was then the end of the line and therefore the place at which one needed to collect and equip a caravan to take the five hundred mile trip further to Addis Ababa. His train consisted of about fifteen mules for riding and carrying tents, food, water and a dozen men, some of whom were muleteers, others were guards, and two or three personal boys to cook and carry his guns and other valuables. There was difficult country to pass through, hot, waterless and unfriendly. They passed through the land of the *Danakils* one of whose tribal customs forbade any young man to marry until he had achieved a 'killing'. In such an area it was very necessary for travellers to remain compactly grouped. During this trek one of Dan's men did stray and was killed. As well as unfriendly locals, there was also danger from lions, leopards and the desert hyenas, who hunt in packs. Dan was expected to shoot for the pot, for him and his men, and there were many species of gazelle and table birds to choose from. After three or four days in the hot plains the track began to wander slowly upwards through the foothills of the plateau, passing the still smoking mass of Fantale volcano, whose base is surrounded by a black, rocky lava flow. Once through the foothills, the land began to change, and instead of nomads, there were people living in small groups of huts, growing coffee, *teff*, and keeping animals. The scrub acacia trees gave way to much larger and shadier acacias, and the terrain was easier to travel over. Water became more easily available from rivers and springs, and food could be bought when it was needed.

Dan finally reached the capital city, Addis Ababa or 'New Flower', and was kindly allowed to make his camp within the British Legation. The city had been founded at the foot of a semi-circle of hills, 10,000 feet high. Two or three foreign legations, those of Britain, France and Russia had already been established. The Emperor Menelik and his wife Taitu were in firm control. The title of *'Neguse negist'* or 'King of Kings' was a fitting one for all the different provinces had their own 'kings' or *'Rases'*. The feudal system prevailed at that time and each *Ras* rendered fealty to the Emperor but expected and received service from their own vassals as did they in turn from those below them. When the *Ras* of a province came into the capital, he would bring some two thousand men with him, not only to parade his own strength but to show the support he could give to his Emperor. Dan would have had to pass through territories belonging to these *Rases*, and it was important to gain permission for passage before going on with the second part of his venture. He stayed in the capital for more than a week and had great kindness shown him by the legation staff. He paid off the caravan taken on in Diredawa and engaged a new set of pack animals and muleteers. The country they now passed through was very different from the lowlands he had just left, being in the main, high plateau interspersed with gorges. He crossed the ridge of the Entoto hills behind the capital and then headed northwards towards the deep gorge of the Muger River. Fifteen years later he was to build the family house of Mulu Farm on a tongue of land that thrust out towards this gorge. He then headed on to Fiche, where the Kassa family were the *Rases* of the province and from there he made his way into the vast canyon of the Blue Nile. Whereas a caravan would normally cover twenty miles in a day, it took three and a half days to complete the descent to the Nile and the ascent out of the gorge. The river itself was full of crocodiles, and the swim across took ten to fifteen minutes before all the animals landed safely on the other side. The cliffs on either side of the river itself were bright red sandstone, along the fissures of which thick vegetation came down to the edge of the Nile. On the other side of the Blue

Nile lay the province of Gojjam, where the people were *Amharas* and not *Oromos* as in Shoa and further south. The area was a stronghold of early Christianity and many circular churches were to be found on the tops of hills, surrounded by their groves of wild olives and sycamores. Dan's notes on the topography of this region were to be put to good use some thirty years later by the War Office. While passing through the area around Mount Belaia, he observed the importance of the place, from a military viewpoint, and it was to be there that the Emperor made his first headquarters in the campaign of 1941. Having passed through Gojjam, Dan's route led him northwest towards the Sudanese border to Roseires. He had to pass down off the plateau and once more into the steamy valley of the Nile. His brother Ruscombe, met him there, and together they headed home for their period of leave. It had been a wonderful and momentous journey, full of interest and enjoyment, but it fixed in Dan's heart a strong attachment to this beautiful country and its people. During his leave in England and a short period in the Staff College at Woolwich, Dan took yet another language examination. This time it was in Amharic, the government language of Ethiopia. He only just passed, but it was an indication of where his interests lay.

Dan returned to Aden in the following year, 1909, and was there until 1910. During this period he took a short hunting trip into Ethiopia, on which he acquired two fine leopard skins in the country beyond Harar. The Governor of Aden also asked Dan to buy him a string of polo ponies while on the trip. He went up, as before, to Diredawa by train, collected a much smaller caravan, and trekked to Harar, the Egyptian built city in the south-east which Menelik's general, Makonnen, had conquered for Ethiopia. It was given him to govern and it was there that his two sons, Yilma and Tafari, grew up. Tafari was later to become Emperor Haile Selassie. From Harar, Dan moved to the wide plains of the Ogaden, watered by the Fanfan River. Hunting one of the leopards, he saw it moving among the bushes and fired. It leapt off and was lost to sight, but he felt pretty certain that he had hit it, so carefully pursuing their way through the bushes for a hundred yards or so, he and his men came upon the leopard but could only see its tail. It had plunged down a hole that was not big enough to go down, and there it was, stuck. Was it alive or not? Signalling to his servants to seize the tail and pull, Dan stood with his loaded rifle ready. At first it seemed to resist, but when they pulled it clear, it was dead. The two fine skins that he acquired were later to be seen hanging over screens in the living-room at Mulu Farm until they disappeared, along with all his other possessions, in a wave of looting that followed the arrival of Italian troops in Addis Ababa in 1935. One of the leopard skins was returned in a very moth-eaten state along with other odds and ends when the family returned to Mulu in 1945.

At the end of 1909 came the fulfilment of Sir Reginald Wingate's promise to give him an administrative job in the Sudan Political Service. He was seconded from the British to the Egyptian Army and in 1910 took up his first post at Gedaref, a town of some importance lying close to the north-west border of Ethiopia. It was the centre of a growing trade, largely in gum arabic, the product of a type of acacia. Dan found the work of his administrative office intensely interesting. His predecessor had been called Postlethwaite, a tongue-twister of which the local people could make nothing better than 'Puzzwuzz'. He became involved in problems of developing trade, liberating slaves who were being settled in that area, and administering justice in cases that involved the buying or stealing of wives or cattle. After eighteen months in Gedaref he was transferred to Nuba country where some of the cave-dwelling tribes were giving trouble. One or two skirmishes at the head of his police force gained him recognition, and he was given the 4th Class Order of the Nile. He set to work to make himself acquainted with these attractive and finally amenable people. Their caves were accessible by a low passage, through which the only method of entry was to bend double. This was an exciting and somewhat hazardous performance if there were as many as thirty hostile tribesmen inside.

Dan's time in the Sudan was of great value and interest to him. It gave him an insight into, and practical experience of, British methods of local administration among peoples of varying cultures and interests. The personal involvement and responsibility of a DC were enormous. Many decisions had to be taken on the spot, but at the same time there were, in the background, the steadying rules and codes of past experience to fall back on when help and advice were needed. The three years he spent in the Sudan Political Service were to stand Dan in good stead when he became an adviser to the Ethiopian Government in later years.

1913 marked another change in Dan's career. The British Legation in Addis Ababa asked for a liaison officer between themselves and the Sudan Political Service, and Dan was selected for the job as he had some knowledge of both countries. The Gezira cotton scheme was being promoted, and negotiations were starting for the building of a huge dam on Lake Tana in Ethiopia, so that the Sudan could benefit from a constant high level of water flowing down the Blue Nile. Accordingly, in January Dan took up residence in Addis Ababa as Honorary Consul and Liaison Officer with the Condominium Administration in the Sudan. It was an interesting moment in Ethiopian History. The ageing Emperor Menelik had a stroke in 1910 which incapacitated him, but his wife, the Empress Taitu, never admitted to this, nor was his death formally announced. She held the reins of government until 1913, by which time everyone was sure that the Emperor had indeed died. A grandson, Lij Yasu, was called to the throne but was never totally accepted. There was a prophecy that he would die on the day that he was crowned, and so he refused to go to the ceremony. Many of the provinces were engaged in petty warfare and tribal vendettas, and government control was enfeebled.

Mr Wilfred Thesiger was the British Minister at this time. He was the father of the explorer of the same name, and the Thesiger family developed the same deep affection for Ethiopia and later for The Emperor Haile Selassie as did Dan and his family. During the next two years, Dan had many opportunities to meet influential Ethiopians as well as the legation staffs from Italy, France, Russia and Germany. Besides the foreign legations there were also a certain number of foreign traders, mainly from Greece, India and Armenia. There were no cars, and all movement, whether diplomatic or social, was conducted on horseback. There were tennis afternoons, polo, shooting trips and race meetings to while away time that could be spared from political negotiations on trade or the waters of the Blue Nile, or intrigue and manoeuvring for position among the Ethiopian provincial rulers. The start of the First World War was to change all this.

As soon as war broke out in August 1914, Dan applied to his immediate military chief, Sir Reginald Wingate, Sirdar of the Egyptian Army and Governor of the Sudan, for release from his secondment to the Egyptian Army, so that he could return to the British Army. At first he was refused permission. However, two months later, because of a shortage of Royal Artillery Officers and on request from the War Office, Dan was released from his secondment and made all speed back to England.

2

CHRISTINE LUSH'S EARLY LIFE

Christine Lush was born on the Isle of Wight on 23 September, 1893. Her earliest recollections were of a large and exciting garden, with a swing under a holm oak, and shrubs so planted that they made ideal places for hide and seek. There was a pink-walled house and a wooden-handled copper kettle. She had an older brother, Cecil, who was to make the navy his career and a younger brother, Maurice, who was in Dan Sandford's battery in the First World War and then spent twenty years of his life in the Sudan Civil Service. During those 20 years he also spent some time in Ethiopia. During the Second World War he played an important role first in the Military Administration of Occupied Enemy Territory, including the Allied Administration of Italy. After the war he was part of the Governmental Committee on Refugees and the International Refugee Organisation.

Christine's family stayed on the Isle of Wight until she was seven years old. She once saw Queen Victoria as she drove through Ryde and heard the church bells ring out for the Diamond Jubilee. When the family left Ryde, they went to Brighton, and Chris went to the Brighton and Hove GPDST school as a day girl. Money was not very plentiful and the pleasures of childhood had to be those where you entertained yourself. Chris's father was a solicitor who never became very successful, and for large parts of her childhood he was away in Canada. The mother of the family taught the three children the love of walking and bicycling on the Sussex Downs which were free and could be very enjoyable.

Chris loved school life; she had a very competitive spirit, a great capacity for hard work and a wide range of interests. She excelled at games and used to play hockey for her school. She swam with her brothers in the sea-water Brill Baths in Brighton, and in the holidays at Twickenham she learned to play tennis, at which game she eventually represented Cambridge. She often used to say that she would have liked to have been a doctor, but there was too much opposition in her childhood to the following of such a career by women. But perhaps her deepest love was for music. She was a very gifted pianist and legend has it that her piano teacher was very averse to her marriage. She promised Chris that she would make her a famous concert pianist if only she would dedicate herself to the piano instead of marrying and having a family. While still at school, she was one of ten aspiring musicians who won the opportunity to play to an audience in the Albert Hall. Alas, her brother, Maurice, developed mumps at the critical moment, and quarantine prevented her from playing. Though only one of her family ever showed the same spark of musical genius, she gave all her children a love of music and a knowledge of the fun and joy that music can give. When out at Mulu Farm in Ethiopia, she had taken on the education of her own children, they marched and skipped, sang, and danced to the tunes of Mozart, Beethoven and Schubert. Later on, when Addis Ababa was to be educated in the enjoyment of Gilbert and Sullivan Comic Operas, it was Chris who played the piano accompaniment and was able to coach the participants in both acting and singing.

Holidays were often spent at the home of her maternal grandmother in Twickenham, together with a beloved aunt, Nell, and while there she became well acquainted with the pleasures, sounds and sights that London could offer. There were frequent visits to the Tower, the Abbey and the Zoo and, above all, the Queens Hall in the great days of Sir Henry Wood. Another holiday adventure was to go to the Lake District with a Brighton family called Smithers. Her elder brother, Cecil, was to marry the daughter, Marjorie, and Chris would be in charge of her younger brother when the three of them were sent by train to Windermere. These events and pleasures provided a perfect counterfoil to their rather restricted and uneventful life at Brighton.

At nineteen, when she gained entry to Girton College, Cambridge, with an organ scholarship to study Classics and Music, she came fully to realise the enormous awakening of mind that a university supplies, in spite of the contemporary prudery and anti-feminine discrimination. Her deep interest in music continued at university, and she often used to play the organ in the chapel at Girton. She used to tell the story of the note on the organ that none was ever allowed to play, because it set up a series of sound waves that shook the whole edifice, threatening to bring the place crashing down in ruins if played often enough and long enough.

Having gained her tripos at Cambridge, her first teaching post was at Church High School in Newcastle-on-Tyne, when the First World War had just started. She was there for the first Zeppelin raid on the city, and in 1916 she went down to Tyneside to see *The Lion* and *The Tiger* come in for repairs after the Battle of Jutland. She found Newcastle a lively and interesting city and made many friends, and it was there that she came to know Dan Sandford. She had met his brother, Dick, and his parents on previous occasions. Dick had joined the navy as a cadet in the same term as her elder brother, Cecil, at Osborne, and on various occasions the parents of both families had met at Cowes to go to an Assault at Arms at the Naval College. Dick had often come and stayed at the Lush's and on one occasion he had been asked for advice on the best way for Chris's younger brother, Maurice, to join the army. Dan, having been consulted, said that a shortened course at Woolwich followed by field training would be best, and Maurice's headmaster had concurred and sent in his name. So it was that, when Dan was training Battery 94 near Newcastle and was asked to choose two junior officers from Woolwich to join him, Maurice Lush was one of the two selected.

There must have been many a merry evening in Newcastle during the early part of 1916 and many friendships formed. Dick Sandford was supervising the building of a new submarine in Blyth. Dan Sandford was training Battery 94 and in his company there was Maurice Lush and Fred Grant, who later became QC in the 1950s. Also among the group was Maurice Platnauer, who later was the Principal of BNC Oxford when Chris and Dan's elder son was an undergraduate there. Ruscombe Sandford came up to visit his two brothers while on sick leave from the Sudan, and at one moment Chris's landlady was driven to admonish her when three young men had called to ask her out. After two years teaching in Newcastle, Chris moved further south and took up the post of classics lecturer at St. Gabriel's Training College at Culham, near Oxford. It was here that she formed another great friendship that was to last for over forty years. This was with Miss K.T. Stephenson who was Principal of St. Gabriel's at the time but who later came to visit her in Ethiopia on several occasions and finally made her home there with the Sandfords. In January 1918 Chris and Dan became engaged and were married in November of the same year. They moved into Box Cottage in Iffley, a house which lived up to its name. One could lean through the door in the dining-room and lift a saucepan from the stove in the kitchen, and the sitting-room scarcely accommodated the piano bought at Broadwoods on Armistice Day. For all that it was a happy house in which to start their life together.

3

DAN IN THE FIRST WORLD WAR: 1914–1918

Once Dan had been granted permission to return to active service in England, he lost no time in leaving Ethiopia. He rode down to Diredawa, and caught the train to Djibouti and reached home by the end of October. Although adventuring into other realms of service during peacetime soldiering, the whole of his training since 1899 impelled him to make use of his skill in gunnery. In December 1914 he was posted as Captain to 10th Siege Battery, Royal Garrison Artillery under the command of Major C.W. Collingwood. This battery was in the process of being formed at Lydd, in Kent, and was the first battery of the new 9.2" howitzers, affectionately called *Mothers*. There was only one of these guns in existence and that was in France. The others were being made in the Woolwich Arsenal. It had accuracy at 10,000 yards, heavy shell power (290 lbs) and mobility. The carriage and bed-plate were all hauled by a tractor and together weighed nearly fourteen tons. When the first guns emerged from the arsenal they were sent to Bristol for them to be taken to France. The first mounting of their howitzer was carried out by 10th Siege on the football ground of Bristol Rovers on a Saturday afternoon while a match was in progress.

One of Dan's subalterns wrote of him thus: 'I remember Dan Sandford joining 10th Siege at Lydd. I was a young subaltern, terribly keen and anxious to be the model officer. I had many things I wanted to know and ask about and I soon found that Dan Sandford was the sort of person one could approach and ask a silly question without being laughed at. He was always helpful and sympathetic and had a dry sense of humour. He himself was a most dedicated and efficient officer and we all said that he would never get married as he was wrapped up in soldiering. He had a Sudanese medal which was unusual to see and had the background of service in the Sudan and Abyssinia. At that time he had the nickname of *Menelik*.'

Finally 10th Siege reached France and were allotted their roles and targets. Dan's section was ordered to support the attack on Neuve Chapelle; this was the first major operation in which 9.2" howitzers took part. The equipment behaved well, largely due to a skilled mechanic from Vickers whose name was J.H. Bottomley but whose suave and impeccable manners earned him the pseudonym of 'our Mr Bumley'. 10th Siege's action in the battle of Neuve Chapelle was an important *first time* in the art of battle planning. It was the first time an artillery barrage was ordered; the first time specific objectives were laid down for the advancing infantry; and the first time the Royal Flying Corps was used for dropping bombs on prearranged targets and for military observation. The British artillery bombardment, before the battle, was extremely accurate, and only delay in the follow-up by the attacking troops allowed the Germans to bring up their reserves. By the end of March shortage of ammunition, among other things, forced the offensive to be called off. After two months of rather dull routine in the South of France, 10th Siege took part in the battle of Loos with a most effective bombardment of Hohenzollern Redoubt, and it was for action during this part of the war that Dan was awarded the order of Chevalier of the French Legion of Honour and the DSO. His service in France was described thus by a fellow officer: 'When we went to France he was just what we expected him to be. A ball of fire, full of energy and efficiency and ready for the many tasks which came our way. We had calls for all sorts of fire which meant an enormous layout of telephone cable, and very uncomfortable reconnaissance to find the best spot whence the target could be seen. Dan was always the one who found the answer, and it was he who went a long way towards showing everyone that the 9.2" was a formidable and accurate weapon. I don't think I have ever met another who matched all his qualities.'

In November 1915 Dan left 10th Siege and returned to England where he was to form his own, new battery. This took place at Tynemouth Castle and he had the good fortune to start with a nucleus of regular NCOs from Tynemouth RGA and a detachment of Durham RGA Territorials. The latter included a number of Durham coal miners who later ensured that the battery had the best dugouts in France. Also from this detachment came Maurice Platnauer, a notable Oxford scholar who provided classical erudition for the officer's mess and taught the members to play good bridge. At the same time Dan was fortunate enough to be given two newly commissioned young officers from *The Shop*, Cassidy and Lush. The latter was the younger brother of Dan's future wife. Christine Lush was then on the staff of Newcastle Church High School, teaching classics. Her elder brother, Cecil, was already a friend of Dan's younger naval brother, Dick, and during the time when the battery was training at Lydd, there was a great Sandford-Lush gathering at The Mermaid Inn in Rye.

While training 94th Siege battery, first at Tynemouth and later at Lydd, Dan used the experience that he had already gained in France. He knew that a regular and accurate supply of information from the front line to the battery, a mile or two to the rear, was as essential as good shooting, so not only were his men trained as gunners and signalmen, but his officers became good observers, map readers, and reporters. He was a good instructor and knew his subject, which was war, not just gunnery and drill. He was adept at delegation and expected every man to know his subject and a good many others as well. Members of his battery became experts at reconnaissance of every kind and learned to be resourceful. Dan was respected both as commander and instructor; he was known to dislike dishonest or shoddy work and was regarded as slightly eccentric in his methods of training. He once ditched, quite deliberately, two large and heavy guns, belonging to some other battery (who complained loudly), in the Sussex mud and then ordered two sections to extricate them by night without any mechanical aid. It rained all night, but the guns were back in the gunpark by dawn.

After four months of training, the battery took its four guns, its caterpillars and thirty lorries and landed in France on 30 May 1916 to take part in the coming offensive on the Somme. Dan's qualities of courage, sympathy, determination and patience with subordinates (perhaps not always with superiors) now came to the fore. He taught his officers and young telephonists the difference between the 'whizz bang' and 'the crump'; between H.E. and shrapnel; he was seen to be fearless but never foolhardy. He was careful of his own life and expected everyone else to be the same but never to the extent of immobility. He taught the young telephonists working from observation posts well forward of the guns to lay and maintain their lines courageously under fire. Colourful or emotional comments such as "By God, we've hit the bloody tower and there's an enormous great cloud of dust" were barred. He insisted instead on tersely matter-of-fact reports, such as, "Direct hit" or "Near miss, short." Throughout the rest of the war, 94th Siege earned the reputation of being the most expert collectors of information about the enemy, his defences and activities, and of communicating this knowledge to the right centres.

When the Battle of the Somme opened, 94th battery joined in the heaviest barrage the world had yet known, firing fifty rounds per gun for the first hour; twenty-two tons of high explosive shell left the battery in that time. The first part of the battle achieved little except to inflict incredible casualties on both sides. During the second stage of the battle Dan moved half his guns to positions very near the front line and ahead of the field artillery guns. While in the forward position Dan and another officer were almost totally buried in mud and debris when four rounds from a neighbouring British battery landed in their trench. The language which finally emerged from the mud-filled mouth of the 'Old Man' transcended even the most hardened telephonist's expectations; "Ask No. 288 battery kindly to increase their range by two hundred yards." It was a great tribute to the young telephonist that his line was intact; it probably saved their lives.

Up to the end of the first year of their service in France, the 94th Siege had been extremely lucky in avoidance of casualties, but in the next stage they fared less well. They were sent to the coast near Nieuport to support a combined operation planned to turn the northern flanks of the Germans away from the sea. The Germans were alert and ready, and on 10 July, one hundred and eighty-two German batteries opened fire on thirteen British batteries and attacked the infantry in Nieuport, capturing the town and stopping any further thought of a combined operation. Every gun of the battery was knocked out at some time or other during the day and casualties were heavy. The battery ammunition dump was set on fire during the evening but this was extinguished by a party of volunteers, who risked their lives to some purpose for two hours. Dan had the greatest delight in recommending one of them (among others) for the Military Medal, for he was the arch defaulter of the battery, always in trouble, often drunk and insubordinate; that was his finest hour. He received his MM and survived the war. During the six months while the battery was near Nieuport, Dan's younger naval brother, Dick, obtained permission to spend some of his leave from his submarine with his gunner brother. The guest's arrival at the battery position was greeted by a very large enemy shell which interrupted introductions to be followed by a second crump which effectively blew in the dugout prepared for the visitor. The battery was to hear more of this young naval officer when news came of the attack on Zeebrugge on St. George's Day in 1918 when Dick rammed his submarine into the structure of the mole and blew it sky high, a feat which won him the VC.

By the end of six months, with nearly two-thirds of the battery listed as casualties, 94th Siege was sent out of line to refit and retrain. In the New Year of 1918 the battery was sent south to the Somme, there to try to stem the German offensive in March. This once more turned the static warfare into a campaign of movement and pushed the battery back some thirty miles in eight days. At dawn on 21 March the battery realised that the German offensive had begun and Dan had his plans ready. The prearranged defence bombardment was carried out, under heavy, harassing fire. The enemy infantry were not far away, somewhere in the mist and pressing forward. At noon Dan received orders to prepare to retire; the big howitzers, hot with firing would take a good hour and a half to dismantle; two hours later the orders came to quit quickly. Each officer and gun crew knew exactly what to do and did it. By sunset the six monster loads with their caterpillars and four lorries apiece were on the road to their reserve positions. Next morning the reserve positions themselves became untenable and the battery was ordered west of the Somme. Dan placed the retirement of the battery in the hands of his Captain and remained with the foremost British troops. The citation for his bar to the DSO which he won on that day reads 'for conspicuous gallantry and devotion to duty, especially on the first day when he succeeded in bringing successfully out of action his widely separated sections of guns – and on the following day when, after sending his battery back, he went forward into a village and stayed there until noon sending back valuable information.' When he was finally reunited with his battery, he found that they had managed to retrieve a complete 9.2" howitzer and had ended the retreat with an additional gun. The battery dug firmly into position west of Villers Bretonneux and stayed there helping to build the last barrier of the defence of Amiens and to stop the German advance.

In August 1918 the Allied offensive began. Dan was given command of a mobile sub-group of heavy artillery ready to take advantage of any breakthrough. He was then put in charge of the heavy artillery brigade during the commander's absence and had the satisfaction of moving his six batteries including 94th Siege across the great Hindenburg Line. The batteries of the brigade were in constant and often hazardous action against the retreating enemy until 4 November, when his battery fired its last round of the war and moved no further forward. The last record of his activities in World War I read 'The Major, who later in the day went out with British patrols chasing the enemy into the forest, received a machine-gun bullet through the strap of his respirator just as night fell; reflecting that the joys of peace were close at hand, he withdrew.' Dan was later made Brevet Lieutenant Colonel for his conduct during the latter stages of the war; he was also three times mentioned in dispatches.

Having heard the news of the Armistice with his battery

and having not taken leave for over a year, Dan quickly asked for permission to take some of the leave due to him. This was granted and he hurried off, early next morning to Boulogne, arriving at the quayside just as the gangway to the ship had been hauled up. When he shouted across asking the seaman to stop and let him on board, they asked, "What's the hurry? What are you going home for?" When his answer came, "To get married," the gangway was let down again and he was on his way home. At 10 pm on the night of 10 November he arrived at Cross Deep in Twickenham, where his fiancée, Christine Lush, was living. They were married on 14 November.

4

MARRIAGE AND LIFE IN THE EARLY DAYS

When the Armistice sirens were sounding on 11 November, Chris and Dan were up in London, outside St. Paul's Cathedral. A lucky chance brought them in view of the headmaster of the Choir School, who was a relative and friend. Although the Cathedral was full, he let them in and they sat in two empty seats in the choir stall for a wonderful service that they never forgot. From there they went to Broadwoods to order a piano and to Buzzards to order the wedding cake; later they joined the cheering crowds outside Buckingham Palace to celebrate the peace. They were married on 14 November at St. Mary's Parish Church at Twickenham. Dan's leave was extended from a fortnight to a month but their happiness was greatly marred by the death of Dan's VC brother, Dick, on 23 November. He had been hospitalised on shore for what was thought to be Spanish flu but turned out to be typhoid. His friendship with Chris's elder brother, Cecil, had been the first link between the families. Chris and Dan found a cottage in Iffley, near where Chris was teaching, and after the month was over, Dan returned to his battery in Cologne to keep the watch on The Rhine. Three months later he returned to England to take a short course at The London School of Economics in business studies, and also to sit for a first class interpretership examination in Arabic. With weekdays in London and weekends at Iffley, a long and happy summer was passed. After the course was ended Dan returned to regimental duties at Shoreham and the couple moved into a furnished house in Brighton.

As before, when Dan was in Aden, he felt the need to change from peacetime soldiering to something more demanding and stimulating. At the end of 1919 a stroke of luck intervened and gave him the chance to return to Ethiopia. The Abyssinian Corporation was a business company with plans to explore the unknown possibilities of trade in Ethiopia. One of the directors of the company was Lord Lugard of Nigerian fame, and he had been asked to go to Ethiopia to look into some difficulties that had been experienced by the company. He needed a secretary, preferably one with experience of the country and Dan was released from the army to go with him. They left England on 14 January, shortly after the birth of Dan's first child, a daughter. In the six months that followed, Lord Lugard found out that the company had spread its wings too far and too fast and that considerable curtailment was necessary. In the event, he suggested to his board that Dan should stay in Ethiopia as manager, with firm instructions to withdraw from such large projects as the mining rights in Harar province or coffee plantations in Goré, and to cut down on any unnecessary expenditure. His appointment was not wholly approved of by the board, and so right from the start Dan was working in strained circumstances in this, his first business venture. He returned briefly to England to arrange for Chris and the baby to come out to join him in October, accompanied by a Scots secretary and an Irish nurse.

Their first house in Addis Ababa was the disused Russian Legation, abandoned by the Tsarist regime and not yet adopted by the Bolsheviks. The previous manager of the Abyssinian Corporation had leased the compound and had furnished the residence at great expense. When Chris arrived, there were no fewer than twenty servants awaiting her. One of the first tasks of the new manager was to reduce expenses, in both house and office by at least a half, and to set about seeing what else of the expansive programme could be rigidly curtailed. So in January 1921, when an accountant had been sent from England to control the financial aspects, Dan set out on a journey of more than two months, to visit Goré and scrutinise the firm's interests there. For the first hundred miles of this journey, Chris accompanied him. With them also was Maurice Lush, Chris's younger brother, who had been in Dan's battery, and was now secretary to the British Minister at the legation in Addis Ababa. Dan was away for three months, and when he got back to Addis Ababa he found that the London board had changed its mind and decided to close down the Corporation. They cancelled his appointment as manager and ordered the accountant to wind up the company's affairs. Even before his arrival from Goré, Chris had been asked to vacate the house because the British Legation had offered to lease the building for their new consul. Rather incensed by this high-handed manner of treatment, Dan returned to London to see if he could persuade the board to change its defeatist attitude, but to no avail. Chris and Dan moved into the small consulate at the bottom of the Russian Legation, and in January 1922 their second daughter was born there. While in London, Dan had been advised by his naval brother to retire from the army, rather than wait to be axed, and this he did, deciding to return to Ethiopia and make his own way to a successful livelihood in any reasonable way possible.

During their occupation of the larger house on the Russian Legation compound, the Regent, Tafari Makonnen, had visited the Sandfords. The house had a large hall with a good parquet floor and the Regent had asked to see some dancing, both European and English and later in the evening had suggested that some of his young officers might take a few lessons. What better than to start then and there? At first men only were involved so that they could play their part at functions where foreigners were present. During the next few years Ras Tafari and the Sandfords, Dan in particular, grew in acquaintance and knowledge of each others' ways. There was no official connection, only a growing understanding and mutual friendship. On one occasion Chris was invited up to the Palace, together with Connie Watson the nurse and the children, to unpack a crate of toys from Hamleys in Regent Street and explain their use and manipulation. A very happy afternoon was spent with the toys, soft and squeaky, clockwork and wheeled, and they had just reached the highlight of the railway line, rails, signals, bridges and all, when the Regent passed through. He looked as if he would have liked to stay to help, instead of dealing with affairs of state.

Once Dan had sent in his papers, he and his wife had to reach a decision on how to start a new life in this land that they had both come to love. They felt that it was a mistake to have all their eggs in one basket in this unaccountable country. They believed that good business could be done on a small scale in the export and import trade of hides and skins, coffee and beeswax. With the kind advice and help from older traders, such as Mr Abel and Mr Low, they opened an office in the town under their own name and made a successful start, but at the same time, they realised that the real wealth and strength of the country lay in its agricultural potential, although in this it would take them longer to achieve success. They started to look for a small piece of land near a river but not too far from Addis on which they could base a mill. It was suggested to them that an area about thirty miles north of the capital where Mr Zapphiro, Oriental Secretary at the British Legation, had some land might be suitable. When they rode out to inspect the land suggested, they felt that the plot on the west side of the river Aleltu might be better. On enquiry they found that this land belonged to the Regent, so Dan went to him and asked if he might lease a small piece. The Regent suggested that a larger area would be better, but Dan replied that there was not the capital available for proper development. The Regent offered to assist with an equal contribution, and so Mulu Farm came into being. In November 1922 tents were pitched on a property of eight *gashas* (three hundred and twenty hectares), overlooking some of the finest scenery of the Blue Nile basin, about thirty-five miles from Addis Ababa. The Regent's share of the capital subscribed was invested in the farm buildings and the living house. Chris and Dan's share was to be allocated for tools and machinery, livestock and fruit trees. During the six months needed to build the house, Dan spent his weeks in Addis Ababa, attending to business there, and Chris and the two girls superintended the initial steps on the farm. The Regent rode out in October 1923 to inspect the new house, to take a first look round the farm boundaries and to note what the first harvest was producing. He left Addis Ababa at six in the morning, rode a mule over the range of the Entoto Hills and then galloped over the long plains to see the farm, sleep the night and ride in again the next morning on his Arab horse. With him, but trailing behind, came his army of about eight hundred men.

5

MULU FARM 1923

The rainy season of 1923 saw the completion of the house at Mulu Farm. It was built in the shape of an 'E', without the centre piece. The walls were made of wooden stakes tied together with rope and then plastered on both sides with a mixture of chaff and mud. The door-posts, the main beams, and the roof joists were made of cedar that had been brought by donkey and mule from the Jum-Jum forest on the mountains to the west of Addis Ababa. The roof was thatched with the local *sambaleet* grass, and only three rooms had wooden floors – the sitting-room, the main bedroom and the nursery. The other four rooms had beaten-down mud floors with a smooth coating of dung that could be renewed from time to time. Over them were laid reed mats. In front of the house were two porches, which led onto the lawn that Chris and Dan tried, without much success, to turn into a smooth green sward. The most trying problem with the lawn was the presence of termites under the surface. They would make enormous underground chambers to live in and then swarm in their thousands. They also made a home in the floor of the house and on a peaceful night they could be heard chewing and fluttering their wings. Every now and then the queen would have to be dug out of the lawn and this required a very large, deep hole which would then have to be filled in and new grass set. The kitchen, laundry rooms and store rooms were in a separate building, at the back and behind them were the servants' quarters. Two Indian carpenters were employed from Addis Ababa to oversee the building and to put in the doors and windows, but the rest was all done by local labour.

Chris and Dan camped out during this period across the stream below the house. While Dan looked after the building of the mill on the Aleltu river and the construction of the stables and pig sties, Chris attended to the laying out of the flower garden round the house and to the beginnings of the vegetables and fruit trees in the area below the house. One day, Chris was sitting in her camp chair at a table in her tent during a thunderstorm when the tent-pole was struck by lightning and she received a very bad jolt right down her arm. It took her some time to recover the full use of her shoulder and elbow.

The decision as to where to build Mulu Farm was guided by the question of water, and it was one of the most fortuitous pieces of good fortune ever to fall into Dan's lap that just below the house was a spring that never ceased flowing in all the years they lived there. It was carefully dug out so that there was a pool of about three yards in diameter and a depth of eighteen inches. A stone parapet was put across the front to hold the water in. An opening was put in the parapet with a pipe leading out of it, and from the very beginning the servants were trained never to put any vessel into the spring to draw water, but always to take water from the pipe outlet. As time went on a great mass of pink and white roses were grown round and above the spring, so that it could only be reached from below. The overflow was channelled down into the vegetable garden and was used through the dry season, for irrigation. Clothes washing was done below the spring, on a grassy bank and the water, heated in big square tins, was then poured into large round tin baths. The water did not need to be boiled for drinking as it was totally uncontaminated. By contrast, when Chris and Dan had a house in Addis Ababa, fairly near the British Legation and needing pure water for the young children of the family, a 'boy' used to be sent up to the Legation every day to draw one bucketful from a specially constructed and reputedly uncontaminated well. However, Maurice Lush, Chris's brother, came riding over one day, with the news that, on doing a routine investigation of the well, the very decomposed body of a sheep had been found lying on the bottom. History does not relate if this ever happened at Mulu.

In later years, as the gardens grew larger and more water was needed for irrigation, several more springs in the hill behind the house were tapped and canals were made down the hillside, so that any available water could be used. When needed, a water-diviner would be invited to come out and find where the springs were and the children certainly tried their hands with Y-shaped willow twigs to see if they were blessed with the gift of water-divining. On the top of the hill behind the farmhouse was a wonderful grove of trees, mainly wild olive and a little lower down was a huge wild fig tree that was hollow. These trees were sacred to the local people and must have been planted hundreds of years before. In Biblical terms, they were the same as The Groves of Baal, that Gideon was commanded to cut down. They always had strings of beads and pieces of cloth hung on them and libations of coffee and other remains of sacrifices could be found there from time to time. It was a favourite picnic spot because it had a wonderful view of the farm, and it is quite likely that the local inhabitants thought that the Sandfords were also joining in some form of tree worship when they took their guests up there for lunch or tea. The trees were marvellous to climb and if you were thin enough you could climb up inside the hollow fig tree and get out onto a branch higher up. It was a wonderful place for children to enact Robin Hood and his Merry Men. Another feature of this hill were the large holes occupied by the porcupines, where one could usually find a sprinkling of their quills lying about. They were amongst the creatures that found the vegetables grown below the spring very delectable.

The River Aleltu on which the mill had been built ran all the year round and had steep sides to it along much of its course. In fact, several times over the years animals would fall in and be unable to get out because the banks were undercut by the water. In order to utilise the water to run the mill, Dan had to build a dam on the river above and direct the water through a canal into the mill. This dam was viewed with great interest by the local farmers but also with some dismay because they thought there might not be enough water left for them. However, in 1923 the construction of the dam was started and all went well until the very last gap was ready to be closed. At this point there was a deputation from the dam-builders to request money to buy a black goat to sacrifice to the spirits of the water. Dan refused, saying that he was a good Christian and did not believe in such practices. Twenty-four hours later there was a big storm, the dam collapsed and the locals felt justified. When the dam was rebuilt, it was almost certain that somehow the spirits were placated and the dam-builders had their share of a feast with money obtained from the Sandfords. In later years, dams were built up and down the river, first by the Sandfords in order to irrigate their strawberries at Mulu Farm, then their coffee on the plantation in the Boli Valley, and then by many of the local farmers who benefited from watching how things were done at the farm. The mill project was abandoned in the 1930s, but whether because water was short or for some other reason, history does not relate.

In addition to seeds for the crops both the Regent and Dan bought cattle in order to start a dairy herd. These were chosen from breeds from within Ethiopia itself and were all humped. They did not produce much milk according to European standards, though it was very rich with cream. Cows from the north-west, with their long curving horns, were among the best milkers. Once a dairy herd of some kind was established, butter was sent regularly into Addis Ababa. This meant that separators had to be imported and set up. One of the back rooms behind the house was always busy with the hum of the hand-turned separator. The dairy business benefited the local farmers too, because many of them would bring their milk in to the farm in bottles or tins provided for them and would then be paid for it. Chitties would be issued and as long as funds were available they would be honoured at the end of the month. Just occasionally, when business was bad, they would have to wait a while. The separated cream was churned in wooden barrels, the butter was patted into shape with wooden scored patters and wrapped in butter-paper with the hallmark MULU FARM in blue letters. Sixty of these pats would be loaded into a rectangular plywood box with a sliding lid and carried into Addis Ababa on the head of a willing carrier. It took him ten hours to get in and this included a thousand feet up the side of the Entoto mountains that lay between Addis Ababa and the farm, and travelling thirty-two miles. For the return journey they would carry back the mail, groceries and anything else required from the capital city.

Butter was not the only produce of the farm and these early years were very exciting, because Dan and Chris never stopped experimenting, whether it was with what they grew or business projects they embarked upon, or schemes to improve the lot of the local residents. To many of their friends and relatives they must have appeared rash and improvident, and certainly there were times when money lent to them was not repaid on time, or at all, but material wealth never had any great meaning for them, and they would never exchange the excitement of trying out new ideas for the comfort of physical well-being.

Experiments on the farm were numerous, some paying off and some having to be left to fade out. Pigs were one of the first trials. These were kept on the far side of the stream below the house. Bacon and ham were produced, as well as fresh pork. The market for this product was the foreigners who lived in Addis Ababa because the Orthodox Ethiopian Christian does not eat pork. For a while the enterprise proved fairly successful, but the market was restricted and later on when other people kept pigs nearer to Addis Ababa the project was abandoned. In a letter written home in 1924, it is mentioned that the bacon of that month had gone bad, so it had to be thrown away. The ability to store produce and also to transport it with reasonable speed always created a problem. Live pigs would be carried into Addis Ababa on a pallet, with twelve men sharing the task.

Strawberries were one of the success stories of the farm. Chris and her gardener, Zoldi, were the main experimenters in this area. Some of the first strawberries that were grown were from runners given to the Sandfords by the French Minister's wife. To these were later added Royal Sovereigns, brought from England. The French variety was usually used for making jam, while the English kind looked and tasted best when fresh. One of the favourite desserts for visitors going out to Mulu would be a delicious dish of strawberries mashed with full cream and sugar and looking almost like a mousse. Served with small meringues, it slipped down very easily. The cook gave it the name *jib uccat* and children of the family and guests both used the name with all the innocent assumption of propriety. It was not until many years later than Dan and Chris admitted to knowing that the word meant: *hyena's diarrhoea* . . . If duly irrigated and carefully tended, the strawberries would produce fruit for nine months of the year, and there was always a ready market for them. Like the butter, they had to be carried in forty cardboard punnets to a box, over thirty odd miles. This entailed scrupulously careful picking and packing, all of which had to be learned by the Sandfords themselves and then handed on to their labour force, constantly supervised.

Chris was in charge of the vegetable garden and through the years almost every vegetable that ever existed was tried out. They were never of real marketable value as the local *ghurages*, living close to Addis Ababa, were always able to provide cheaper vegetables but they added to the general picture. During the latter years of the twenties, there was a time when money was really short, and the Sandfords imposed a shopping embargo which meant that about the only grocery they bought in Addis Ababa was tea. Everything else was either produced on the farm or bought in the local markets. Vegetables, fruit, meat and dairy products were all there on the farm and the rest were luxuries that were not needed. At Mulu Farm they tried to grow plums, peaches, apples, figs, pears, quinces and soft fruit. The most successful were a Japanese variety of plum called *Myrabalan* but these only lasted a short season. Once the farm in the valley was acquired, bananas, pineapples and citrus fruit enriched the family diet.

On the more agricultural side of the farm, the crops were equally varied. Wheat, barley, oats, linseed, maize, beans and chick peas were all grown. A plantation of eucalyptus trees was set up for building and for fuel. As ever, on a farm, there were the various pests, scourges and plagues, but they were reasonably intermittent. Locusts were the plague least controllable. On one particular occasion there had been warnings of the possibility of a plague, and sure enough, one morning a dense black cloud appeared far away over the mountains on the other side of the Muger gorge in front of the farm. The wind was taking the swarm westwards and it looked as if it might pass by. However, precautions were set in train. Piles of grass, reeds and weeds were piled up round the strawberry fields, the vegetable garden and the fruit trees. It was impossible to surround all the crops. About midday the swarm started turning south towards the farm and at about four in the afternoon they were there. All smoke fires were lit and every man, woman and child was out with branches to beat the ground and create every conceivable variety of noise. The locusts descended in their millions like a living blanket. People moved up and down, beating the ground with their branches, shouting and whooping, but the locusts would fly a yard or so and then land again. They flew into the people, they crawled over their feet, and clung to their clothes. Where the smoke was thickest they moved on a little further and as night fell all just dropped out of the sky and settled. At sunrise the next morning, the main swarm rose and moved on, but plenty still remained on the ground for another three hours. The Sandford children, taking their ride after breakfast cantered over countless bodies and the crunch of insect under the hooves of the horses was an unforgettable sound. Many of the trees in the plantation of eucalyptus had their top branches broken off by the weight of thousands of locusts, and fruit trees, grassy plots, and crops had been stripped bare. There is little that man can do against such a force.

When considering the amount of time and energy involved in the setting up of the farm, particularly as neither of the Sandfords had been brought up as farmers, it is amazing to think that in the early 1920s, they actually lived in Addis Ababa for more than half the year and lived a totally different sort of life when in the capital. Occasionally Dan would ride out and deal with farm matters for a week or two while Chris and the family stayed in Addis Ababa. At other times this situation was reversed and Dan would come out to the farm for weekends. Certainly, in the early years, he felt that his business prospects in Addis Ababa were financially more rewarding than the farm. After the Abyssinian Corporation ceased trading, he started out to build up an export trade in coffee, beeswax, honey, hides and skins.

While the Regent, Ras Tafari, and Dan had a common interest in their partnership on the farm, there was another way in which they met to share and exchange views. The Regent found it convenient to use Dan as a liaison with outside contacts and as a mouthpiece for English Press utterances. In the thirteen years that followed the formation of their farm partnership, Dan worked at journalism. He wrote articles for *Reuters*, *The Times*, *The Daily Telegraph*, *The Daily Mail* and *The Near East and India*. Many special articles, particularly in the last-named paper, were written at the Regent's request to explain and publicise his own political views. Dan was Special Correspondent to *The Daily Mail* in 1928 when Ras Tafari was crowned King of Abyssinia.

There was another facet to life in which Dan's experience in the Sudan could help him. He became involved in court cases, especially where foreigners had to go to court with Ethiopian opposition. There was a big Indian firm of Mohammedally and Co., who played an important part in financing and encouraging trade, and between them and the Ethiopian Government, there appeared to have existed a reciprocal business agreement. They had helped many important people in business enterprises and maintained a steady import trade of cotton goods for the common people, silks and velvets, skilfully made up and embroidered, for the ceremonial garments of officials and the nobility. They had specialised in the extremely ornate vestments of the church dignitaries and in the brilliant gold and velvet umbrellas with their tasselled fringes that were so striking a part of church ceremonies and festivals. One of their most important clients was Fitaurari Hapte Giorghis who, as Minister of War, was very influential and had an enormous current account with the firm. When the time of reckoning came there was a big discrepancy between what the Minister of War thought he owed the firm and the firm's own account. The case was taken to the mixed courts and the firm brought Indian lawyers over from Bombay. These lawyers found that

Dan Sandford: The First World War
Royal Garrison Artillery.

Dan Sandford on holiday in Kashmir, 1905.

Glaciers on Mount Kolahoi, Kashmir, 1905.

Dan Sandford on the breakwater, Aden, 1907.

Chris Sandford and eldest daughter, Christine, 1919.

Chris Sandford on Moody in the 1920s.

Photograph by Tony Boyajian.
Emperor Haile Selassie I.

The Empress Zauditu on her mule,
with escort.

A wayside station on the Franco-Ethiopian Railway, near Diredawa in the 1920s.

Camping at Mulu Farm while the house was being built, 1922. Chris, Dan and Maurice Lush.

The first thatch for Mulu Farm.

Mulu Farm buildings, with vegetable and fruit gardens below.
Circa 1930.

they were totally disregarded and flouted and gave the case up in despair. Knowing he had served as a magistrate in the Sudan, the Mohammedally firm came to Dan and pleaded for his help. He took up the challenge with vigour, even at the expense of good relations with his own legation. He thought that they were not giving enough support to one of their nationals and fought the case, tooth and nail, finally being instrumental in increasing the amount due to be paid to Mohammedally by two-thirds. He earned their lasting esteem and gratitude, and not only did they pay him a substantial fee for his services and present a glittering gold necklace to his wife, but they let the news of his success spread through the city. This produced a stream of clients anxious to make use of the abilities of the new English lawyer.

One strange case was that of a Jewish client who sued another of his own faith for trying to exclude him from reading the Talmud in the town's synagogue and usurping his functions. On another occasion he was acting on behalf of the family of a murdered man. His body had been found, in a state of good preservation, in a heap of salt that was due to be packed up and sold. Dan was conducting the case against the reputed murderer and was making good progress, he thought, when the case was closed for lunch. Dan had forgotten his brief-case in court, and when he went back to retrieve it, he found, to his astonishment, that the alleged murderer was sitting at the judge's bench in close confabulation with the judge. It is said that Dan gave up the case before it ended. In 1925 a conventional English lawyer called Gardiner, came to Ethiopia to see if he could set up a practice, Dan sold out to him, using the money from the sale to help towards paying for seven months leave in England for himself, Chris and the children. Cases were conducted in French and the story goes that Gardiner, listening to a case in which a French advocate was opposing Dan, said, "You speak very good French. I could understand every word you spoke, but nothing the other chap said."

6

PERSONALITIES AND SOCIAL LIFE IN ADDIS ABABA

If the Sandfords worked hard, they also played hard, and the social life in Addis Ababa in the 1920s was full and exciting. In a foreign community that was not very large everyone knew everyone else, and social affairs were normally conducted strictly according to etiquette. Ladies and gentlemen dropped their visiting cards in the correct way, at the correct time and on the correct people. There were lunch, tea and dinner parties. There were perhaps two cars in the capital in the early days and everyone either rode or went in a carriage when visiting. If you were an Ethiopian dignitary, the higher your rank, the more retainers it was necessary for you to have in your retinue. Foreigners did not ride by themselves; they always had grooms with them. At night, when you went out to dinner in your long evening dress or dinner jacket, you rode sedately along with your syce in front of you, carrying a hurricane lamp. One night Chris and Dan decided to race each other home after a party. Chris urged her horse ahead, reached the steps of the house first and felt she was the winner, but Dan rode up the steps of the house as far as the front door and claimed victory. If you were doing your shopping, you might walk a short distance between shops but you had your retainer behind you. Most of the roads were not paved and there were plenty of potholes to be avoided. Chris was a very good pianist and on one occasion she was requested to come up to the palace and give a concert. This meant bringing her own piano, so during the afternoon of the performance, about twenty coolies carried it up to the palace on their shoulders, ready for the evening performance. In those days the coolies were supposed to come from a particular tribe – the Ghurages. When it was necessary to have some unskilled labour done, one of the Sandford servants would go out into the street and shout, "Ghurage, Ghurage." In a short time there would be as many as ten men at the gate waiting to be employed. When the work was finished, there were occasions when the Ghurages did not think they had been adequately paid and they would sit round the house or at the gate, refusing to go. The only way to ensure their speedy departure was to start whistling for the dogs, real or fantasy, and the call would go out, "Here, Zeus, Boadicea, good dog, come here." This would rapidly clear the compound, and everyone was satisfied with the outcome, except, presumably, the Ghurages.

Other social activities included tennis, polo, races, snipe-shooting and riding out for picnics. On the top of the Entoto mountain range above the British Legation, there was a very popular picnic site which was called *The Portuguese Ruins*. It was the remains of a rock church carved out below ground level and was an exciting place to investigate. Much of the roof had fallen in, but there were still passages and dark nooks and crannies for the children to explore. The level top of the mountain made very good riding country, and it was not too far for the picnic to be carried up the hill. Britain, France, Italy, Germany and Russia all had legations with numerous personnel and there was plenty of rivalry when it came to sports. Chris, having played tennis for Cambridge was an eagerly sought partner on the courts, and Dan was a stout heart on the polo field. He broke several bones during this activity but this did not seem to deter him. The foreign community tended to come and go according to their contracts of work, but there were a few who, like the Sandfords, made Ethiopia their home. Perhaps one of the longest lasting friendships they formed was with Elli and Otto Singer, an Austrian Jewish couple in the export/import trade. Elli was very musical and a good tennis player, so the families shared common interests. She lived in a big compound with a high wall round it, and she kept several *medakwas*, a type of small gazelle, roaming round her garden. She was always superbly dressed in the height of fashion. There was Mr Fred Abel, also Austrian, and also in business. He was a stickler for decorum and correct behaviour and was very upset once when the chair he was sitting on in the Sandford's house tipped over backwards and left him with his legs in the air. It is related that Fred Abel had conversation lessons with Dan and Chris in the early days and had to be delicately told that one didn't say, "Thank you, this is a bloody good tea," at a tea party. During a game of polo Fred Abel's horse went lame and he was about to retire, so Dan said, "Have one of mine." Fred mounted, and the horse lay down. Fred stormed off in a fury because he thought Dan had staged the whole thing to embarrass him. When he died in Addis Ababa in 1981 it appeared that he had written notice of his own death, without, obviously, the date. It read: 'The late Alfred Abel, born 1890 in Vienna, wishes to inform his friends that he has departed for good, without any regrets in Addis Ababa. His future address presently unknown,' leaving his executors to insert the appropriate date, 13 July 1981.

During the twenties there were several Ethiopians who joined the family household and became an integral part of it. There was Tziggie, nanny and confidante. She had an interesting history. Captured as a child, somewhere in the west of Ethiopia, by Arab slave traders, she and several other children had been forced to walk through to the Red Sea coast where they were put on an Arab dhow to be taken east. The dhow was intercepted by a British destroyer and the children were taken to Aden; from there some of the girls were sent to South Africa to be trained as nannies by a missionary society. Ras Tafari heard about the girls and asked for them to be returned to Ethiopia saying that he would guarantee finding jobs for them. So with their training done, they were returned to Ethiopia and were naturally very sought after by the foreign community. Tziggie was beloved by all the children she looked after and was a force to be reckoned with. Her worst punishment was to pinch you on the inner thigh with the knuckles of her fist and second finger, a painful experience.

Another likely lad was Wolde Mariam. He was a groom

in the stables to start with, and very early on in his association with the Sandfords, he saved the elder daughter, Christine, from a very nasty accident, at considerable danger to himself. He was leading the pony on which she was riding in a wicker chair made as a saddle. They were moving along a very narrow footpath between two rough stone walls, when Wolde realised that there was a runaway pony approaching them with insufficient room to gallop past. He turned the pony he was leading round and gave it a slap on its back. He then stood in front of the runaway animal, and forced it to slow down and grabbed its reins, in the meantime sustaining considerable cuts and bruises himself. Much later on, in 1935, it was Wolde who accompanied Dan down to the south-west to Maji and stayed with him until Dan left the country a year later. After the liberation of Ethiopia from the Italians, Wolde once more joined the Sandford family and they found him a fascinating person from quite another point of view. He knew all the ramifications of kinship and marriage of the Imperial family and most of the nobility, and could hold forth for a long time on the whys and wherefores of family feuds and alliances. On rejoining Dan's service in 1941 he would also – but only after drinking too freely – claim that Dan owed him his pay for all the years between 1936 and 1941.

The gardener, Zoldi, was another outstanding figure of the early days. He and Chris together managed the flower, fruit and vegetable gardens. There were three beds of flowers of all varieties just in front of the house, while on either side there were beds of roses. On the west side of the house there was a bed of arum lilies and at the back creepers were encouraged to grow up the trellis of bamboo outside the back verandah. There were passion fruits of various kinds and rambling roses, while along the bank in front of the kitchen was a long stretch of sweet peas. Down below the spring were the vegetable garden and orchard. Dan and Chris together shared in the learning of expertise in the orchard, with constant experiments carried out in pruning and grafting. Through the whole area ran a maze of little channels carrying water to flowers, vegetables and fruit. There was a real art in the damming and releasing of the water at set times so that all the plants got their fair share and Zoldi was the person who masterminded this. Later on, when they rented the lower farm for coffee and citrus fruit, Zoldi was put in charge, and there the irrigation was a much more complicated affair, needing water to be channelled from the top farm as well as from springs below. Zoldi's sense of levels was not infallible. According to Dan, he used to dig short cuts along Dan's carefully contoured alignment and hope that the water would flow down one slope and up the other side. The first foreman on the farm was Jema, a Somali, whom Dan had picked up on a trip to Harar. He was much feared and disliked by the *Galla* work force.

A brief mention of three others. Guadu was the laundry man who washed, dried and ironed the clothes. He was an expert in the use of Reckitts Blue, starch and the old, heavy iron filled with red-hot coals of charcoal. This gentleman, whose foul temper, largely due to rheumatism and manifested in a vitriolic vocabulary concealed a most loyal heart, was a master of his art, and ladies could leave the most delicate of creations from London or Paris to his deft fingers. He waged a ceaseless war of words with Tziggie. In 1924 the menage was joined by a cook, called Hapte Michael or, as Dan christened him, 'Help-to-make-it-boil'. He knew an apparently unlimited number of dishes to be made from eggs and this was useful, because in the 1920s the price of eggs was 100 to the dollar. In later life Hapte Michael took to drink, which would make for some awkward moments if there was a sedate dinner party in progress, because he might easily invade the dining-room and proclaim his problems to all. The last friend to be remembered here was Haile. Later a general factotum he started life as a kitchen boy. His first moment of fame was when he was discovered sitting on a stool in front of the kitchen stove, preparing toast for the family breakfast. He had both feet up on another stool and between his toes he held the bread to be toasted. Retribution followed very swiftly. As he progressed up the scale of the Sandford staff, he learnt quite a bit of English but this was always personally coloured. He had the greatest difficulty with pronouns. Once, when telling Dan some of the farm news, he was heard to say, "Last night my wife, it borned a baby. Him's a she." On the other side of the language barrier, it was to Haile that

Dan, intending to advise him to wash his ears *(joro)* out, used the word for chickens *(doro)* instead.

In 1923 there was some correspondence between Dan and his cousin Emma Awdry as to the possibilities of her son, Vere, coming out to help on the farm. He was waiting to join the Rhodesian Mounted Police when he was old enough and Dan needed help in the supervision of the farm, although he realised that he could not offer much in the way of financial inducement. The contract was for a year and renewable for two if it suited both parties. Vere would get board and lodging and ponies to ride and a salary of $50 a month which was the equivalent of £5. A further $50 a month would be put aside to pay towards his passage home. For this Vere would supervise the farm with its dairy, pigs, horses and mules and would gain experience in keeping some of the farm accounts. Dan asked him to do a quick course on the slaughtering of pigs and the produce of bacon. The contract was accepted and Vere came out in early November. He was actually to stay until after the coronation of the Emperor Haile Selassie in 1930 and for his first three years at least, stayed at the farm all the time, while Dan concentrated on his business affairs in Addis Ababa. Vere was immensely popular with the Sandford children. He had a gramophone and a few records and taught them songs such as *No matter how young a prune may be, it's always full of wrinkles*, *Abdul Abulbul Amir* and *My Sweetie Turned Me Down*. He was always a source of admiration because he claimed that he ate twelve fried eggs at each breakfast. At the weekends he would ride into Addis Ababa and join in the social affairs there, but out at the farm he settled down to learn Gallygna, the local language, and organise farm affairs to his and Dan's satisfaction. The Sandford's gave him a horse called Gama in early 1924 and with this horse he won the Duke of Gloucester's cup for jumping during the Emperor's Coronation celebrations. Ras Tafari still took a great interest in the farm and at one moment sent out two hundred head of cattle and several mares. Mules, worth $300 each were bred from these mares, using the Sudanese donkey, Pasha, as sire.

A few months after the birth of their first son, Richard, or Dicko as he was called, their second daughter, Eleanor, caught pneumonia, and the family took a trip to Harar once she had recovered, to spend some time at a lower altitude. Here, the story goes, her diet was bananas and bull's blood, a fact frequently referred to when she lost her temper in future years. This incident made Chris and Dan think seriously about the question of home leave and whether it could be afforded. It also brought up the suggestion that Vere's mother, Emma, should come out for some months and keep him company. In this way Emma could get to know more about the financial prospects of the farm and a decision could be reached as to whether Vere would like to become manager for the farm with some money invested in the project and make this his career. She arrived in February 1925 and stayed for nine months. Chris and Dan took her on the social rounds in Addis Ababa and they called on the ladies of the British, French, Italian and German legations and watched the polo, tennis and races. They went to church at the American Presbyterian Mission on the other side of town and met Dr and Mrs Lambie who were setting up the American Mission Hospital. During the day they went out in the carriage which Emma thought to be very insecure along the rough, rocky roads. At night they rode astride and followed the groom with a hurricane lamp. At some moment during this time, the road across the Entoto range was improved and the carriage could actually go part of the way towards Mulu Farm. Two reliable ponies called Sankey and Moody were trained to pull the carriage, though they were also used as riding ponies. Chris's piano was also carried out to Mulu by twenty-four men. This was a wonderful sight for the local inhabitants who had never seen a piano before, let alone one carried along for so many miles by so many people. It was ironic that this piano, the only insured piece of their property, was the only thing to survive the burning and the looting in Addis Ababa in 1935.

So several changes took place in the early part of 1925. Dan sold his legal practice and the goodwill to an Englishman called Gardiner for quite a substantial sum. This enabled the family to go on leave during the year and was also used to give a boost to the farm and Dan's business prospects. The status of the joint partnership over Mulu Farm altered at this time. The Regent had given the farm to his wife, later Empress Menen, and the Sandfords made a thirty year lease agreement with her for the land. In this way it was hoped that they would benefit from the profits of the farm and could be more independent in choosing how to use the land. At the same time Dan, with Vere to back him up, became interested in looking at land for leasing in the valley below Mulu Farm. This valley lay 2,500 feet lower than Mulu, and with the difference in altitude and temperature, there were good prospects of growing cotton, bananas, citrus fruit and pine-apples. There was also the opportunity to grow coffee, where the valley spread out and became more level. While the family was on leave in England, Vere and his mother, Emma, made several trips down into the Boli Valley and work was started on coffee growing.

While he was in England, Dan made opportunities to make business contacts there, to have personal interviews with the newspaper editors whom he served and to work out plans to extend his trading beyond the Addis Ababa market using the orthodox export route by train to Djibouti and cargo boat to Europe. Having himself a knowledge of trade with the Sudan, he had begun to consider the possible openings for diverting some of the produce of the northern districts of Ethiopia in that direction. With this in mind, he approached the African Trading Company in their London offices and suggested that he should merge his private business into their larger one, being paid by shares in the new venture; he would open a branch for them in Addis Ababa and would be the manager. Then coffee, hides, skins, honey and wax from the north could go on a route to the Sudan. The African Trading Company were interested and agreeable, and it was arranged that Dan should make an exploratory trek into the north, along the suggested trade route, once he had finished his leave and returned to Ethiopia. So it was that Chris and Dan left the three children in England with her mother and returned to Addis Ababa to prepare for the journey. They made ready a caravan with several mule loads of Maria Teresa dollars and salt, which served as the only currency for amounts less than a dollar. They went along the route of Dan's first trip in 1907. They crossed the gorges of the Muger and the Blue Nile and moved on through Gojjam. There Ras Hailu, who was Governor General, expressed interest in, and approval of, the scheme. At Danghaila they met the British Consul, Colonel Robert Cheeseman. Thus began a friendship that was to last many years. Finally they arrived in the Sudan, and there they split up. Dan spent a month maturing his plans, seeking interest and support from the Sudanese side and playing games of polo. Chris went on back to England via Khartoum and Cairo, collected the three children and returned to Addis Ababa by boat. But once Dan had trekked back to Addis Ababa he found to his chagrin, that his plans for expansion were completely upset by the agreement made with Italy by the British Government. This agreement left the whole sphere of influence and trade expansion in the north of Ethiopia for Italy, in return for the right to raise the level of Lake Tana and use the water for irrigation purposes in the Sudan, where a new dam was being constructed. Dan's trip had been in vain and this wrecked his planned trading partnership with the African Trading Company. They closed down, only to open a year later but with another manager, under a new name, and with no shares in the new venture for Dan.

It is interesting to note that there was an immediate reaction from the Regent at this high-handed and insensitive agreement between Britain and Italy. He appealed immediately to the League of Nations, of which Ethiopia had recently become a member. The agreement was cancelled and the two signatories were justly rebuked for their improper and unjustifiable interference in Ethiopian affairs, but this all came too late to help Dan in his business affairs. He continued on his own and was always on the lookout for new ventures, but it must have been about then that the time of *the family embargo* was put in train. The family spent more time at Mulu Farm, the Addis Ababa household was reduced to a minimum, and they lived on the produce of the country only, with fruit and vegetables from the farm. Vere continued to be a very active member of the farm team, and his grand-mother, 'Aunt Margie', invested some money in the project.

7

LIFE ON THE FARM, HOME AND SCHOOL

When the plans to open trade towards the north and through to the Sudan faded away, the ever hopeful Sandfords looked elsewhere to see what other openings there might be. This time they turned eastward. Salt is a commodity that never loses its value and in those early days in Ethiopia, it was not only bought and sold as a vital part of food, but bars of salt, wrapped round with thin pieces of palm leaf, were often used in the countryside as a subsidiary currency. The silver Maria Teresa dollar was the only acceptable coin, and no paper money could be used away from the towns. There were lesser coins than the dollar, but they were not freely available and so bars of salt were very handy as change. Dan decided to buy a salt concession in British Somaliland on the coast of the Gulf of Aden. In May 1928 Chris and Dan took a trip to see the concession and to try to start a trade route in that commodity, not only within Ethiopia, but also spreading towards India. Chris's account of the journey gives a fascinating insight into the intrepid sense of adventure that the two of them shared.

'In May 1928, my husband and I set out to inspect our newly acquired concession for making salt on the Somaliland coast and to sign the documents appertaining to it, at the British Government Headquarters, now up at Sheikh, for the summer months. We took the train to Djibouti, a three day's journey, with night stops at Awash and Diredawa, the first an isolated building on the Awash plain where the wind blew ceaselessly and the same seven o'clock dinner was served continually week by week and year by year. Awash breeds a particularly venomous mosquito and strict precautions are necessary when staying there. After a roll and a cup of coffee at six-thirty the next morning, the train set off for a long and hot ten hours' run, through typical lion country. Many years later I saw a couple running alongside the road. The track went over dry water courses that have water only during the rains when the midday storms come down from the hills above. By four-thirty we were in Diredawa, a thousand feet higher than Awash, with a high ridge of hills to the south, across which the road to Harar winds its way. The pleasant hotel was a few hundred yards from the station and was built around the green and scented courtyard of orange and lemon trees. Black beetles rather marred the luxury of a hot bath after the day's dust and sweat. A much more varied supper was offered than that of the previous evening, the table set out under the orange trees and the evening cool and serene.

'We started at seven the next morning for the four thousand feet descent to the coast, at first through green and shady groves, but later, having passed through the only tunnel on the line, we found ourselves in the arid, rock-strewn wilderness of the Danakil Desert. We stopped for lunch in the shady gloom of the frontier station with its meal of lentils and inevitable pineapple chunks, then on down through the wilderness of the real desert; with an occasional camel train, carrying the wicker tent frames of the nomad *Afar* tribes, threading their way across the landscape. We arrived at four-thirty in Djibouti where a wall of heat confronts you as you step out of the train. The town has little to recommend it, save the blueness of sea and sky, and more practically, the deliciousness of lobster, crayfish and cantaloupe melons. Even the drinking water is too brackish for decent tea or coffee, so you drink endless varieties of mineral water and sweat out again all you drink in.

'We stayed for one evening only, making arrangements for a taxi to take us to Zeila, in British Somaliland, some 40 miles south, along the coast. We stocked up in tea, lemons and some hard boiled eggs for the sea voyage of fifteen to twenty hours, and then boarded our taxi for a run along the sandy track beside the sea, with one or two plunges through the incoming tide as it filled up the creeks. We met with a comfortable reception at the British Consulate in Zeila and arranged our own private dhow to take us that evening, after we had supped, to our destination, Berbera. We did not board her as I had supposed by climbing up from the sands, but were hoisted on consulate chairs and carried some several hundred yards out to the dhow through the shallow water by sturdy Somali coolies. We clambered from the chairs over the side of the dhow where the only person visible was the helmsman. He sat in the stern with his hand on the rudder while the great, single lantern sail swung lazily to and fro. Our beds were spread on the poop in front of him and made ready for us and we lay down watching the stars above us. Our bags were dumped between us, and half way down the boat our Somali boy made a cup of tea to sustain us through the night. Two or three of the crew members were moving around until, with a huge shout from the coolies, we pushed off. We slept and woke, slept and woke until the dawn, and then they set to work to rig up an awning above us before the sun grew hot enough to be unpleasant; then a breeze sprang up from the south east and we realised we were in for a blow; the first strong wind of the monsoon had struck us earlier than we had hoped. My recollection was that of a very somnolent day, lying on our camp beds on a strict diet of cantaloupe melons and tea, while the boat rocked up and down over the bumpy waves and the sail relentlessly flopped this way and that overhead. We seemed to make no headway along the low cliffs to the west of us. The morning and the evening were one day and as we slid into the night we seemed no nearer our destination. However we did reach Berbera, the capital of British Somaliland at 4 pm on the second day, rather jaded and windswept, but greatly relieved to be there.

'We had tidied ourselves up as we entered the harbour and a cup of tea at the Club soon restored us. We went out to see the location of our salt concession, a strip of the sea-shore about a quarter of a mile wide and a mile in length. Here we should have to make the cement wall about eighteen inches wide to contain the incoming tide; then it would be closed at about a depth of twelve to eighteen inches, and evaporate during the day, leaving a carpet of white salt all over it. This would be swept up, sacked and borne away, ready to be refilled and the process repeated.

'We slept the night in Berbera and the next morning went up by car to Sheikh, the summer residence of the Governor. Signatures and seals were attached to the documents and the concession was ours. Alas, it was of little use to us. Ghandi exhorted his own people to make their own salt, himself taking part in the project, and the East Africa India trade in salt was killed and dead by the following year.

'We planned to return overland and hired a truck to take us up to the border at Burao, where the firm of Mohammedally had arranged to send ponies to meet us from Jijiga, over the border in Ethiopia, but when we arrived at sunset there was no sign of them. Mr Walsh, the DC at Burrao, very kindly came to our rescue. He gave us a wonderful supper and at midnight, on ponies lent by our host, we rode off through the night until five in the morning, when we stopped for an early breakfast and a rest. We then rode on through the cool of the early morning until we reached Jijiga at noon. The Mohammedally employees came out to meet us, full of apologies for sending no ponies, but explaining that the general state of famine and shortage of grain had rendered the horses incapable of travelling long distances. "Come and have lunch with us," they said and we went in to a delicious meal of curry and chapattis and made plans for mounts for the following day to go half way to Harar and complete the journey the day after.

'As we came out from their compound we were met by the White Fathers Mission from the opposite side of the road. "We saw you riding in and we never meet white people; we have lunch ready for you," they said. We could not disappoint them and so we were treated to a second lunch, this time of thirteen courses with their home-made liqueur to finish it off. We staggered to our tents which had been pitched just outside their lovely garden and sank onto our camp beds; but after twenty minutes there was a discreet tap on the tent and a face looked in, "I am the lay brother who works in the kitchen," said he. "We do not have tea but I know the English take theirs at four o'clock, so here is a cake I made for you," and a large and beautiful cake, twelve inches in diameter was handed in. Of course we supped with them, but not with quite so many courses, though with many little glasses of different liqueurs brewed in their different monasteries.

'It rained that night and a rifle, leant against the side of the tent, brought in a stream of water onto my bed, with the result that, next morning, I climbed on to my large and very raw-boned stallion with great difficulty, and soon decided that walking was more suited to lumbago than riding. By four in the afternoon we had reached the house of an Arab who offered to put us up and lay on piles of beautiful carpets in the warmth of the tropical night. We discarded our mounts the next day and sent them back to Jijiga; for the last climb up from the Farfar Valley into Harar we paid for a couple of mules from one of the caravans and rode up to the British Consulate. We had tea and bathed, had supper and were lodged for two or three nights by Clifford Plowman and his wife. They then lent us their ponies for the thirty-seven mile journey to Diredawa, where we took the train for Addis Ababa, having been away for the space of three weeks. So ended the excursion to claim our salt concession, but the salt trade faded into nothingness and that strip of coast may still be waiting to be worked.'

Chris never went there again, but Dan visited it years later in the company of General Wavell and then the talk was on military matters. But what a wonderful three weeks it had been and what an experience, particularly for Chris, being the only woman on so many occasions. When recounting the story of the trip, she explained that there were no arrangements for toilets on board the dhow; one simply sat over the side of the boat – not easy, if you are the only woman. She was justly proud of her ability to last the voyage without needing to resort to this indignity.

Thus it was that another business venture faded away and though Dan continued to diversify his activities, there is no doubt that the farm began to be the more rewarding part of his life. He continued to trade in hides and skins, extending his buying areas to Mojjo and Hadama, and the particular goatskins that he traded in all bore his mark 'D.A.S.' up to the time of his death, though he had long since given up the trading.

Once the children began to reach school age, the question of their education became a matter of vital concern to both parents. There was nothing in Addis Ababa for them and as Chris was herself a teacher, she took on the task. The Parents' National Education Union, started by Charlotte Mason in England, was the system to which Chris applied for help. It was an invaluable institution for parents who lived abroad or in isolated conditions and who wished their children to have a British education that would enable them to fit into the school system when they came back to England. Not only did the PNEU give a syllabus and a time-table for parents to use, but they also supplied the books that covered the work and suggested ways of teaching. The PNEU set examination papers and then marked them, so that a parent could judge each child's progress by marks given by a third party. The curriculum was far-reaching, though perhaps a little old-fashioned, and it insured that the children were encouraged to acquire a good general knowledge. Latin and French were taught at an early stage and there were two wonderful subjects called Picture Study and Music Study. In these courses each term a different artist and composer were studied, their lives and six of their most famous pictures or compositions. And so it was that life at Mulu began to take on a time-tabled existence, particularly for Chris. The children would be up and given their breakfast by Nanny Tziggie and they would then go out for their morning ride, to be back in time to start school by nine. Each child was naturally at a different level and had to be kept occupied while another was having the teacher's attention. Each child was taught the piano as well, and because Chris was herself a classical scholar all the children became familiar with the ancient myths and legends of Greece and Rome. It was in the evenings that Dan joined in the teaching process whenever he was there. He would do his share of reading stories before bedtime, starting with the brothers Grimm and Hans Anderson and progressing through

Robin Hood, *Winnie-the-Pooh* and *The Wind in the Willows* to *Treasure Island* and *Robinson Crusoe*. Later on came Scott and Dickens, with Dan's preference for Scott. On many evenings there would be singing games and dancing, starting with *See the Bunny Sleeping* and *Here We Come Gathering Nuts in May* and progressing to Sir Roger de Coverley. Then Sunday evening was hymn time with sometimes a Bible reading and prayers. The hymns were chosen by each of the family in turn, but always ended with hymn five hundred and ninety-five, for *Absent Friends*, and twenty-one, *The Day is Past and Over*. As the children grew older, they learned each collect on a Sunday by heart, and if it happened to be a rainy day, the more competent were allowed to paint the pictures in *Darton's Sunday Book*.

It was some time during the latter part of the 1920s that Miss K.T. Stephenson started to come out as a regular visitor. She had been the Principal of the Training College where Chris lectured in Culham, and to begin with she came out for a few months at a time. She joined in the teaching and took particular interest in mathematics, poetry and drama. She also used to join in the evening story reading time when Dan was not available. She did not suffer fools gladly and could be very sarcastic if an unlucky pupil did not immediately understand all that she was saying. When other visitors occasionally came out to the farm, they were usually asked to help with the teaching and the children played up, as children always do. Padre Austen Matthew, the chaplain of the Anglican Church came out to spend some days at the farm and to give a service to the Sandfords. He agreed to give a Latin lesson to Dick and Eleanor and during the lesson had to show them the difference between *ero*, I shall be, and *erro*, I wander. The two miscreants knew that one of the things that Austen Matthew could not do was to pronounce his 'r's properly and with feigned misunderstanding they got him to say 'ewo' and 'ewwwwwwo' for a long time until he realised that he was being victimised.

Padre Matthew first came to Addis Ababa in 1927 as chaplain and became a very dear friend of the family. The Anglican church was a small building, with a house for the chaplain attached, very near the Imperial Hotel, in the heart of Addis Ababa. Austen had spent some time in Nyasaland, where he had a bout of black water fever he barely managed to survive. He stayed in Addis Ababa and worked there, but once a month he would set out and walk the thirty-two odd miles out to Mulu Farm to give the Sandfords their service and communion. They always sent a mule for him to ride, but he did not often use it. He would walk up and over the 10,000 foot mountain range of Entoto, with his servant riding the mule provided behind him, and arrive at the farm somewhere near sunset. He would be greeted and left to indulge in a large beer or whisky in silence. Before he started his drink, he would always check, on his large pocket watch the time he had taken to complete the walk. After that he would go to his bath and change and was then able to join in the general conversation. He was a distant cousin of K.T. Stephenson and they were very fond of disputing cultural topics. He stayed in Ethiopia until the Italians invaded Addis Ababa in 1936, and he then went to Jerusalem where he helped with many of the Ethiopian refugees until 1942. Then he returned to Addis Ababa and was there until he died in 1969. He was greatly loved and respected by the Ethiopian people. As a scholar of Amharic he helped translate the Bible into that language. The local people would often say that his Amharic was so good that they could not understand what he said. His pronunciation was Anglicised and with no 'r's. This baffled them completely.

Apart from the education of the children, Chris had another great interest that she started. There were no medical facilities whatsoever in the countryside around, neither hospital, nor clinic. So she decided to set up a small clinic in one of the outhouses of the farm to deal with the injuries suffered by the farm labourers and with the children of the villages around. Many of these were fairly routine and simple, but there were times when she dealt with horrifying conditions, including burns. She did not have a large number of complicated medicines, and what she used aimed to ensure simple hygiene. Gastric troubles were dealt with by castor oil or epsom salts. Occasionally the local remedy of the cosso flower was used. Sores and cuts demanded potassium permanganate, iodine or lysol. Colds were treated by crushing eucalyptus leaves, inhaling friar's balsam, or sipping honey and lemon. In 1927 there were fears of a smallpox epidemic and it was then that she tried to get a regular routine of inoculations given to all the local people. Her children were inoculated regularly and she used them as guinea-pigs. Every six months or so, she would start another campaign of inoculations and one of her children would always have to be done first for all to see, whether they needed the jab or not. There were, of course, many diseases that she could not cope with at all. Then she could only hope to get the patients into Addis Ababa before it was too late. Leprosy was fairly common in the countryside and in those days, nothing much could be done about it. There was a good deal of rabies around among the animals, both wild and domestic, but people were on the lookout for it and danger could usually be avoided. There was a story told about a European riding from Gojjam to Addis Ababa and spending one night on the farm. He had been bitten by a rabid dog in Gojjam and had to get to help within the twenty-one days between the bite and last deadline for the course of twenty inoculations. Burns were a frequent hazard as the customary place for a cooking fire was on the floor in the centre of the house, and all too frequently children would fall in.

The clinic started slowly as the confidence of their neighbours had to be gained, but gradually, as mothers found out that they could get something for their children and the workmen on the farm found that their cuts and bruises were quickly dealt with, there came to be a regular stream of patients to be found coming along during the day. Eventually Chris trained a local deacon of the church to take charge and deal with the common treatments. Patients had often been to the local witch doctor first and had not been cured. The witch doctors themselves were quite well-disposed to the clinic. When the Sandfords started growing coffee and citrus fruit on the farm in the lower valley, they found another enemy, malaria, to combat. They gave regular doses of quinine and also built their labourers' huts five hundred feet above the floor of the valley to be out of range of the mosquitoes.

The acquisition of the lower farm was quite an important

step in the family life. Finances were not going to permit home leave of any kind for some time and the 'house' for the farm in the valley was an ideal place for the family's yearly holiday during the rainy season. First there was a two mile ride from Mulu to the edge of the gorge. Then a descent of 1,500 feet by foot along a very narrow, overgrown track for half an hour. There was only one piece of this track for about a hundred yards where it was level, but it was actually the most dangerous bit of all, because it was along the edge of a sheer cliff of two hundred feet high and at no time was the track wider than two feet. This was the only piece of the trail going down where silence was imposed upon the children, so that they gave their full concentration to the task in hand. Interestingly enough, at the end of this piece of track there was an old acacia tree that had been cut about until its trunk was in the shape of an upright backed seat. Whenever the family passed, there on the seat were offerings of flowers or blades of grass put there by the local people, perhaps as a thanks offering for dangers passed. At all events, the family would always add their bunch to the rest, placing it on the fairy tree as it was called. If one was lucky, there were baboons to watch as one went down or even a klipspringer standing on a rock on the horizon. Near the end of this descent occurred a flatter promontory, not more than two hundred yards wide and about a quarter of a mile long.

It was here that the Sandfords built their wet season residence consisting of a thatched rectangular house, with a bedroom on either end and an open common room between. There was no front wall to the middle room, and it had steps leading down onto a grassy patch with trees round it, and in the middle of the patch there used to be a nightly bonfire. Behind the house there was a small hut for a toilet and another for a kitchen. Some of the workers had huts built further back behind the house and water had to be fetched by donkeys from a spring about ten minutes away. One of its greatest assets from the childrens' point of view were *the red rocks* just out of sight behind some bushes and below the grassy patch. These rocks were a curious outcrop of huge red sandstone bubbles that produced a kind of clay. These bubbles were about the size of a small balloon and the hillside gave the impression of thousands of red sandstone coloured balloons, all hardened and tightly packed together. All round this area of about a thousand square yards the bushes grew, dense and impenetrable. On the lip of these rocks was some white clay that could be softened with water and moulded into pots and plates and then left in the sun to harden. Baboons frequently came through the bushes, sat on the edge of the rocks and watched the humans at play. One morning, very early before anyone was up, there was considerable screaming and chattering from the rocks and when the older children leapt out of bed and ran down to see what the commotion was about, they saw a leopard running across the rocks and chasing the baboons. Once the Sandfords lost a pony to a leopard down in the valley. The ponies had been used on the flat ground in the bed of the valley and were being brought up to the summer home in the dusk. The first one was being led but the others were coming along wearily, on their own. The leopard was waiting up in a tree until the last animal, Dick's pony, Dama, came past, and then he sprang onto its back.

To reach the bed of the valley, where the coffee was grown, one had to descend a further five hundred feet from the house, either by a precipitous short cut or a more circuitous path which could be used by ponies and donkeys.

Being at a lower altitude, the valley was much warmer and the daily thunderstorm brought a welcome coolness. From the house there were many places and things to visit. There were the coffee plantations under enormous shade trees, there were bananas, oranges, guavas and even pineapples to eat; there were swimming pools made from enormous rocks making a natural dam on a stream and, if you were prepared for a hot and sticky trek, there was the bottom of the great six hundred feet waterfall to visit. For wildlife there were baboons, colobus monkeys, leopards, jackals, guinea-fowl and many other creatures, and for flora there were wonderful orchids, ferns and delicate red fairy-cup fungi. Every day a carrier or two would come down the hill from the top farm with fresh milk and bread, fruit and vegetables and anything else required. It was an ideal holiday for adults and children alike, and, if for some reason, the climb up to the upper farm seemed rather daunting, then there was always the possibility of going home a longer way and riding a mule up a wider, less dangerous track.

In 1927 the Sandfords bought a truck, a Ford. The government had by then built a road of gravel over the high Entoto range and along the Selulta plains towards Fiche. Mulu Farm was some fifteen miles off this road and the van could also manage to go across a grassy track towards the farm. This made the bringing of produce into Addis Ababa much easier. Even if the van stayed on the gravel road, the carriers had a much shorter distance to carry their boxes and could get there and back in a day. This did not mean that the riding into Addis Ababa was stopped but that there were several options open. With the family spending a longer time at the farm than before, more visitors would come to the farm, rather than wait for the family to come into Addis Ababa. Both Chris and Dan enjoyed the visits of other families, especially if they had children who could come and play with the young at Mulu. There was a missionary family called Russell who had children of a similar age; there were the Plowmans whom Chris and Dan had met in Harar on their trip to British Somaliland; and there were the Hardys, a French family that ran a general store in Addis Ababa. These children came out from time to time with their parents and almost without exception were given a hard time by the Sandford brood. They quite enjoyed their company but the games were already made up with the principal actors knowing their parts. The only thing that visitors could do was to be the enemy and the unsuccessful enemy at that, who perforce were captured and tortured. On one occasion the Plowmans' two daughters were taken to *the point*, a small hillock overlooking the expanse of the Boli Valley, by their hosts. There the eldest was tied up with rope and left on the top of a fairly steep incline, with the threat of falling to her immediate death if she moved, because, as Sheriff of Nottingham she had flatly refused to give in to Robin Hood and His Merry Band. History does not relate how she was rescued, but her being tied up was her own fault for being plucky and not cowardly. The tables were turned on Dick, a few years later, when he was about ten, when Wilfred Thesiger, the explorer and David Haig-Thomas, who was to die in the Second World War, came out to do some research on flora and fauna and showed the children of the family an infallible way of tying up a victim to a pole by twisting his arms and legs round the pole in such a way that he could not break loose.

Dan's business interests in Addis Ababa were going ahead and his trade in hides and skins was doing quite well, but he was no longer involved in as many side issues and was thus able to concentrate on marketing the produce of the farm. This never seemed to hold so much interest for him as did his previous trading ventures. It was probably because the experiments in what to grow and how to improve production proved to be more of a challenge to him than how to sell more butter or strawberries. He tried a shop and he tried having agents selling for him, and though both were moderately successful, there was no great change for the better in their financial affairs. Dan still spent quite a bit of time in Addis Ababa, riding out to Mulu for the weekend or for a few days at a time. On one occasion he had a hair-raising experience. He left Addis Ababa rather late and rode over the range of mountains and on to the plain beyond, changing his horse when he was about half way home and dusk was approaching. He told the groom to stay the night in the house where he had met him. He decided that the horse he had just been riding could canter along beside him and get home unridden. All went well and Dan moved quite fast over the plains, with the loose horse following at its own pace behind him. The sunset and then darkness came, although this was mitigated by a moon and some starlight. About five miles short of Mulu Dan realised that the loose horse had moved close in towards him and seemed to be very nervous. Suddenly it shot past galloping fast into the night and Dan saw two hyenas chasing it in hot pursuit. Dan cantered forward, shouting and yelling, and the hyenas moved off to the side. The horse came in close again for protection. The hyenas tried again three times and each time Dan's shouting prevented their moving in to kill the horse. He was very relieved to come over the brow of the hill and reach the stables with the horse unharmed, but it was interesting that at no time did the hyenas try to attack the horse that was ridden. Hyenas could be a nuisance to the cattle and at night the herd was always kept in a thorn bush *Buret* or *Zereba* with a night guard. In spite of these precautions there were times when the animals were taken from the herd. The sound of a pack of hyenas chasing and bringing down their prey is one of the most eerie and soul-shivering noises ever made.

The experiments on the farm went on. Some succeeded and others had to be discarded. Vere Awdry was still on the farm and was very much part of the family. He managed the workers on both the upper and the lower farm. The pig industry was discarded as keeping the meat from going bad was not easy. Great experiments went into using the river water for irrigation. More than one dam was put up on the Aleltu River and even the small stream below the stable was utilised. One of the largest projects to be started was named the *Corinth Canal* and came right across the promontory which made the farm. The dam for this was made up the river and the final cutting across the highest part of the farm was very deep. Small bridges had to be constructed over it at several places for people and animals to cross. The other big irrigation project was to get water from a stream on the upper farm and take it all the way down the side of the Boli Valley to the coffee and citrus trees below. This was quite a masterpiece and needed constant inspection and repair.

Chris experimented with all types of fruit. She discovered that apples and pears were not worth growing because the atmosphere was too dry. She had considerable success with plums, peaches, guavas, and quinces. The strawberries, however, were the major success and they could only be kept in fruit for nine months of the year with irrigation. Raspberries and gooseberries were only moderately successful, though the cape gooseberry grew like a weed. With the fruit also came jam making and at one moment a small canning machine was purchased with the intention of producing jam that could travel easily. In 1933 or 1934, there was an agricultural exhibition, and Mulu Farm showed its butter, fruit and jam. There was also a suggestion that the canning machine could be used to can *wat* for the army, but nothing came of the idea. The invasion of Ethiopia by the Italians halted experiments like these.

e

8

CHANGES IN ETHIOPIA

At this point a digression must be made from the story of the Sandfords to the history of Ethiopia, because so much that happened to Dan and Chris was directly the result of the rise to power of Ras Tafari, the Regent. In 1913, when the Emperor Menelik died, the heir apparent was his grandson Lij Yasu. He was not a man suited to lead a country into modern times. He was weak, vacillating and morally corrupt. When, in 1916, he announced that he was going to become a Muslim, the Council of Ministers decided to depose him and declared Zauditu, a daughter of Menelik, to be Empress. It was at this moment that Ras Tafari was made Regent and heir to the throne. During the twelve years that followed, the Regent had to move cautiously. Not all the great Rases and warlords were going to agree whole-heartedly to the modernising of Ethiopia or to a change in conservatism and tradition. But Ras Tafari was a man of infinite patience and steadfast perseverance. He knew that eventually the older men would die and time was on his side. He spent much time thinking of the future and planning the course to be taken. A young Ethiopian who was employed at the Regent's palace was once asked by Chris how he liked his new work. "I like it very much and His Highness treats us very kindly, but there is one thing that is a terrible trial," replied the lad. "One of us, of course, has to stay up until His Highness goes to bed, and he never goes to bed until the early morning. He sits alone in his study, just thinking and thinking and thinking."

The Regent realised that education was the first thing that

needed to be encouraged. He founded and equipped the Tafari Makonnen school himself and in his opening speech, he made his desires clear: " . . . Knowledge must be sought and found whereby Ethiopia, an African state which has preserved her independence, may be led towards progress and may obtain political stability and the well-being of her people. Before this task can be undertaken, the tools must be prepared . . . Education is the tool . . . Everyone who loves Ethiopia should concern himself with founding schools." Not only did he found schools himself but he also sent many young Ethiopians abroad and paid for them from his own resources.

In 1924 Ethiopia was admitted into The League of Nations and this had much to do with the Regent's growing reputation. This added yet another problem to be resolved. The League of Nations demanded that firm steps should be taken to abolish slavery and Ras Tafari was very aware that Ethiopia should be seen taking these steps.

In 1926 two of the toughest of the old guard reactionaries died of natural causes, and the Regent began to see his way clear to push for some of the reforms that he had waited for so patiently. But the last of the reactionary party saw that their position was becoming untenable, and in 1928 a last stand conspiracy was formed to depose the Regent.

The story of the failure of this plot shows up the courage and resourcefulness of the young man. He had gone, as usual, to the central palace, where affairs of state were conducted and was in the presence of the Empress, when all the palace gates were shut and troops stationed outside to hold him prisoner. The Empress asked him about rumours that had been started that he was trying to usurp her power and take over complete control. He denied that he was in any way disloyal to her and said that he was only working for the good of Ethiopia. He left the Empress and walked out and down the steps of the great hall. There he ordered that the main gates of the palace be opened. Outside, his own retainers had assembled having been sent, hastily armed with what weapons could be found, by his wife, Waizero Menan. With the crowd still held by the force of his personality, he mounted his mule and rode slowly towards his own house.

Shortly afterwards, when the rebel troops had been disarmed and placed under guard, the Council of State met and after discussion, petitioned the Empress that the Regent should be raised to the status of *Negus*, or King, thus giving him the real power.

Dan, who was the special correspondent to the *Daily Mail* at the time, reported the coronation. He had a private audience with Ras Tafari on the eve of the occasion, and the Regent told him that he wished it to be made known to the British people that he ascended the throne and assumed full powers at the express desire of his people. It was their wish to strengthen the Central Government of Ethiopia by bringing to an end the evils of divided control. The ceremony took place in a silken tent outside the palace. The Empress, wearing a crown, was seated under a scarlet canopy, and Ras Tafari, in a dark blue mantle, was seated on her right. After a short religious ceremony, the Regent was led before the Empress and she handed him a crown and the sword of state. After receiving the homage of the grand dignitaries of the Empire, the King went in his carriage drawn by six horses to the Church of the Trinity for a solemn mass, while the Empress remained behind, surrounded by a few personal attendants and watched the procession from the silence of the silken tent.

During the two years between his coronation as King and his coronation as Emperor, there was only one last attempt to overthrow the King. This conspiracy was led by Ras Gugsa, Governor of Begemder Province and a former husband of the Empress Zauditu. He had been forced to separate from her when she was called to the throne and had great influence in the north of Ethiopia. It was essential that a great battle and loss of life should be avoided if the King's position was to remain stable. The emissaries of the King were sent to Ras Gugsa's friends and allies to persuade them to refrain from fighting and the Ras was excommunicated by the church. Leaflets were dropped from an aeroplane, unknown before in those parts and thought of as *a messenger from the sky*, giving the news and the Church's condemnation of those supporting Ras Gugsa. As a result, the overwhelming force of the King quickly overcame the small personal force of Ras Gugsa's and he was killed on the field of battle. Meanwhile, the Empress, whose health had been failing for some time, became seriously ill and died when news of her husband's death was brought to her. Immediately a proclamation was issued and his accession as King of Kings took place smoothly and quietly. The last part of the proclamation reads:

'The passing of Her Majesty the Empress is grievous for myself and the whole of the empire. Since it is the long-standing custom that when a King, the Shepherd of his people, shall die, a King replaces him, I being on the seat of David to which I was betrothed, will, by God's charity, watch over you. Trader, trade; Farmer, plough; I shall govern you by the law and ordinance that have come, handed down from my fathers.'

This was in April 1930, and on 2 November of the same year King Tafari was crowned Haile Selassie, I, Elect of God, King of the Kings of Ethiopia. It says much for the reputation that the Emperor had gained, both for himself and his beloved country, that so many foreign countries sent important representatives to the ceremony. The Duke of Gloucester represented Britain, The Prince of Savoy, Italy, and Marshall Franchet d'Esperey, France. Three British aircraft flew up from Aden, the coronation coach came from Austria and the Governors of Aden, Somaliland and the Sudan were all there.

The coronation of the Emperor on 2 November 1930 was a great time for rejoicing, not only for the Ethiopians but also for the foreigners living there. With so many foreign representatives arriving for the occasion, living room was at a premium and Chris and Dan did what they could to help the situation. They loaned their two small contiguous houses in Addis Ababa to the government so that the entourages of government representatives could be housed. They also ran a camp for themselves and any other people in need of accommodation. This was on an open space quite close to their two houses and folk were fed and given beds. In the houses, among others were three Italian Air Officers and Percy Philips, the *Daily Telegraph* correspondent. In the camp there were RAF sergeants and consuls' wives and several others. The story goes that one of the people to whom house room was given by the Sandfords was Evelyn Waugh, who had come out as correspondent for some paper. He had expected to be put up at the legation and was slightly put out when he found that all space there was taken up by the Duke of Gloucester and his entourage, other governors and distinguished dignitaries, and all he was given was house room with an English couple in town. However, he was grateful for small mercies, because when he wrote *Black Mischief*, his famous novel based in Ethiopia, many recognisable characters from the British Legation fared badly and the daughter of the Minister was even eaten by a lion, but Chris and Dan were not among the caricatures in the book. At the actual ceremony of the coronation the Sandford's eldest daughter, Christine, was the only foreign child present and this was an exceptional honour to be given to her parents.

There was, of course, much feasting and entertainment at the time and some visitors even managed to get to Mulu Farm. There were also the Races and Jumping Competitions held at *Jan Meda*, in which Vere Awdry and Dan took part. There was great jubilation when Vere won the jumping competition on Gama, for the Duke of Gloucester's cup, presented to him by the Duke himself. The events on Jan Meda were always great occasions for the children of the foreign community and the Ethiopian nobility. At some moment during the proceedings, when the Emperor was present, he would have little bags of gold and silver coins which he would throw out to the crowd of children below the steps, and there would always be a great rush to try to pick up as many as one could.

One other story must be related in regard to the coronation period and the people that were looked after by Chris and Dan. Three RAF aeroplanes had been flown up from Aden for the occasion and when the time came for them to depart, the Sandfords went up to Jan Meda to see them go. The race-course was used as a landing field as well as for equestrian events. As the first plane tried to lift off, it was found out that it was too heavily laden to take off at 8,000 ft. The three planes would have to jettison some of their cargo. On board they had several drums of castor oil and these they decided to leave behind, so they were donated to Chris and

Dan, and carted off in their Ford truck. As the planes left Addis Ababa, they flew over Mulu Farm and dropped a farewell banner. The castor oil eventually found its way out to Mulu and there it was used for a long time in the clinic. In fact Chris discovered that castor oil was an infallible cure for a great number of unrelated illnesses and it was handed out with great zeal to all and sundry.

Once the coronation was over and the Emperor established on the throne, Dan was often to be connected with the changes and plans that were made for the country. He became a writer for several newspapers and it was at this time that the Emperor would use Dan's writing in order to make his ideas and plans known to the world. Perusal of Dan's contributions to *Near East and India* gave a good idea of the trend of ideas in the Emperor's mind and their influence on the history of his country. Within a year the Emperor had granted Ethiopia a written constitution which was a remarkable and voluntary innovation. In granting it, he spoke of the moment having come 'to establish a constitution whereby the whole people may be made to share our labour in accomplishing the heavy task of government, at which former Emperors laboured alone.' Ministries were set up, and foreign advisers were chosen to help them. The Emperor, then and later, after he returned from exile, always followed the policy of choosing advisers from several nationalities and this proved to work very well. His first legal adviser was Swiss; there was a Swede for Foreign Affairs and an Englishman for the Ministry of the Interior; an American was adviser on financial affairs and the police were trained by a Frenchman. It was this use of foreign advisers that was to take Dan to the south-west province of Maji later on in 1935.

9

1930 to 1935

For the Sandfords the period between the Emperor Haile Selassie's coronation and the invasion of Ethiopia by Italy was a time for consolidation. The upper farm at Mulu had settled down and was providing a regular income from strawberries, butter, cream and other fruit when in season. The local population was closely integrated with the farm, providing much of the milk for the dairy, producing the labour needed on the farm and benefiting from the clinic and its activities and from the small school that had started under one of the large sycamore trees on the farm. This was run by a lame deacon called Teffera from a neighbouring church and he was assisted by the Sandfords when certain rudimentary teaching aids were needed. The lower farm was beginning to produce coffee and citrus fruits that could be turned into marmalade, if not sold as they were. Dan still had to be in Addis Ababa fairly frequently to attend to his other business interests. His hides and skins were bringing in a steady income, he was still writing articles for various magazines and papers and had to keep in touch with the marketing side of the farm produce. The buying of the Ford truck made the journey to and from the capital a great deal easier for the transporting of butter and fruit, and in the dry season the truck could reach the farm.

Shortly after 1930, Vere Awdry left Ethiopia as there was not enough money in the farm to give him any sort of permanent career, and he went to Madagascar, where he was to die tragically not long after of black water fever. Dan decided to manage the farm himself but to try to get someone to take over the selling side in town. For Chris, life on the farm was very busy indeed. There were four children in the family, one son and three daughters and their education took up a large part of the day. Besides that, she supervised the flower and fruit gardens and was in charge of the jam making sessions. After ten years, much of the farm activity was supervised by well-tried and devoted foremen, but as has been said before, Chris and Dan never stopped experimenting with everything they did and experiments could not be left to others. In the dairy there was the question of cheese making and whether that would be profitable. Dan found a Swiss gentleman, M. Ossent, who had been doing some work for the government in this field, and negotiations were opened up with him into the possibility of him coming to the farm to do this. When the Sandfords had to leave Ethiopia in 1935, the Ossent family were asked to become managers at the farm and to keep the place open until better times. Jam making was another experimental outlet. When the work was first started the jam was stored in twenty litre paraffin tins and carried into Addis Ababa. Some jam was even sent to Diredawa in the same way.

The four children settled down to a wonderfully happy life on the farm, and with that number they never seriously felt the need for other children's company. The youngest at that time, Audrey, was a happy-go-lucky child with a placid disposition and very much her Daddy's darling. At one picnic, when she was quite young, Dan was tenderly feeding her a hard boiled egg, which he had carefully 'peeled'. He put it to her mouth, waiting for her to bite a piece and instead she sucked it hard and managed to get the whole egg firmly wedged into her mouth where it was too large for her to bite or swallow. There were panic stations and she was held upside down by her ankles until the egg was persuaded to pop out again. At other times the three eldest children would taunt her with not being as expert on horseback as they were. Nothing daunted, she allowed them to tie her on her horse, facing the tail, and would be carted off home by the animal, totally incapable of directing it. Christmas at the farm was always a great excitement, and Dan as Father Christmas had the most imaginative ways of appearing. The tradition was that carols were sung round the tree and then presents were opened. After tea and the Christmas cake there was the game of snap-dragon, in which the children were utterly absorbed in trying to pick up prunes from a burning plate of brandy. This had to be done in semi-darkness, and just as the last prune was disappearing, Father Christmas came. Once there was a great sound of digging from behind the screen and spades full of earth came onto the wooden floor. Father Christmas had just been to Australia and had to come through the earth to get there on time. On another occasion he appeared by cutting a hole through the cotton ceiling and assured the children that his reindeer were sitting on the roof. When it was time for him to disappear, Haile would rush madly down into the vegetable garden blowing a hunting horn and the children would go outside to try to catch a glimpse of the reindeer galloping away, while Dan would go to his bedroom, hide away his costume and join the search for Father Christmas. Very often the screen behind which he appeared had a dual purpose. The children had to fish for the presents as Father Christmas put them on the hook. They were not always what they expected; sometimes an old boot would be dragged up rather than a present from an uncle or aunt in England. Boxing Day, always a picnic for Christine, the oldest daughter's birthday, often included a paper chase on horseback with guests from Addis Ababa.

1932 was an eventful year in the family history. In January Chris and the two older daughters, Christine and Eleanor, set off with Miss Stephenson or K.T. as she was called, on a two months trip to Lake Tana, in the north of Ethiopia. Christine was aged twelve and Eleanor ten and the four women had several servants with them and a caravan of about a dozen mules. There were ponies to ride on as well as sure-footed mules for the rougher parts of the journey. K.T. had a special white pony, called Swank, lent to her by the Sandfords, and for the most part it was very quiet and well-behaved. The only thing that upset it was horseflies, and it must have had a particularly sensitive skin because it would rear and kick out if one was biting its underbelly. On this particular trip it went quite frantic once, with K.T.

on its back, and she had to be rescued and dragged off while it was frenziedly kicking out.

The party set off from Mulu Farm on 15 January 1932 and went first to Debra Libanos, a famous monastery overlooking the steep escarpment of a tributary of the Blue Nile. Audrey, the fourth child had been left with a member of the British Legation, to be looked after, while Dick, the third child was left with his father and Tziggie, the nanny. The plan for Audrey's stay broke down, because she utterly refused to stay with the Taylors and Dan had to keep her with him. The result was that the whole family spent the first night under canvas and then Dan returned to the farm with the two youngest children. Christine, the eldest daughter, kept a diary of the trip and it makes interesting reading, because at no time does it show that she thought such a trek anything but quite normal. She comments on the generosity of the local chiefs, who came to the different camps, bearing milk, eggs, chicken and even, on occasions, a sheep. She mentions the birds and the beasts they saw and the camp-fire at night. A normal day would see an early rise, followed by the packing up of the camp and the setting off of the whole entourage. The four ladies, with a couple of grooms would soon leave the caravan behind, but they would take a lunch break somewhere pleasant and wait for the rest to catch up. Then they would go and find a camping spot with water and, if possible, firewood. There the caravan would catch them up once more. Some time during the afternoon, there would be a couple of hours of lessons for the two girls, and during the evening the adults would have conversation with the local chief.

The crossing of the Blue Nile was an interesting experience. It took a day and a half to get down the escarpment and reach the actual Nile and the riders and the caravan all went over together. There was no bridge and the river was nearly a hundred yards wide. Shots were fired into the water and into the air to frighten the crocodiles and then the animals were pushed on through the water, with the men holding onto their sides. The water came up to the knees of the riders as they sat on their ponies and everyone shouted and yelled until all were safely over. They then sat on the rocks on the opposite bank to have their lunch and watched the crocodiles come up to bask on the sand below them. It was the dry season of the year, otherwise the river could not have been crossed.

The party reached Lake Tana on the 9 February, having, on the way, seen the Chisissat Falls that are south of the lake, where the Blue Nile starts its journey towards the Sudan. These falls are not very high but are spread out like a great arc of black rock, and the water pours over a stretch of three hundred yards. It falls into a deep pool and then the river takes a very sharp bend and the whole mass of water thrusts through a narrow chasm, only a few yards wide. In one place the overhanging rocks are less than two yards apart and history has it that an Emperor gave a horse to a man who leapt across. There was an ancient Portuguese bridge that spanned the gorge a little further down and the party crossed it in order to gain a fully frontal view of the falls, an unforgettable sight. While staying at the lake they used the papyrus reed boats, called *tanquas*, to visit some of the islands and see the hippos and other wildlife abounding in the area. The diary states that the water became quite rough at one point when the two girls and a rower were in a boat by themselves and it must have been quite frightening to be sitting on a pile of reeds inside a boat made only of reeds, with water lapping your feet. The boats are made of papyrus reeds which are laid out in bunches and tied tightly at the prow and stern and then opened out in the middle and laced together with thin rope to make the shape of a boat. Amidships a large bundle of reeds is then placed athwart to help maintain the shape of the boat and also to make a seat for passengers. Water laps in and out of the boat all the time as it is unsealed and one sits just above the water level. The boat is propelled by a long straight bamboo pole which is used in the same way as a modern canoe paddle. Balance is essential to keep the boat trim.

Little of the lake's shoreline skirts shallow water and most of the way round one clambers over sharp lava rocks and can then plunge straight into deep water. There are several rocky islands, some large enough to be inhabited. There are some monasteries built on the islands and no woman is allowed to set foot there. In 1951, Eleanor, the second daughter, returned to the shores of Lake Tana to spend her honeymoon. She and her husband went across the lake in style in a motor-boat run by a cheerful Italian. During the Italian occupation, he had been instrumental in taking some of the giant monolithic stones from Aksum to Italy, only to be forced to return them. Dan, as Adviser to the Ministry of the Interior had tried unsuccessfully to have him deported for this crime. Now the honeymoon couple were treated to champagne and great courtesy by the same gentleman, who told the story against himself with great glee.

Chris and her fellow travellers returned to Addis Ababa by a slightly different route and saw the real source of the Blue Nile, a place called Minch Abbai. At one moment they tried to get in touch with Dan in Addis Ababa by telephone, a most haphazard business with the odds heavily weighted against making a connection. The operator picked up the telephone and never knew whether he was going to speak to someone to the north, south, east or west of him. The ceaseless cry of "Allo Metalia" went on and on until at last someone answered him further down the line.

Two other events happened in that year; the first was that Chris had a serious attack of jaundice and had to be admitted to the American Presbyterian Hospital in Addis Ababa to recover. She stayed in for quite some time under the careful hands of Dr. Lambie and his wife. The only thing she wished to eat was grapes, and alas, Mulu Farm could not produce them. Instead she was given pineapple and Jacob's Cream Crackers, which her children always helped her eat when they came to visit her. The second event was the visit of Maurice, Chris's younger brother, and his new bride Diana. Maurice already knew Ethiopia as he had worked in the British Legation shortly after the war. He was now in the Sudan Civil service. There were times when Chris and Dan left the young couple at the farm in charge of the four children, and they gave the young bride a hard time when she tried to make them clean their teeth more than once a day and when she tried to give the only son a bath. At eight he considered himself quite capable of taking a bath unaided and had no desire to have this young lady interfering with his rights.

Their fourth daughter, Philippa, was born in February 1933 and the older children were delighted to have a baby to look after. Chris and Dan rented the house of one of the Emperor's advisers, a Mr de Halpert, and for the period immediately before and after the birth, two or three of the older children went to stay at the American Presbyterian mission on the outskirts of Addis Ababa. This was one of the few times when the children had stayed in someone else's house without their parents, and they made every effort to behave in an exemplary fasion. Strange American ways, however, coupled with missionary discipline caused them quite a few anxieties. One of these habits was the curious idea of eating sweet things with a meat dish and when some chicken stuffed with prunes was put before the young guests, it took a geat deal of resolution to follow the strict parental orders to finish everything on their plates. The other anxiety was Sunday evening prayer meeting, at which old and young sat round the room in one of the missionary houses and sang hymns, heard Scripture readings and prayed. The first two parts were endurable but when the whole room turned round and knelt, facing their chair backs, and everyone in turn was supposed to utter an extempore prayer out loud, then real panic set it. The Lord's prayer and the Creed were known and even some of the collects had been learnt by heart, but the children had never been required to compose their own prayers. The terrible time of reckoning grew nearer and their bodies tenser. Their relief when prayers stopped two places away and the meeting ended was indescribable.

Shortly after the birth of Philippa, the eldest daughter, Christine, departed for school in England and thus a new financial anxiety arose, that of school fees. The problems of school fees lasted a long time in a family of six with the oldest and the youngest being fifteen years apart, but it must be said that the education the children received from Chris bore wonderful results. The whole family earned a considerable part of their fees by gaining scholarships, and Wycombe Abbey School in particular was most generous in helping parents with uncertain incomes. As well as the generosity of the schools, there was also the wonderful rallying round of family in England. Advice, financial and other aid, love and interest abounded and did much to keep the incurable optimists ever optimistic, even when the clouds seemed very dark. The departure of Christine was a sad moment and marked the beginning of a period of separation that was to last a long time. It was fortunate that both Chris and Dan had such sanguine and trusting characters, because the next ten years were to test their faith in each other and in the ultimate winning through, to the very limit. 1935 was heralded by the birth of their second son and last child, Stephen, and this event was soon followed by the departure of their second child, Eleanor, also to school in England.

So, at this time in their lives, both Chris and Dan endured anxieties and sorrows over family separations and commitments, but by far the greatest source of disappointment and discouragement came from world affairs. During the time leading up to the Italian invasion of Ethiopia, the attitude of The League of Nations and, more especially of their own country Britain, to the aggressive machinations of Italy against a much smaller and to them beloved country, Ethiopia, was something that they both found incredibly hard to bear.

It is as well to take a brief look at the situation between Italy and Ethiopia at this time. In 1928 a treaty of friendship had been signed between the two. This was in the main to enable Ethiopia to have the use of the port of Assab, which was in the coastal strip of Eritrea. Ethiopia had no access of her own to the sea, and with Italy having two colonial frontiers (those of Eritrea and Italian Somaliland), Britain having three (British Somaliland, Sudan and Kenya) and France having one (French Somaliland), it was vital to her to keep ties of friendship with all three powers. There was perpetual jealousy and bickering along all these frontiers, but it became obvious to the Emperor that Italy was deliberately fomenting these incidents and building up a series of complaints. At one time the Italian Consulate in Gondar was attacked and the Ethiopian Government made full reparation. It was then that the Italian Government reaffirmed the Treaty of Friendship. In December 1934 there was a clash between Italian and Ethiopian troops at Wal Wal, which the Emperor protested was well within the Ethiopian border. The Ethiopian Government asked for the matter to be put to arbitration but the Italians refused. The Emperor reported the incident to the League of Nations, believing in all good faith that the matter would be dealt with fairly and justly. There followed nearly a year of vacillating and damaging inaction by the League. Throughout the year Italy sent arms and troops in ever increasing numbers to Eritrea and Somaliland and the Ethiopian Government protested to no effect. The British and French Governments refused to issue any further licences for the export of arms to either Italy or Ethiopia, but Italy was not buying arms from those two countries and so in effect the sanction lay heavily on Ethiopia alone. On 4 September 1935 The League of Nations stated that it stood for the steady and collective resistance to all acts of unprovoked aggression and Sir Samuel Hoare declared that Britain stood firm behind the League. Only six days later he and M. Laval of France privately agreed that no action should be taken of any kind which would involve any risk of war with Italy. In October Italian troops crossed the Ethiopian border and the invasion began.

To Chris and Dan, as to many of the foreign residents in Ethiopia, these pusillanimous efforts of The League and in particular, those of Britain and France, seemed almost incredible. They had begun by sharing the Emperor's conviction that the members of the League of Nations, and among them Britain, would meet their obligations to a member state, obviously threatened by another member so much larger and stronger. They began to realise, however, with sick shame, that nothing was going to be done. In January 1935, just after the birth of his second son, Dan was called to an audience with the Emperor and from that time on he was constantly at the Emperor's bidding. Finally he was asked to undertake a job which would separate him from his family and send him as adviser to the newly appointed young Governor of Maji, with the double task of countering Italian propaganda charges of slave-trading and raiding on the Sudan frontier and the creation of a model province. Unwilling to leave his wife and family alone in Addis Ababa or Mulu, when the clouds of war were so indisputably gathering, he arranged for them to leave for England. He arranged that M. Ossent, the Swiss agriculturalist with whom he already had an agreement over the making of cheese, should take over the management of the farm. He also asked the Rev. Austen Matthew to take over the work of reporting, particularly to the paper *The Near East and India* and to be the point of contact to whom he could write while in Maji. There followed a period in which hope alternated with despair, a time of anxious waiting and crucial decision-making. Chris had to make the journey back to England, with four young children, by rail and by sea, with the ship forced to make a passage along the Red Sea where ever-growing movements of ammunitions and troops were being made by the Italians. Both of them had to leave a home that they had built themselves over twelve years and where their undertakings were just beginning to succeed. They had both of them stood behind the Emperor in the belief that the League of Nations, and especially their own country, Britain, would honour their obligations to another League member. One can imagine their sense of impotence, of degradation and shame, when they realised how their own country was betraying the trust put in it. At a conference of reporters which Dan attended, a young Ethiopian bitterly attacked him as an Englishman whose country was betraying its duty as a member of the League of Nations. The next day, after reading Sir Samuel Hoare's assurances: 'The League stands and my country stands with it for the collective resistance to all acts of unprovoked aggression,' the young Ethiopian publicly apologised for what he had said. But, alas, the previous day Hoare and Laval had made their private agreement that no action was to be taken. When this became known, Dan felt that his degradation in the eyes of the Ethiopians could go no lower and, as Ethiopia declared war against the aggressor nation, Dan left Addis Ababa and proceeded south to Maji to do his best in the assignment that the Emperor had given him.

10

JOURNEY TO MAJI

The information for this chapter comes from a description of his trip by Dan. It is quoted here in detail, because it is one of the few documents in which Dan writes on a whole range of subjects. It is a good indication of his feelings and his tremendous ability to observe what was going on.

On 2 October 1935, The Emperor Haile Selassie proclaimed a general mobilisation of the manhood of Ethiopia to meet the invasion threatened by the Italian forces. Dan writes: '. . . I left Addis Ababa on 9th October to take up a post in Maji, in the extreme south-west of Ethiopia. To reach my destination, I had to march across a good half of the country through those provinces which lie furthest from the coming conflict. I had over three hundred miles to cover and the journey would take me at least five weeks. When I left the capital the Italians had already bombed Adua and Adigrat in the north, most of the Italian population had left Addis Ababa and many European families with children had departed to their own countries, as had my own family. There was no need for me to take a large staff of servants and so it came about that most of our old servants were left behind in positions of trust, pending my return some time in the future. There was Nanny Tziggie, who ruled our children with a rod of iron and had, on occasion, been entrusted with sole charge of them during prolonged absence of their parents. Old Zoldi, the grey-bearded foreman of our small coffee plantation in the Muger Valley, who trots down to his work at dawn and returns in the gloaming often carrying a log up the six hundred feet from the plantation to the workmen's hut, so that the children can enjoy a camp-fire. Tesfaye, the foreman of the labourers' gang on the farm, who started life as a syce but really found himself when his eagle eye and envenomed tongue were put to the service of making others work. The last of the stay-behinds to mention is Guadu the washerman. This old gentleman, whose foul temper and vitriolic vocabulary are the camouflage concealing a most loyal heart is a genius with soap and iron. I left him doing his bit for his country washing and ironing for The Red Cross. The only one of "the old guard" who is going with me is Wolde Mariam, one time children's syce and bodyguard, now my major domo and personal valet combined. He once saved the life of our eldest child. When I told Wolde that I was uprooting and going to Maji for several years and asked him whether he would come with me, his brief comment was, "If Master says come, I come."

'My caravan consisted of fourteen men, seventeen mules and five ponies. I have never yet learned to ride a mule with satisfaction to either man or beast. Our natures do not agree and there is never any desire on either side to become better acquainted. When I was not walking, I rode one of my five ponies; Moody, Gama, Tango, Curragh and Lux. Moody is a veteran traveller and has turned twenty. In his youth the perfect polo player, he is, in his old age, the trusted friend and riding-master of the family. I recall an incident of two years ago. I was taking an evening stroll along the edge of a eucalyptus plantation on the farm. There was a sudden thunder of hooves and three ponies went careering past. First mad-cap twelve-year-old-being carted as usual by her pony, Tango, as wild as herself; then ten-year-old on Curragh, sitting down to his gallop in a business-like way; and last a seven-year-old imp, bare legs, rag of a cotton frock and hair streaming in the wind, yelping ecstatically, perched high on old Moody, sweeping past at a fine pace but just *not* all out – in a word mindful of responsibility and watching his step . . . Allowed? Certainly not . . . But there are times . . . And anyway Moody is safe . . .

'I was driven out of Addis Ababa by car, some forty miles along the Addis Alem road to the west and joined up with my caravan there, to do a half day's journey through the foothills of the Mecha Mountains. Next day we crossed the Belcho Plain, a densely cultivated area that acts as the granary for the capital. It was in the middle of the plain just short of a rickety bridge of logs that spans the Awash River, that I saw the first signs of mobilisation. Amhara soldiers are settled in the plain and many of the Galla inhabitants have enlisted in the Addis Ababa militia which does the policing of the capital. These men normally do a month's service once a year. Added to these are the Gallas who hold their lands upon terms which entail certain forms of military service during wartime. Next night I camped at Busa. There was a colony of the Emperor's father's old soldiers there. One offered me a camping site and brought a present of grain for my beasts. He had been there some forty-five years and said that lions and elephants had abounded in the area.

'Early on 11 October we passed the chief of the district, Fitaurari Felleke, on his way to Addis Ababa with his party of soldiers escorting the Minister of War's war drums – ten mules with two drums apiece, made of rawhide stretched across large wooden bowls. The next day we stopped by a telephone place and there heard that The League of Nations had applied sanctions on Italy, and all the time there came through news requesting greater urgency in the mobilisation of troops. On the 15 October we reached the ferry crossing of the Ghibbe River. It was some fifty yards broad and running deep between mud banks. The ferry station was a scene of feverish activity with the Governor of Kaffa, with a consignment of dollars and an escort of soldiers, on the far side and my caravan waiting to go the other way. There were four dugouts conveying people and baggage to and fro and the animals had to swim. Horses show more individuality when swimming than at any other time. Some swim strongly with heads and necks well out of the water; others quietly and equally without any apparent fuss. Others look as though they would sink at any moment, only a nose and a resigned-to-my-fate eye showing above the surface; while others again crash along in a desperate panic, snorting and plunging, glaring at the far shore with frantic eyeball.

'There was no mistaking Jimma province when we reached it on the morning of 17 October. We were quite suddenly among crops and villages. A brown limbed lad leaning on his spear watching us answered my question, "Can you get everything you want here?" by saying proudly, "Barley, maize, milk, eggs, everything. This is Jimma." Riding on to Hirmata, I found the Governor of the Province camped on a ridge, engaged on making arrangements for his march to Addis Ababa with three hundred and fifty men and choosing four saddle mules as a present for the Emperor. Two clerks seated on the ground were receiving money – I gathered payments that were being permitted in lieu of certain personal services required on mobilisation. The Governor told me that many of the men of Jimma province, not already in the army, would be called up for transport services and the rest would be excused on payment of sums of money in lieu. The Governor had attended the coronation of King Edward VII and had also fought at the battle of Adua. I spent a week in Hirmata, staying with Mr & Mrs Piepgrass of The Sudan Interior Mission and left them on 28 October to travel on towards the province of Kaffa. This meant passing from a very fertile province inhabited by energetic, industrious and tractable people whose standard of cultivation was of a high order to a province where successive Governors had settled a number of their soldiers and had tried to administer the territory through the hereditary landlords and a short-sighted and uneven method of feudalism. We stayed four days in Bonga, the present capital of the province. It was nothing more, as yet, than a rather larger clearing than usual in the forest. We were invited to join in the celebration of the Emperor's coronation and there was a feast given by the Governor. The *tej* supply was kept in two hollowed out tree trunks screened off in a corner, and as fast as it was emptied by attendants, maids would replenish it from large *gombos* that they carried in.

'While I was at Bonga, the newly appointed Governor of Maji province arrived and we agreed to continue the journey together. He had several hundred men with him to provide the new garrison. The old garrison was being sent back to Addis Ababa as they had been there for some time and had vested interests in the old feudal system. As we started off on a day's march my men and their animals would try to get a little ahead of the main cortege to keep up their momentum. The first day out we all came down to the stream below the camp which had a rickety old wooden bridge across it. Half my animals got safely across and then someone else's donkey inserted itself, put its foot into a hole in the middle of the bridge and stuck fast. My next mule, carrying two rather heavy boxes, tried to walk over the donkey, straddled him and also got stuck. The most energetic of the mulemen rushed forward to help, but the mule stood on his hind legs, spun round on his hocks like a polo pony and crashed back off the bridge. Four strong men then hauled the donkey's foot out of the hole and we proceeded.

'In spite of the crowded situation, there was no incident of any kind in the camps. The preparation of the evening meal and its consumption is a scene not easily forgotten. Scores of camp fires were ablaze, lighting up the trees, the billowing smoke, the heads of the baggage animals tethered round the bivouacs and the faces of men, women and children sitting round, and the camp was alive with songs and laughter. I take my hat off to the women of the army; they tramped the whole of the four hundred miles from Addis Ababa, mostly carrying heavy burdens, they did the cooking and the chores and yet they were always merry and bright. In the three weeks I accompanied this migration, I never once saw a quarrel take place. We crossed from Kaffa into Shoa-Ghimirra on 9 November. The Amhara governor and his troops had left some weeks previously and the province was being administered by the local *balabats* or landed gentry. We stayed two days in this province and then crossed into Tishana country where the local people had a poor reputation of banditry and resentment against the oppression of the Amhara garrisons. However, no attempt was made to attack us and those whom we met were friendly and helpful. The Tishana are fine specimens of humanity physically. The men are mostly naked with a strip of cloth round their waist and the women wear a skirt of strips of banana leaf or leather thongs.

'We made our triumphal entry into Maji on Saturday 23 November, the women and children and baggage being sent ahead. The soldiers, in formation, escorted the *Fitaurari*, who was proceeded by musicians playing the flute. We had passed through 'the Home' provinces, where in every household one member at least was answering the call to arms; we had passed through Jimma where the permanent garrison had been called up, half to fight in the north and half sent south for garrison duties, but with the mass of the population left unmolested. We had passed through districts where the war in no way affected the local peoples and only the garrisons were being withdrawn or replaced; and lastly and at the limits of this great Empire we had come to a province where a policy of reform, long projected, was being quietly pursued, as though no war was taking place at all.'

11

DAN IN MAJI AND SUBSEQUENT EVENTS

Dan was in Maji for less than a year, from 23 November 1935 to 28th May 1936. He was away from his family, and Ethiopia was being overrun by the Italians. The Emperor had to make his most difficult decision, that of leaving the land of Ethiopia to plead its cause before the League of Nations; and in all this turmoil Dan felt a tremendous sense of loyalty and duty to do what he had been asked to do, to help the young Governor of Maji to organise and run a model province. Throughout these few short months, Dan was consumed with a desire to find out all the facts about the province and to write down suggestions for the Governor, Fitaurari Zaudi Ayelle, as to how the different parts of the province could be governed, taxed, garrisoned, protected from raids, learn to live peaceably among themselves and with neighbouring countries and improve their standards of living in many ways.

His contract with the Ethiopian Government was that he should be Adviser to the Governor of Maji Province and should receive five hundred Ethiopean dollars a month and fifty pounds sterling. It is doubtful whether the contract was ever signed and it is certain that Dan received very little of the salary promised. Communications with Addis Ababa were never very good, and with the ever increasing threat of Italian supremacy, the last two months of his stay were hampered by a cloak of silence.

The Emperor's intentions were clearly to have a trusted European Adviser in that part of south-west Ethiopia most vulnerable, on account of maladministration, to accusations of slave raiding, poaching, and tribal unrest. A real attempt was to be made to deal with slavery and to be seen to be doing so by the neighbouring governments of Kenya and the Sudan. Dan was quite clear as to his role and mission and was fully aware of the tremendous difficulties that would surround the new Governor and his adviser. It is ironic that the fall of Ethiopia should have been added to this burden.

Right from the start, the main difficulty was lack of money. Throughout his time there all government officials, including himself and the soldiers of the different garrisons, were not paid on time, and this did not augur well for a disciplined and honest organisation in control of a province. Dan was not idle in trying to raise money locally. He collected much information about supplies of cash and grain and of the whole system of taxation. Dates and notes made on memoranda show how urgent the problem of money and taxation was, and also the complexity of what had to be understood, before it could be put right. On 27 November he asked for information on past budgets and said that the budget for the next year had to be drawn up. On the 29 November he was told that the tax on produce and work had produced nothing; the poll tax had raised only a third of what was expected; the amount of tax collected on cultivation was still unknown; there were no records of revenue in past years and no one was sure how much was owed to the soldiers in the various garrisons. On the same day Dan produced a memorandum concerning the main principles of taxation. This was to show how to simplify the collection of tax, so that the payer should not find that he was paying several different taxes overlapping each other. Tax collection should be made at a sensible time of year and by the local *balabats*, who would be duly salaried. On 2 December Dan wrote to say that increased dues had been charged in the market and this would frighten away the traders. On 18 December Dan produced 'Notes on Taxation' for the Governor. In these he set out what a man would be expected to pay as comprehensive tax in Kenya or the Sudan, compared with what was expected from a taxpayer in Ethiopia. He pointed out the current confusion of the different taxes that a householder had to pay: poll tax, tax on cultivation, the provision of grass and wood without payment, the days a man had to work on roads and maintenance of telephone lines, etc. He suggested ways in which things could be simplified. On 26 February there was a meeting where Dan produced a draft budget to start on 10 March 1936. During all this intense period of policy making and effort to curtail and wipe out the old, bad systems, the whole process was hampered and delayed by the lack of ready cash, the inexperience and hesitation of the new Governor and the blocking tactics displayed by the suspicious and not-over-energetic Director of the province.

Other concerns that Dan interested himself in while at Maji were questions regarding ownership of land, the municipality of Maji and the construction of permanent buildings and government offices. He wished to build a house for himself and Chris when she came out and, at the same time, he asked if he could plough up some waste land and grow grain for his servants and his animals. He wrote to the Civil Secretary in Khartoum and asked if he had instructions for clerks, accountants etc; also instructions for DCs and notes on taxation. He was sent eight books with the remark, 'You will, of course, appreciate that Sudan Government documents of this kind should not be allowed to get into Ethiopian or other hands; otherwise we might be accused of taking over Maji.'

On 15 April he wrote to Sir Harold McMichael in Tanganyika for copies of books and instructions on taxation, land settlement and tenure and indirect rule. Dan wrote, 'We have to deal with subject races in all stages here, from primitive tribes to highly organised communities . . . The Emperor knows that he has got to satisfy the League and World opinion over his plans of reorganisation and reform, and, in copying Tanganyikan methods, he would know he was copying something which already had the approval of the Mandate's Commission of the League.'

From 3 to 20 January 1936 Dan toured the province and visited Beyrou, Tirma and Tid country. The governor was unwilling to let him go and wished to see that he had enough soldiers for his protection. Dan replied that he would pass on any relevant information he collected and would take a small escort where he thought it was necessary, and these soldiers should be paid before the tour started. His reports covered most aspects of interest. In Beyrou he found the road had been kept in good order; the people were industrious and friendly. There was plenty of cultivation and coffee. There had been a cattle raid six months before, perpetrated by the Tishana. He recommended taxation at the Maji rate. At another place, Duku, he reported that the road was cleared but not the mountain track. The people were friendly, and there was firm authority. The people were industrious, but there was no coffee. Six Duku women had recently been abducted by Tid raiders, and government help was asked for in securing their release. The Tirma country was friendly and the chiefs were glad to be able to state their case to the government. They wished to be friendly with the government, live in peace, pay taxes and keep their young men from lawlessness. They wished to pay their tithes in honey, due to lack of money and cattle. They wished to pay direct to the government, not to the local Amhara governor. It is interesting that in another comment Dan says that he has had a reply to his report of his travels to Governor Zaudi, and in the main his requests had been granted and his suggestions had been put into train to be carried out. It is sad that so few of the reforms could be carried out, because everything halted once the Italian invasion was complete.

In Maji at this time lived Major R.C. Whalley, serving in the Sudan government and given the local rank of British Consul. His job was to protect British and Sudanese interests in south-west Ethiopia with respect to slavery, poaching and border raids, and to foster trade. His intense loyalty to the government that he served made him distrust the Ethiopians among whom he lived, and on many occasions there was distinct conflict of ideas and opinions between the two Englishmen. This in no way affected their personal relationship, and Major Whalley was kindness itself to Dan when he most needed encouragement and sympathy. As ever, in matters dealing with tribal squabbles and raids, it was almost impossible to get to the absolute truth as to who was helping whom. Boundaries fixed by government meant nothing to tribes hunting or poaching lion skins, and rhino horns. When cattle were taken, or women abducted and sold for some bullets and a cow, one could never be sure as to whether it was Ethiopians versus Sudanese or family, in which cases the prevalence of intermarriage made it likely that there were Ethiopian and Sudanese strains on either side. Many of the complaints from Major Whalley to Zaudi the Governor were in fact, dealt with very adequately, but only after some time had passed, since Zaudi felt that the Ministry in Addis Ababa had to be informed and permission to act granted, before he would use his authority to put things right.

As a military man Dan was particularly interested in the garrison of the Maji province. Many of the soldiers were used for police work and Dan felt that this should be changed. The local chief should be in charge of policing, using mainly local people. Another point of dissension that came up in discussions was that the soldiers, who were not receiving their pay regularly, were driven to sell ammunition locally in order to buy themselves food. They had also run out of medicine and it was reported that eighteen had died of malaria. Dan offered to buy the quinine himself for four hundred odd soldiers until such time as money came from Addis Ababa. On 21 May Dan wrote to the Minister of War offering to train a force of men that could stay in Maji province, deal with security, maintain law and order, and act as information agents in the face of the continued advance of the Italian invasion.

Dan was kept very busy, both mentally and physically. He was ever optimistic and this shows through all his correspondence, but he was also realistic and knew that any reforms would take time and would need the real desire of the government, the local chiefs and the people to make any real headway. In a Christmas letter to his brother, Tom, who was in Rhodesian Government circles, he wrote: 'Maji itself is peopled very thinly by a gutless, mild people who have been mal-administered almost out of existence. Beyond a three mile radius, the province is in a state of passive revolt. And the whole thing is due to the *gabar* system, i.e. a system by which soldiers are supported by allotting them so many serfs. With a firm and wise Governor the system functioned adequately, but when control slackened the serf rapidly became a slave. The stronger tribes revolted, the weaker were ground out of existence. Slavery had been kept going by the natives selling their own children to pay their masters . . . Please send me any odd reports on taxation. I want to know the latest on the subject of house, poll and cultivation taxes . . . I start training the army tomorrow. Hush – the police. I am in a delicate position as you can imagine.'

The eternal problem of money, both for the Province of Maji and for Dan's personal needs, must have been a great burden to bear. In all his administrative work he was concerned that failure to pay their salaries obliged garrisons to pay for food by selling cartridges, taxes could not be paid by the local people, and there was virtually no support from central government. And yet he was conscious that with Ethiopia being at war against a much better equipped enemy, it was useless to expect a miracle of efficiency. Finances affected his own private life in much the same way. His contract with the Ethiopian Government was theoretically for five years with the expectation of quite a good salary, but having been in Maji for less than a year he had still not received his full salary even for that period, because the Emperor's Government had fallen and the country had been conquered.

The changes in family circumstances and anxiety over finances were enormous burdens for both Chris and Dan. The farm, which was beginning to show some signs of prosperity, still owed money to the loyal group of generous relations who had helped with loans; a manager and his family were now installed and needed to be paid. The two older girls were at boarding school, and the son, Dick, had started Prep School. The family at home had to be supported and his sojourn at Maji paid for. And over and above all these, there was still repayment needed on loans previously taken out. If it had not been for the fact that relations on both sides of the family had been so heart-warmingly generous with their support, both morally and financially, Chris and Dan would not have been able to keep things going at all. Dan's sister, Ethel, supported the school expenses of the two girls at Wycombe Abbey School and Dan's brother, Temple, paid for Dick at Brightlands Prep School. Chris's brothers, Cecil and Maurice, not only lent money but provided homes and holiday attractions for the family. Maurice, himself in Cairo, was the person with whom Chris stayed on her journey to join Dan in Maji. Emma Awdry took on the formidable task of looking after the two youngest children while Chris started out on her journey to Maji with the third daughter Audrey. Far more lastingly important than all this financial help was the moral support given by all their friends and relatives, even though some of them were quite obviously not in complete accord with what was going on. Dan, in his often lonely position in Maji, was hungry for news and comment and advice on his three eldest children at school. In letters written to Temple, a housemaster at Marlborough, and to Ethel, also a teacher and headmistress, he expressed his anxieties and fears for the future. He wrote, 'The more I hear of life in England these days, the more I wonder that the product in young men and women that is being turned out is so good. It is good, isn't it? But the rush, the ceaseless demand for entertainment and the competition can't really be the proper surroundings for sound character building.'

The idea of living in separate countries for any length of time did not appeal to either Chris or Dan, and soon after the family had arrived back in England and Dan had reached Maji, plans were started to enable Chris to return to Maji. They both had far too optimistic a faith that the war against Ethiopia would quickly be resolved, and that, in spite of being far less well equipped than Italy, Ethiopia would regain her sovereignty with the aid of countries that were members of the League of Nations. For this reason they saw nothing hare-brained in their planned reunion in Maji. Again, finance was the major obstacle and Chris was indefatigable in her efforts to raise the cash for her journey out. It was not only the money that she worked for. Both she and Dan were loyal believers in the ideals of the League of Nations and both were loving advocates of the Ethiopian cause. The degrading shilly-shallying of the League of Nations and its failure to support weaker nations in these early days of Mussolini's aggression made them feel sick with sorrow and anger. Chris spent many hours campaigning for supporters who would urge the League of Nations to stand by its stated principles without fear or favour, and to help foil the aggressor. She lectured, she spoke at small gatherings of church congregations, and she even addressed a meeting at The Mansion House, side by side with the Archbishop of Canterbury. In a letter Dan wrote to his sister, Ethel, he said, 'Tell me if you think Chris is overdoing herself. She is very strong but she appears to be on the go from early morning to one and two at night every day. Looking after the kids, making money by lecturing, etc., because I have miserably failed to make enough to keep us going, helping the Red Cross, rushing round – she never seems to have half an hour to sit down and have a rest.' By January 1936 Chris was making plans to go out to Maji. She had the three eldest children in boarding schools, she had accepted the kind offer of Emma Awdry to look after the two youngest, aged one and three, and she intended taking the eight year old Audrey with her. She was to travel to Kenya by ship and then make her way to Kitale, where Dan would meet her and then they would go trekking to Lokitang and so north to Maji. Dan was desperately trying to get a six-roomed house built for her and she was due to arrive in Mombassa on 12 May. By early March there had been Italian planes flying over Maji, and Dan heard that they had taken the province of Sidamo, only two hundred and fifty miles away, by mid-March. Inside Ethiopia itself, news of the progess of the war was scarce, and all that was heard in Maji were rumours from the Sudan and Kenya. Dan still felt that the danger was minimal but wired to Chris to tell her of the flight of the Italian planes. On 13 April he wrote to his brother, Tom, that his last letter from Chris was dated 11 February and he still did not know whether she was going ahead with plans. In a letter to Emma on 15 February he said that he would go to Kitale from Lokitang by lorry, kindly lent by the transport officer there. They would then drive back to Lokitang together and proceed by mule to Maji, arriving in the middle of June. A letter to Austen Matthew on 6 May, told that Dan had a wire to say that Chris was leaving Audrey behind, because the Foreign Office was concerned with the situation, and though they were prepared to allow Chris to go, they thought it unwise for her to take a child with her. Furthermore, the situation in Maji had deteriorated. There had been two raids, in which women and children had been abducted, and both Sudanese and Ethiopian tribes had been involved. This meant that Dan would not be able to meet Chris in Kitale or Lokitang and she would have to make the journey on her own. Wolde Mariam and thirty porters had already been sent to Lokitang and Dan hoped he might just be able to rush down there in time. He actually left Maji to go to Lokitang on 7 May but received a telegram from Chris saying she had been delayed on the 11 May while he was still travelling. He then returned to Maji on 14 May. A week later Dan received a telegram which told him that Chris had stopped before reaching The Red Sea, and had stayed in Cairo with her brother, Maurice, and was waiting for Dan to join her there. The next month was a wretched period for Dan. On the 24 May he received telegrams which spoke of the fall of Addis Ababa and the departure of the Emperor to Jerusalem. He comments: 'It would be incredible in any other country that the Emperor and Government could have disappeared and the capital be taken weeks ago, without our having the least idea of it here.' He was now in a terrible dilemma. Should he stay to help the Governor and Director control and keep the province calm? Should he offer to help Ras Imeru with the continued fighting further north? Or should he leave the boat sinking and go back to his family in England? After he had discussed all this with his Ethiopian Governor, he went south to Lokitang, first of all to try to establish a surer method of information and communication for the Governor. He also wanted to assure the British Authorities of Governor Zaudi's very real desire to co-operate with them over border issues.

Dan left Maji for good on 27 May, arrived at Lokitang on 5 June and was there until 22 June. During that time there was a feverish exchange of messages and telegrams, some coded and some free. Dan was desperate to have confirmed news of the situation in Ethiopia, the plans of the Emperor, and what help and advice Governor Zaudi could expect from the Sudan and Kenyan authorities if he continued to govern and control Maji province. As well as these problems, he was concerned for Chris's safety and what he should do as a loyal employee of the Emperor. Naturally, the information and advice he received were contradictory; a message from the Emperor requested him to go to Gore and join Ras Imeru, together with the Governor and as many men as could be mustered. The Foreign Office was not in favour of a British national's returning to Ethiopia. If Zaudi were to leave Maji with unpaid troops left behind and no one in real authority, the province could very easily forfeit any progress it had made and decline into tribal anarchy. Nothing was resolved or decided upon, and Dan left for Nairobi. When he reached there, he did not have enough money to pay for a flight to Cairo, but eventually, thanks to the kind officers of the RAF, he reached Cairo on 29 June. If after-dinner yarns are to be believed, this flight was not without its hazards. Chris, waiting impatiently in Cairo, had been told that two RAF planes were due to arrive there during the day and Dan would be on one of them (from Khartoum). To keep up the suspense, someone cheerfully told her that one of the planes had been forced to do a crash landing somewhere in the desert, but no one knew if it was the one carrying Dan. It was not, and they were finally united. Extracts from Dan's letters to Chris during June show how unhappy and fearful he was: 'I am petrified with funk over the money side of it . . . As far as personal affairs are concerned, I just feel all numb . . . I don't want to go home and become a pensioner of the rest of the family. I couldn't bear it.' He wished to get someone to save Maji from anarchy. 'It's horrible to contemplate, and yet all the powers-that-be seem to contemplate it without a quiver and think only of avoiding complications.' Over the general situation he wrote, 'What a jolly muddle everything is in. Old Baldwin is pathetic and Eden in an impossible situation.' But in another letter he says that Chris's letter to him was perfect – 'You always know how best to help me.' He says of his brother-in-law, Maurice, and his wife, Diana: 'They are real rocks in a land of quicksands.'

While in Cairo, Dan wrote to countless people. He wrote to the High Commissioner for Egypt and the Sudan trying to state a case urging the authorities to keep a paternal eye on Maji and its people. He wrote to Lord Lugard and asked that he might put in a good word for him if he looked for work in the UK. He wrote to Dr Martin, the Emperor's secretary, to ask him to advise what he should be doing to help the Emperor, but explaining that his personal situation was financially critical. In the end, it was clear that the only thing to do was to return to England and try to start a new life until the way was clear again. He saw the Emperor in Bath on his return to England, but plans to help Ras Imeru keep up resistance in Ethiopia were thwarted by the Foreign Office.

To digress a little, but to add another item of interest, the story of Dr Martin was a fascinating one. When General Napier was attacking the fortress of Magdala in 1868 where the Emperor Theodore eventually committed suicide rather than be captured, some of the troops under Napier's command were Indian. After the battle was over, one of the Indian officers found a small Ethiopian boy wandering, quite lost, amidst the carnage, took him back to India and brought him up as his own son, giving him the name Martin. He was educated to be a doctor and returned to Ethiopia where he married and had a vast family. Once when Chris and Dan visited him in the early days, a small boy passed through the sitting-room, and Chris asked whether he was Dr. Martin's son. A servant had to be called, and his master asked him whether the child was indeed a Martin. Only thus could the question be settled in the affirmative.

12

CHRIS AND THE CHILDREN RETURN TO ENGLAND

Dan's departure from Addis Ababa and his work in Maji have been described in the last chapter, but the journey Chris made back to England also needs to be recorded. It was June 1935 when Chris with four children under the age of twelve left Addis Ababa by train for Djibouti. The children were allowed one small case each for their toys and belongings, although Stephen, the youngest son, was only six months old. Audrey, then aged eight, remembers getting down off the train at the border with French Somaliland and filling a matchbox with the soil of Ethiopia, her motherland, to take with her. At Djibouti they boarded a Norwegian cargo boat sailing to Barcelona and were the only passengers. They were allowed the run of the ship, from bridge to crew's quarters and practised riding one of the crew's bicycles, and the eldest girl was briefly shut in the ship's cold store by the ship's cook, as a joke.

The journey back to England was most exhausting and demanding. The weather in the Red Sea was oppressively hot, and looking after four children single handed must have been a nightmare. One child caught mumps and the baby's nappies had to be washed every day and hung like flags across the deck. As they steamed northwards, they passed ship after ship of Italian soldiers and equipment, sailing to the Eritrean port of Massawa, although Ethiopia was prevented, by League of Nations sanctions, from buying arms and ammunition. At one moment their boat passed her sister-ship in the Red Sea and sounded off her siren.

Unfortunately the mechanism jammed and it continued wailing for several minutes. This caused the two year old Philippa to cling to her mother in a fit of hysterical screaming that was for a long time quite uncontrollable. Thereafter, for several months, Philippa, already rather spoilt, reacted to the new and violent sounds she now encountered by becoming acutely sensitive to them. She also developed the inconvenient capacity to be sick at will, whenever her will was crossed.

At Barcelona they were met by a Thomas Cook agent and put on to a train for France passing through Paris to reach Calais. After a bizarre journey, memorable for the throwing of eggs at Customs Officers by a Spanish lady, and the dropping of a bottle of Vichy water on her toe, Chris tipped the Thomas Cook agent at Calais half-a-crown. He looked embarrassed and said, "Are you sure you can afford it Madam?" Their journey ended with an appropriately choppy Channel crossing.

Once landed in England, Chris and her children received the warmest possible welcome from the entire family. Her elder brother, Cecil, gave her the use of his house in Lindfield, and there the rest of the family joined her for the summer holidays and later for Christmas of 1935.

The year that followed was bleak indeed for both Dan and Chris. They were separated, with Dan alone at Maji and longing for his wife to join him. Their farm was looted in their absence and many things taken away by the local people. Their possessions in Addis Ababa had also been looted and burned. Dan had earned a good salary but received virtually none of it. They owed money in Addis Ababa, in Maji and in England. Chris concentrated first on settling the two elder girls into their places at Wycombe Abbey School and getting Dick into prep school in Gloucestershire. She taught Audrey at home, but sent her to classes in Lindfield for one or two additional subjects. She went round wherever possible lecturing and giving talks on Ethiopia and writing articles for newspapers. At the same time she was looking for ways and means of joining Dan in Maji, possibly taking Audrey with her and leaving the two youngest in the charge of Dan's cousin Emma and her daughter Diana. What a daunting and frightening position for a family of eight!

Two major factors overcame the problems and routed the adversary, misfortune. The first lay in the boundless strength of family loyalty. From both Chris's and Dan's sides of the family came help of all kinds. Mother, father, brothers, sisters and cousins rallied round and gave unstintingly. During the holidays the family stayed at Plymouth, Lindfield, Brighton, Dursley and Marlborough in turn. School fees were paid by relatives on both sides along with immeasurable gifts of love and advice. The second factor was the indomitable characters of the two of them. They never gave up and they never abandoned their beliefs that, ultimately, things would come right.

Once home, there came the unenviable task of finding work to pay for living expenses in England. Dan first went to see the Emperor and discuss with him whether there was anything that Dan could do that would be of benefit to both of them, but, with the League of Nations and the greater powers unable to deal with the increased aggression shown by Italy, there seemed to be little hope of this. Dan's sister, Ethel, was Headmistress of the high school in Beverley at that time and she offered Chris a job teaching classics in the school there. Teaching PE at the same school, was Muriel Ward, or, as she became known to all the family, Gym Ward. She was to become a very loyal friend of Chris and later when they were all back in Ethiopia, used to come out to stay, rather as K.T. had done. The two youngest children, in the charge of a formidable lady known as Nanny Reagan, spent some time in Beverley with Chris and some time with Dan staying with Emma Awdry. It was from there that Dan applied for several jobs. The dossier of things that he had done so far would sound impressive to someone who was looking for help in an administrative job abroad, but was less helpful for a man seeking work in England in the hard time before the war. Apart from distinguished military service in the First World War, his work had been: District Commissioner in the Sudan, Liaison Officer in Addis Ababa, businessman (not very successful), lawyer and farmer in Ethiopia and finally adviser to the Ethiopian Administration of an Ethiopian Province, and in addition, some press work for several newspapers. What did he know of England and the way that things worked there? He had impressive references from previous commanding officers and from Lord Lugard, and tried for a tremendous variety of jobs ranging from organising secretary for Physical Training and Recreation Area Committees to driving a butcher's van. It wasn't until 1938 that he finally landed a job that he felt he could put his heart and soul into. He was appointed Secretary to the Special Building Appeal Fund for Guildford Cathedral and was to help organise and carry out a campaign for collecting money to finish building the Cathedral.

The holidays were times when the whole family tried to get together, and once again it was the rest of the family that repeatedly came to the rescue. Christmas 1936 saw them at Chris's brother, Cecil's, house in Plymouth. During another holiday there, younger members of the family were fiercely inducted into the language of yacht racing while crewing for the Lush family. Once on Dartmoor Uncle Cecil thought the Sandford young needed toughening up and decided to leave the older ones in the middle of the moor telling them to find their own way home by compass. When Chris was teaching in Beverley the family spent a short and lovely holiday at Goathland on the moors in Yorkshire. On another occasion the family was invited to spend some time at Preshute House in Marlborough College, where Dan's eldest brother Temple was a housemaster. There was plenty of room there for all of them and some other cousins from Rhodesia, where Dan's brother, Tom, was working. Dan's elder sister, Betty, who kept house for Temple, insisted on total respect for elders. The youngsters could only approach and talk to 'Uncle Temple' if she first found out whether he was available and willing to listen to them. It was at this time that there was a vogue for chewing every mouthful one ate thirty-five times as a health fad. A diet of nuts and raisins was favoured for the same reasons. Uncle Temple was a fervent believer in all this and the young would sit through interminable meals watching him chew his way slowly through such unappetising food. It was a relief when they were allowed to indulge in a more ordinary diet. There was a swimming-pool attached to Preshute House, and happy hours were spent there, when it was warm enough. During one holiday at Lindfield, the Sandford enthusiasm for outdoor drama, passionately performed, earned some neighbourly remonstrance – for which Chris had little sympathy.

Chris did not stay teaching at Beverley for more than a year and it must have been soon after this that Dan's sister, Ethel, resigned as headmistress there. Having disagreed with the Board of Governors on some matter of policy, she was obliged to resign. It was an unhappy time for the family and Ethel in particular. She had been a very successful headmistress in Auckland, New Zealand, and had expected to continue her teaching life in England, but this setback effectively put an end to her career as a headmistress. Chris had found that living so far north meant a wide separation from the family and she accepted a job teaching in Yeovil, Somerset. When starting there, she noticed in the local paper that there was a house to let in Batcombe, Dorset, for the magnificent sum of twelve pounds a year. The house was a 'two up, two down', but it had a large hall attached to it that had been the village school. It now housed the local library that was only open for certain days of the week. It was not too far from Yeovil and she and Dan and the two youngest took up residence there, complete with Nanny Reagan. The rest of the children used the library for their dormitory during the holidays and had to leave it very tidy on days when it was open. There was a large vegetable garden attached to the house and the whole of Dorset to explore. Batcombe was a very small village with a church which the family went to every Sunday. A lady in the choir, a powerful alto, took good care to see that there was no back-sliding in either village or church. A little further away there was a monastic community of 'Brown Brothers', which the whole family, together with cousin Diana from Dursley, visited for carols one Christmas-time. On Christmas Day, squashed into the tiny house, the whole family had a wonderful Christmas, with Dan appearing in his usual role as Father Christmas in a red and orange striped towelling dressing-gown. One of the Christmas presents was sixpence each for the children to walk to the nearest cinema, several miles away, to see a film.

When Dan was finally appointed Appeals Secretary for Guildford Cathedral, the family moved to Brookside in Ewhurst, Surrey. This house was to be the family pied-à-terre for the next fifteen years or more, though Dan and Chris were not there themselves for very long. It was a large house, with plenty of space and had a mobile home for extra room in the front garden. The flower garden, together with a tennis court was at the back, and a small wooden bridge led off into the woods behind. The bridge spanned the brook from which the house got its name and the whole place was an ideal area for a large family. When they left Batcombe, Chris gave up teaching at Yeovil. Nanny Reagan departed and a Batcombe girl called Lily Hansford came with them to Ewhurst. Chris's parents also joined the household, and from time to time an enormous number of people seemed to have taken up residence in the house. Not only did Brookside seem home to many passing friends and family, but Chris's brother, Maurice, had a house called Westlands only three or four fields further up the road. There he and Diana were bringing up their young family. They had Ruth Hill, Diana's mother, with them. So, for a time, life seemed to become more settled and Dan and Chris became part of the village scene. With his job as Appeals Secretary, Dan travelled widely all over the diocese, and very often Chris went with him, and together they got on with the job of raising money for the finishing of the building of Guildford Cathedral. In these tours, the name of Ethiopia would often crop up as well as Cathedral affairs and the two of them never lost an opportunity to plead for an independent Ethiopia under her Emperor and for the reawakening of a positive attitude within the League of Nations towards its less fortunate members.

The family situation in October 1938, before the threat of the Second World War changed everything once more, may be summarised thus. Dan had a satisfying, full-time job as Appeals Secretary. Chris used to give him a great deal of help, but was at the same time teaching the two youngest, Philippa and Stephen, at home. Christine, the eldest had just left Wycombe Abbey School and had decided that she was not really interested in going to Cambridge to read History, that her true bent was for doctoring. She was living at Brookside and going daily into Guildford to take her HSC in physics and chemistry. Eleanor was still at Wycombe Abbey School and Dick was at Shrewsbury. Audrey was still at Plymouth living with Cecil's family and attending St. Dunstan's School as a day girl. Chris's parents were living at Brookside and so was K.T., who shared the teaching of the two youngest. Herbert Lush, Chris's father, was a representative of Pyrene fire extinguishers until he retired. He would go off about his business in a very quiet and unobtrusive way. He smoked like a chimney and was dearly loved by all the children. Somewhat bullied by his wife, he would often seek refuge in the mobile home which was the nursery and listen to the news there. A vivid memory of the younger children was that he had to have hot wax foot baths for a First World War wound.

In holiday times the house overflowed and there was a great deal of fun and laughter. Dan was Father Christmas yet again, in the same towelling dressing-gown and the fetching of the Christmas tree from the top of Pitch Hill was a grand affair. There was skating on the pond of a local Prep School where Chris occasionally helped out with music lessons and in the summer there were tennis parties in the garden and walks over the fields. Rhodesian cousins came to stay, and eventually nannies left and a series of people came to help the older inhabitants. There was a capacious barn attached to the house and cars, bicycles and garden tools were all stored there. Eventually it was also used as a hen-house. Everyone took a share in the household chores, with Granny being in charge of the cruets and keeping them in immaculate condition, and Stephen, aged four, being introduced to the art of boot polishing. When he resisted, his elder brother and a cousin lifted him up onto the roof of the barn and refused to release him until he had done his share.

But, in spite of the happy family times, it was becoming more and more apparent after September 1938 and the Munich affair that war was inevitable and that the family home was going to be disarranged by outside forces. Dan applied to the War Office, offered his services and left in

July 1939 for the Middle East. His work there is dealt with in a later chapter. When he was accepted for duty he was amused to find his name in the Army List not under Royal Artillery, Lt. Col., but under 'Miscellaneous, miscellaneous'. Once Dan had gone and war was declared, it seemed that Chris would have to bear the burden of managing the family affairs on her own. In truth she was far from alone because the dynamic power of the family was behind her. Now, however, Chris was in a position to give as much as she received. Brookside became a place where any member of the wider family could come and stay – and not only family but Ethiopian friends and others anxious to find a haven in troubled times.

13

MISSION 101

Mission 101 was the name given to the small band of British soldiers and their Ethiopian comrades-in-arms that, under Dan's command, spent five exciting and valuable months in the heartland of Ethiopia, stirring up the flames of war which were to end with the freeing of the country and the return of the Emperor. The preparations for the entry of the Mission and the final defeat of the enemy took a good deal longer. Dan and the Mission finally crossed the border into Ethiopia on 12 August 1940, and he handed over command of the Mission to Orde Wingate on 21 January 1941 before taking over the duties of military and political adviser to the Emperor.

In July 1939 when it was becoming increasingly obvious that it was going to be impossible to avert war in Europe, Dan applied to the War Office to be given some kind of military position. He was fifty-seven, and so was not applying for a position in the field, but he felt that his knowledge of East Africa could very well be of some help to the War Office, if Italy came into the war on the side of Germany. His experiences in the First World War had taught him the value of gaining accurate information in any situation and the vital necessity of getting that information distributed to the right quarters. His application was successful, and towards the end of August he was sent out to Egypt, together with about twenty-five officers from all the services, travelling aboard HMS *Shropshire*. He was in Alexandria on the day that war was declared, and went to Cairo to join the Joint Intelligence

Centre there. General Wavell, for whom Dan had the greatest admiration, was in control of all British land forces in Egypt, Sudan, Palestine, Transjordan and Cyprus. If Italy came into the war on the side of Germany, her presence in East Africa would be a threat to Egypt, the Sudan, Kenya and both British and French Somalilands. It was going to be of great importance to keep her troops in Africa contained and busy in that area and at the same time to free Ethiopia from Mussolini's grasp. This would need carefully planned co-operation between British forces and Ethiopian Patriots. It was to this end that Dan was asked to collect information and help to work out plans.

It was a time of great frustration, not only for Dan, but for many others. In London there was a deep feeling that as Italy had not yet joined the war, nothing must be done to dislodge her from her position on the fence. At various times Dan was able to visit Kenya, the Sudan, British Somaliland and to meet up with important Ethiopian personages. At other times the balance would alter and headquarters in Cairo would be told that there were to be no agents in Ethiopia and no contact made with Ethiopian Patriots. As war had not been declared against Italy there were many Italians working and living in Cairo, and Dan and his friend Clayton actually had a flat below the headquarters of the Italian Fascist Club. A second source of frustration and non-co-operation that Dan felt acutely, lay in the attitude of many of the British officers when expressing their opinions about the value, or more frequently the non-value of the Ethiopian Patriots and with them their Emperor. Many felt that the help the Patriots and the Emperor could give, in the battle against Italy, was negligible, and that there was no need to plan joint action. Towards the end of 1939 there was such a strong feeling in the War Office that Italy should not be aggravated, that General Wavell felt that he had to take Dan out of the intelligence section where he was working and put him in 'personnel' as a gesture of reconciliation. At the same time he personally urged Dan to get on with the job. Meanwhile Dan had 'acquired' an Ethiopian secretary, Merid Mengesha. He had also made contact with Lorenzo Taezaz, who had been in Gojjam at the Patriots' Headquarters and had a great deal of invaluable information. A small printing press had been set up in Gojjam by Getahun Tessema. This was producing news of the outside world events and of the possibility of aid and support to the Patriots. Lorenzo went back to England to see the Emperor and give him news of events. He also went to stay with Chris and give her news, much of which could not have been sent in letters.

The first five months of 1940 were gruelling ones for Dan and for those who worked with him. A great deal of paper work had to be kept up with. He often felt that the job he had been given was mere bottle washing, but his reaction was, "If necessary, I'll simply wash the damn bottles." At other times he travelled: to Jerusalem, where he met Austen Matthew; to Aden to see that plans already laid had been followed up and to tighten procedures; and to Khartoum where he met Chris's brother, Maurice, a welcome break from the restrictive atmosphere in which he had been working. He liked the people he worked with and found them very helpful, but he was full of impatience and dissatisfaction with those for whom he worked. Through these critical months, together with all the other British people, his thoughts were often with his family at home, first through the declaration of war, then the taking of the Low Countries, followed by the British withdrawal at Dunkirk. On 10 June Italy declared war on Great Britain, and Dan wrote home: 'The long expected declaration of war was on 10 June. I am sure that a more robust attitude, instead of the weak-kneed or apologetic attempts at appeasement, would certainly not have increased the danger of war and might perhaps have lessened it, and our preparations would have been less hampered.'

Within a few days of the Italian declaration of war, Dan left Cairo for Khartoum, in order to start carrying out the plans made for Mission 101. Almost immediately another quite serious problem arose and had to be dealt with as tactfully as possible. The Foreign Office in London, apparently without the correct consultation with the War Office, arranged that the Emperor should leave London and arrive by flying boat in Alexandria on 24 June. He arrived unannounced, unexpected and unwanted by the political pundits, while at the same time he was expecting tanks, ammunition and a backing force with which to make his entry into his empire. The British Ambassador in Cairo felt that it was impolitic for him to stay in Egypt as did General Platt, the Kaid in the Sudan. Eventually the Emperor was flown to Wadi Halfa, and it was there that Dan went to greet him and to try to smooth things over. He was perhaps the best man to choose for the job. His sympathies lay totally with the Emperor; his duties as a British officer were to General Wavell and the plans that were being laid. He had already been in the thick of the tussle and tangled issues that were being thrashed out between those, on the one hand, who were most inclined to inaction and conciliation and those, on the other, who were actively planning operations in the Horn of Africa. His letters home had used the terms 'petty-minded obstructionists' and 'passive resistance', but, above all, he knew the strengths and character of the Emperor, and though he found a very angry and deeply disappointed man at Wadi Halfa, the two of them were able to work out conditions and a programme that could be accepted by all.

Dan's letter of the 1 July sets it out very clearly: 'Reported to the Kaid at nine o'clock; he took it well. Went with the Kaid to report to the Governor General at ten-thirty and was positively gushed over. He said, "A difficult task, admirably performed," and a few nights ago I was being almost screamed at. They don't understand me and I suppose I don't understand them. Anyway I have got most of my wishes met. The crowning joy was my being sent for at midday to discuss the bombing of Gondar and Gallabat, which I have long been asking for.' General Wavell put pressure on the Sudan authorities to provide suitable accommodation for the Emperor and on 2 July the Emperor moved from Wadi Halfa to 'The Pink Palace', just outside Khartoum, where he stayed under the pseudonym of *Mr Strong*. He was escorted from Wadi Halfa by Maurice Lush who was able to accord the Emperor the respect that he so often felt was lacking from the Kaid and the Governor. During the next two weeks before Dan's actual departure into Ethiopia, matters grew very tense, and feelings of anger, disappointment, hope and despair ran high. Extracts from Dan's letters show the position very clearly.

7 July. 'I am probably off to Gedaref tomorrow though Haile Selassie is very anxious to keep me here until things are straightened out. I should revel in these battles much more if you (Chris), were here and we could laugh at them all. I fell into a slit trench this morning and, as it had been pouring with rain and the trench was half full of water, I looked a funny sight when my car cleaner fished me out.'

10 July. 'A good deal of water has flowed under the bridge since Sunday–Monday. On the whole, to good purpose, but I can't write about it yet.'

14 July. 'A Godless and tiring day. I overslept, did not go to the early service and I've been on the go, till I got back from the Palace, where we had a conference until after eleven at night. I didn't get my point of view accepted, but though I am sorry for that, I said my say and can obey orders. It will be a great relief to get going on definite instructions at last.'

16 July. 'Plans are beginning to crystallise and I hope we are beginning to work on something definite. I can't tell you how glad I shall be to get away from the mental and moral atmosphere of this place.'

17 July. 'All goes well with me but I have had a very difficult time. Things are smoother here and I am almost the blue-eyed boy.'

21 July. 'I left Khartoum about eleven-thirty in the morning and had a most delightful surprise as I was leaving when a man came running up with letters from home. Your letters make me realise, more than anything else, the fatality of the procession of tremendous events. That is not phrased right. What I mean is that there you have on one side the evidence of tremendous, devastating, swift power, the devil triumphant, but on the other there is our own little family and countless other little families where simple love and simple trust are the things that mean everything to me and the power behind all these simple things is much more tremendous and permanent, as time will show. As you say so often in your letters, you and I haven't the slightest reason or excuse for doubt of the outcome of this struggle. At the moment we are stuck at the little station of Duki.

Great interest by the local inhabitants in the forty *Habesh* I'm taking with me. They are the pick of the volunteers who have been arriving and congregating in Khartoum over the past four weeks. I am taking them with me to serve as mule loaders etc. I slipped away from Khartoum pretty quietly and did not even ring Maurice up. I came away leaving a much improved atmosphere behind me. I lunched with H.E. and the same evening the Chief [General Wavell] passed through and I had a twenty minutes talk with him. We are all now agreed on plans and they all wished me luck and said they thought I had a great opportunity for doing good work and promised all the support in their power. It has been a difficult business using up a lot of one's nervous energy in getting things to this point. H.E. went so far as to admit that he had been obstructive, but of course, thought his reasons for being so were adequate. In Khartoum they still look on the little man [the Emperor] merely in the light of a beastly nuisance, or at most, as a rather useless pawn. Never mind, if God wills, I shall make them see reality in a couple of months' time, if not sooner.'

23 July. Dan received a telegram to say that Maurice Lush had been seriously injured in an accident on the railway bridge at Atbara. He was terribly upset by the news. 'Lying in pain and danger at Atbara; I don't want to believe it's true. I cannot go to him as I am actually in process of getting my affairs under way and I can't even send him a direct message from here.' A week later Dan heard that Maurice was out of danger, which was a great relief.

4 August. 'I have packed off the whole lot today and have stayed behind to clear up things and have a final talk with Lorenzo Taezaz. I have a number of important letters to write so I don't imagine I shall get away very early tomorrow. This time next week I hope to be more than a hundred miles away and shall be wishing we were visiting old haunts together, though a little further south than last time. It's going to be a muddy business but otherwise I don't anticipate any difficulties.'

It was the task of the British Mission 101 to give news of the Emperor's arrival in the Sudan, to meet Patriot leaders inside Ethiopia and advise them as to the most useful part

Christine riding in her basket chair, on a mule led by Wolde Mariam, 1920s.

The Boli Waterfall, on the edge of Mulu Farm. The first fall is 600 feet.

Carrying water from spring to home.

The holiday home in the Boli Valley, overlooking the coffee and citrus farm.

The family group, 1931.

Audrey and a baby donkey on the lawn
at Mulu Farm, 1934.

A picnic in 1930, with Chris's mother and
Emma and Vere Awdry.

A caravan of mules crossing the Blue Nile, 1932.

The Chisissat Falls on the Blue Nile, south of Lake Tana.

Coffee trees in the Gulle plantation in the Boli Valley.

A strawberry plantation. The gardener is supervising the irrigation of the plants.

The view from the lawn at Mulu Farm.

Dan Sandford on active service in Mission 101, 1941.

No roads or bridges. Problems for motor transport in the Ethiopian Campaign, 1941.

Dan Sandford during Mission 101.

Dan Sandford, Maurice Lush and Waizero Shoareg, one of the women patriot fighters at a camp at Holleta, outside Addis Ababa, 1941.

they could play, to arrange a route for the entry of arms and ammunition, and to play on the nerves of the Italian forces in Gojjam in order to discourage them from any offensive action in the Sudan. The Mission was not a fighting force and had to avoid contact with any Italian garrisons. They had to rely on the Patriots with whom they came in contact for protection. The five British members of the Mission were Lt. Col. Dan Sandford, Captain R.A. Critchley, Lieutenant C. Drew, RAMC, Sergeant-Major G.S. Grey and Signalman T.W. Whitmore. With them went the Emperor's delegation: Azazh Kebede Tessema, the Emperor's personal representative; Getahun Tessema, secretary of the Gojjam Committee of Union and Collaboration; Assegehein Araia; Gebre Maskal, a first class wireless operator; and Lij Merid Mengesha, who had worked with Dan in Cairo.

The first priority of the Mission was to cross the border and reach the escarpment of East Gojjam, undetected. This meant crossing a main road regularly controlled by the Italians and then finding their way across eighty miles of waterless scrub, before climbing the escarpment, which was 5,000 feet above them. On their way they reached a monastery which was built on the top of a mountain, most likely a volcanic plug, called Mahaber Sclassic, and there Dan and Azazh Kebede were greeted and allowed in. The monks washed their feet, as Christ did the feet of his disciples, and from information they gave, it was felt that Dan's party could safely make for Sarake on the plateau. They reached there on 20 August. Nine days later Dan left Sarake to proceed to Zebist; he left behind the doctor and the two signallers and half of the Ethiopian force. This was because the mules were tired and several had died and they hoped to be able to return the transport once they had reached Zebist. This march was perhaps the most arduous of the whole journey. They had to descend to the plains once more and skirt round the plateau, held by the Italians, and then struggle up the 5,000 feet to the top again. They finally arrived, with only eleven mules and having had to jettison most of their personal kit and stores. The loyal chief Fitaurari Ayellu Makonnen had been out on a sortie and only arrived as they did.

The Emperor's proclamation was read and they were preparing for a feast when a runner brought the news that there was an Italian force moving in. Dan and his party disappeared over the edge of the escarpment, while Ayellu and his men used delaying tactics on the enemy. The Italians reached Ayellu's village and burned his house but did not pursue Dan's band down off the escarpment. The small band spent the night in a cave half way down. At dawn an enemy plane came swooping low along the side of the cliff but could not see into the cave. It was decided to abandon the mules and everything that they could not carry on their persons and descend the escarpment as quickly as possible. They scattered and made their individual ways down some 3,000 to 4,000 feet of rock and collected in the valley below. They then waded for an hour along the river, and spent that night in a village deep in the valley. Torelli, the Italian commander searched the huts on the top and offered a reward of one thousand Ethiopian dollars but was given no information and so withdrew after seizing grain and foodstuffs. On 14 September, the party returned to Ayellu's village and enjoyed the feast that they had been promised. Ayellu and his men then accompanied the Mission over the next part of their journey and they met up with Dejazmach Mengesha on the east side of the Ashwar and little Abai rivers. The crossing of these two rivers was no pleasure; they were very deep and cold. A violent storm during the morning did not help. Most of the members of the party took off their clothes and held them above their heads, but Azazh Kebede, who was a poor swimmer anyway, had to be assisted. To add to the problem of seeing him safely over, he insisted on wearing his clothes, including his army greatcoat.

Having reached Mengasha, Dan was able to begin his real work and by the 25 October he had accomplished most of the task in western Gojjam. He had met nearly all the leading chiefs, and with Azazh Kebede's invaluable assistance a pact of co-operation had been made between Dejazmach Mengesha and Dejazmach Negash, two overlords who had never found it possible to co-operate before. They formulated a plan of action and began to put it into effect. Briefly the idea was to prevent the enemy from reinforcing its troops in western Gojjam, to clear the enemy away from the district bordering the escarpment, and make arrangements for the collection of transport and escort for conveying war material from the Sudan into Gojjam. Dan's successive social contacts with these two overlords revealed at least one of the reasons for their mutual dislike. When feasting with Dejazmach Mengesha, he had commented on the very fine bouquet of the *tej* that they were drinking and with suitable gallantry had sent his compliments to the lady of the house. Several weeks later, when feasting with Dejazmach Negash, he had once again complimented his host on the *tej* remarking that it tasted very like the one he had drunk at Dejazmach Mengesha's table. He realised, from the deathly silence that ensued, that he must have touched on a topic of some delicacy. Later when he tried to find out in what way he had been tactless he discovered that the lady of the house had changed husbands, so the same *tej*-making had been taught in both camps.

The Mission's next job was to move into eastern Gojjam and make sure that the enemy in western Gojjam did not receive reinforcements from the east and from Addis Ababa. Dan left Captain Critchley in charge at Sakala and he and Kebede travelled over two hundred miles along the plateau, often reaching a height of 11,000 feet and once climbing up to 14,000 feet. They met all the leading chiefs and put into operation plans to make as much trouble in the area as possible, so that the Italians could not send any reinforcements to the west. The Patriots were as successful as a shortage of arms and ammunition and a complete lack of cohesion allowed, but they held out and did the job until such time as the British forces from the Sudan and from the north could come to their assistance. The Italians, very uneasy and disturbed, brought Ras Hailu, the most influential war chief in Gojjam back from Addis Ababa where he had been working with the Italians, to Debre Marcos, which had been his capital. By the middle of December Dan was sending messages back to the Sudan to ask for air support and a bold advance of troops to back up and encourage the Patriots and make them feel that in very truth Britain was their ally.

Dan was back in his headquarters at Sakala when in flew Major Orde Wingate, as he was then, in an old Vincent 1930. A landing strip had been hastily prepared, but choosing its position which had to be hidden in the mountainous country, was no mean feat. Enemy fighter planes and bases were not more than fifty miles away. Wingate had been appointed staff officer with special charge for the Gojjam venture; and it was a characteristic step, carried out with a determination peculiarly his, that he insisted on coming to talk things over personally with Dan. The news of the landing of a British plane at Sakala, followed a few days later by the dropping of arms, ammunition, money and stores, spread like wildfire over the country and made an enormous impression. In many ways this seemed to be the turning point of the campaign. Wingate brought the news that an offensive from the west was in train. A mixed Ethiopian and Sudanese force would shortly enter Ethiopia and enormous convoys of camels carrying arms and food would be sent to Mt. Belaia. The Emperor crossed the border on 21 January and reached Belaia on 6 February, after a harrowing journey over the dry plains and then up into the mountains. Motor transport was almost impossible and on one occasion the lorry carrying the Emperor rolled over. On several occasions he and his retinue helped to build up the road and make bridges across dry river beds. They passed hundreds of dead camels which had failed to make the journey. Eventually motor transport had to be abandoned, and the Emperor rode up to his headquarters at Mount Belaia. Here he had a cave for his quarters and it was here that Dan met him, having had to walk from Sakala as there was no alternative transport, covering the sixty miles in a pair of sand-shoes. With the arrival of the Emperor at Belaia the work of Mission 101 was finished. Colonel Wingate, with his 'Gideon Force', and Colonel Boustead commanding the Sudan Defence Force, took over the offensive, and Dan took up his new work as principal Political and Military Adviser to the Emperor.

The presence of the Emperor at Belaia acted as a magnet to the Ethiopian Patriots. The chiefs and their men came to kiss the Emperor's feet and proclaim their loyalty. They told of their brave deeds in the martial *fouqara*, with much stamping and shouting and waving of weapons. Many of these Patriots took part in the battles against the Italians, once they had been given sufficient arms to fight. They, together with Wingate's force and Boustead's battalion, ceaselessly harassed the enemy troops and made it impossible for them to join up with each other and form strengthened units to stand up against incoming British forces. With General Platt moving in from the north and General Cunningham pushing his way up from Kenya, the Italians were caught in a pincer movement from which they could find no way out. Dan stayed with the Emperor and moved with him, first to Buré and then to Debre Marcos on 6th April. Reaching there meant that resistance in Gojjam was virtually at an end. At Debre Marcos, Ras Hailu, the hereditary overlord of the area around came to declare his allegiance and beg forgiveness. He was one of the few Rases who had openly co-operated with the Italians. He came up to the Emperor, walking through lines of Patriots and threw himself at the Emperor's feet. Although the Emperor's magnanimity permitted his eventual reinstatement he was, on this occasion, totally ignored. On the same day General Cunningham's forces from the south entered Addis Ababa. Maurice Lush, now Brigadier and deputy political officer flew to Debre Marcos, a few days later, to confer with the Emperor and Dan on the situation. It was then that the Patriot forces, under four leaders, were assigned to help the British in the four operational areas. Ras Kassa helped in Gojjam, Ras Ababa Aregai in the Dessie area, Azazh Kebede in Lekempti and Gerassa Duké in Jimma. On 5 May, five years after he had left Ethiopia, the Emperor drove into his capital city Addis Ababa, amid scenes of great jubilation and enthusiasm. General Wingate at the head of the 2nd Ethiopian Battalion led the way, followed by the Emperor and his immediate court, and then the British men who had been instrumental in the victory – among them, Dan. He was awarded the CBE and the rank of Brigadier General for his efforts in Mission 101. He was also awarded two Ethiopian medals, Commander of the Order of Trinity and the Haile Selassie Military Medal with palms.

There is no doubt that the success of Mission 101 was,

to a great extent, due to Dan. He was most fortunate in having people he liked and respected to go with him. Both the British and the Ethiopians and the loyal patriots whom he met up with were ardent in their desire to accomplish victory. But throughout the campaign, it was his unshakable belief in the Emperor and the right of Ethiopia to be free, that gave him that calm and cheerful manner that was to be his greatest strength. It is amusing to look at the similarities of expressions used to describe him during that time, both by the Italian propaganda, urging the Ethiopians to capture him and deliver him up as prisoner, and the British war correspondents letting the British public know of the efforts of Mission 101. The Italians spoke of him as a mad, bald and ageing English onion grower who was spying for Britain; the British papers spoke of a bespectacled, bald and cheerful man of fifty-eight. Even his Ethiopian pseudonym of *Fikre Mariam*, or 'love of Mary' was hardly a name to conjure up ideas of a dashing hero performing daring deeds. He never tried to mislead the Ethiopians as to his role, and his remarks at the beginning of the mission were to have profound effect on Azazh Kebede, the Emperor's representative. As final plans were made to enter Ethiopia, Dan spoke to Kebede and explained that, on this particular job, he was a British officer and under British Command, not an adviser to the Ethiopian Government as he had been in Maji. This upset and concerned Azazh Kebede, because he felt that they were no longer equal companions but superiors and subordinates together. He said that in small matters they did not disagree, and because of the common cause, they worked together, but at the same time this blunt speaking by Dan must make them inclined to drift apart. Whether, in truth, this drifting apart really occurred it is difficult to tell, but it had no effect on the successful conclusion of the Mission nor on their future relationship together. Dan was adviser in the Municipality when Azazh Kebede was Mayor, and later on Kebede was to send his children to the school that Chris opened in Addis Ababa.

14

CHRIS IN ENGLAND AND HER RETURN TO ETHIOPIA

When Dan left England in August 1939 both he and Chris knew that war was inevitable. The preparations that so many families put into effect were started with everyone helping. A shelter was dug in the garden near the tennis court and a good strong roof was put upon it. Electricity was laid on from the house and it was made as snug as possible. It was never used but spoke of the determination of so many thousands of ordinary people to be ready for when the time came. Chris had a great deal on her plate and in her imperturbable way took on a great deal more than was necessary. She tried to go on helping with the Appeal for Guildford Cathedral, though she never actually took Dan's place. She brought Audrey home from being at St. Dunstan's in Plymouth and taught her at home with the others. The two children of a Dr. Brown also joined the makeshift schoolroom and had lessons with Chris and with K.T., who became a permanent fixture in the house. Chris's parents were both there as well and needed considerable attention. Christine, the eldest daughter, joined the ATS for a short while before starting on her medical studies at the Royal Free Hospital. The next two were still at boarding school. Chris got down to using the vegetable garden to the full and providing most of the vegetables needed for the family. She bought some chickens to keep the family in eggs, and over the years, many were eaten and others pickled in a liquid called Eggo. The chickens alternatively chose the tennis court or the coal house to live in and often had to be chased from invading the vegetable garden. There was usually some kind of help in the house with a succession of people coming in from the village. There was also a dour gardener rather past the job, called Mr Mitchener. Despite a wooden leg he used to vault onto his bike at the end of the day's work in a remarkably athletic way. A plum fell into Chris's lap rather later on during the war, when a great wave of children were evacuated from south east London and took up residence in a camping site in Ewhurst and this was turned into a school. A mother of one of the boys, a Mrs Hinkley, also wished to come and live in Ewhurst to be near her son. Having been a nursemaid in the Mildmay family, she was also a first class cook. Chris immediately offered her house room and wages, and she became an institution until her family moved back to London.

Once Italy had joined Germany and declared war, Chris seized an opportunity of a different kind. On a Sunday evening, the BBC were in the habit of playing all the national anthems of the allies and then taking each country in turn and playing some of their songs. Accepting this as a challenge, Chris wrote to the BBC and asked if they had any songs for Ethiopia or, if not, whether they would like her to provide some. In due course a response to her offer was received, and Chris and the four eldest children went up to the BBC where they recorded several of the songs they had heard while in Ethiopia. These songs were usually sung by the workmen on the farm round a bonfire on the lawn at Mulu, or by groups of girls who came singing at the end of the rains, bearing bunches of bright yellow daisies. They were traditional folk songs, but many of them, as they were sung, used to include names of the personages to whom they were being sung, in order to earn a few more coins as a present at the end. One would extol the prowess of Sandford who was so strong that he could plough without oxen; another would speak of the weaving done by my lady being as fine as a spider's web and so on. One of the songs involved some leaping into the air, accompanied by grunts of exertion. In another the high pitched ululation of joy had to be added. It was the greatest of fun for the quintet, and must have been at least a remarkable novelty for the engineers who recorded it. A short while later some of the family paid a visit to the Emperor's eldest daughter, Princess Tenegne Worq, who was living in Bath at the time and played the record in the hope of her approval. She was so highly amused that the words recorded may have meant rather more than the Sandfords realised. Be that as it may, the recordings were broadcast several times during the war.

In September of 1940 Chris's second daughter, Eleanor, left Wycombe Abbey and went to The Froebel Foundation to train as a teacher. Cash was always short and Chris went to several places to try to find assistance in paying fees. Discovering that the Drapers Guild had some bursaries to offer she took Eleanor up for an interview and an examination. She told her to wear her second best uniform, while Chris donned a shabby hat and coat. Whether these had the right results or whether her test scores were good enough cannot be known, but Eleanor was awarded a grant out of a fund called 'The Prison Trust' to pay for her training. It took her quite a time to live this down with the family. The third daughter, Audrey, was successful in getting into Wycombe Abbey School in 1940, and she was there for five terms before the United States Air Force took over the school as one of their bases in England. This happened just before Chris was planning to leave for Ethiopia, and entailed a hectic rush to procure her a place at Benenden School, which was evacuated to Newquay. Even Chris's imperturbability must have been hard-pressed by crises of these kinds.

Once the Emperor was back in Ethiopia and the Italians had been defeated, Dan became once more fully caught up in Ethiopian affairs and it was very natural that they should both make plans for Chris to return to Ethiopia to be with him. There was never any question in their minds that her place was by his side, even if it meant that the family would be split up.

In November of 1941 Dan came to England for a brief visit. He was there as the Personal Adviser to the Emperor, to help put the Ethiopian side in the negotiations on the Anglo-Ethiopian agreement. Once the Emperor had reached his capital and the Italians had retreated to other parts of Ethiopia and Eritrea, there arose the important matter of restoring the country to law and order and maintaining essential services. On the British side there was the Occupied Enemy Territory Administration, which had its headquarters in Nairobi. This was a very hard-working and efficient organisation that concerned itself with the setting up of ways and means for Italian families to leave the country, with the upkeep of roads and railways and with many other incidental tasks. The chief difficulty lay in deciding who was the legal power in Ethiopia, how soon the Emperor was going to be the real ruler and how long he would have to submit to the dictates of the British military command. Legal advisers to the OETA said that until a peace treaty had been signed with Italy on Eritrea, the King of Italy must remain the legal ruler of Ethiopia. This was of course an absurd situation, however legally defensible, and the problem of dual control had to be solved at the earliest possible moment. Chris's brother, Maurice Lush, was head of the OETA, at first in Addis Ababa and later in Eritrea. He and Dan had several serious arguments on the setting up of the Treaty and what should be contained in the document. Dan was in England from September to December in 1941 putting the Emperor's viewpoint and it was a great credit to both sides that the Anglo-Ethiopian agreement was drawn up and signed on 31 January 1942. It was a practical agreement, providing for collaboration and mutual assistance between two allies in order to restore order and to provide the Emperor with such assistance as would enable him to re-establish his administration. The agreement was to last for a minimum period of two years.

Once Dan returned to Ethiopia, Chris began to make her plans to return also. Several relatives and friends tried to persuade her against travelling during wartime and against leaving four of her children to fend for themselves in war-stricken England. She never wavered in her purpose, however, and when all found that she was determined, then, as ever, the family accepted the need to give her all the help they could. K.T. Stephenson decided to go with her and to make her permanent home in Ethiopia. Chris took the two youngest children, Philippa aged nine, and Stephen aged seven, with her. Her father had died in December 1940 and her mother had decided to stay on at Brookside. From that time on Brookside held a series of companions to look after Granny Lush and also a succession of older relatives to keep an eye on her and on the four young left behind. This, of course, was in the main regarded by the young as quite unnecessary and often rather trying. What an exhausting but at the same time triumphant period the first half of 1942 must have been for Chris. In England the house had to be settled and plans made for all the occupants. Christine was at medical school, Eleanor was training to be a teacher, Dick was Head Boy at Shrewsbury, in his last year before joining the army, and Audrey was at Wycombe Abbey, a school soon to be taken over by the US Air Force. She had to persuade the War Office, the Foreign Office and several other authorities, that it was right and proper for her to be given a passage on a troopship out to the most convenient port for Ethiopia, and not only for herself, but for an elderly companion and two young children as well. It says much for her determination and her certainty that it was right, that she accomplished her objective. Her success must have been at least partly due to the countless kind friends in high places who were called upon to speak for her. Suffice it to say that some time in April she sailed from Bristol. The story goes that, as she was sitting in the train at Guildford, ready to depart, each of her four older children was called in one by one, to receive her final injunctions before the party of four set off on their adventure.

The troopship they travelled on was part of a convoy going out to the Far East via South Africa. The family sat at the First Mate's table and the inevitable happened during the voyage; K.T. and Chris taught some of the officers either Latin or mathematics. Off Cape Town, German submarines attacked the convoy and the ships in front and behind them veered off as they were struck by torpedoes. As all were standing on deck at danger stations the irrepressible Stephen won admiring glances from the troops by singing, "And if we're parted by a shot, we're sure to meet below," a theme not fully appreciated by his sister. The fortunate four disembarked at Durban, where they were immensely pleased to be on African soil again, where there were tropical fruit and vegetables and no rationing. From there the epic journey continued overland to Ethiopia and it was Chris who had to do all the planning and organisation, and yet one thing stands out clearly in the memories of the two children – she remained calm and imperturbable throughout. They travelled by train and bus and eventually by car.

In Northern Rhodesia, they stayed with Dan's brother, Tom, and his wife, Ray, and their daughter, Madeleine, with her two little boys. On the border of the Belgian Congo in the middle of a forest, one document Chris was asked to sign demanded the maiden name of her grandmother. This was a curious practice in south-west African colonies, because something like twenty years later, one of her daughters was asked to do exactly the same thing when landing in Angola. In Kampala in Uganda the group met Padre Matthew, who had been, and was to be again, chaplain in Addis Ababa. They met the Singers in Kenya. They had been very good friends in the 1920s in Addis Ababa and were to meet there again after the war. Once they reached Nairobi, the hope of any public transport was at an end. The only way that they could get to Ethiopia was either by being given a place in a military vehicle or by buying a car and driving up on their own. Neither of these options seemed to be looked on with great favour by the military authorities, who started by saying that there was no room on the military bus that was going up on the next convoy, which, in any case, was starting almost at once. The time had come for changing into top gear on decision making, and here a piece of good luck dropped into Chris's lap. She went to a bank manager in Nairobi to see if she could arrange to borrow some money in order to buy a car for the journey. As luck would have it, the same manager was looking after the son of the manager working for the same bank in Ethiopia, and was not finding the task easy. He seized the opportunity to make a bargain. If Chris would take the boy as an extra passenger, he would expedite the necessary loan. Nothing daunted, Chris agreed, went ahead and bought a Ford V8 van. It was bad luck that the garage selling the van was so enthusiastic about getting it into tiptop condition for the journey, that they painted it freshly both inside and out without allowing sufficient time for the paint to dry. The whole of the inside, painted milk chocolate brown, had to be covered with newspapers to save both passengers and luggage from the wet paint. A busy day was spent buying six weeks' supplies of food and petrol, with the help of Padre Matthew and Otto Singer. Five passengers and mountains of luggage were then piled in and the party set off on a first most tiring day to reach Nanyuki in order to catch up with the convoy there. A straightforward journey was made even less probable by two further developments. Philippa broke her thumb as soon as they started, and, the bank manager's son threatened to be car sick, whether from wilfulness or whether from the smell of wet paint, none ever knew. Philippa's thumb was bound up and the unlucky boy was told by Chris, in her most determined and compelling voice, that he was not allowed to be sick until they reached camp that night. Such was her tone of authority that the boy obeyed her implicitly. When they reached Nanyuki, however, he demonstrated the reality of his complaint.

Travelling with a convoy of army trucks over poor roads and tracks and through desert scrubland is not an easy task for an ordinary car, and the convoy's low speed combined with the heat of the day forced the Ford V8 to boil at frequent intervals. Their military companions took pity on the overloading of the car and removed the petrol to store in one of the lorries. They also put Stephen into the front lorry of the convoy and Philippa into the back lorry, which itself frequently broke down. At one moment a crisis flared up between the CO and Chris, when he suggested that she and K.T. could travel on the bus carrying ladies and families, on which, earlier on, she had been told there was no room, and that he would drive the van himself. The offer was refused with some firmness. Matters came to the boiling point in more ways than one when the convoy reached the climb up the escarpment near Mega. This is a steady climb of about two thousand feet and the slow pace of the convoy was too much for the van which boiled several times. Chris begged to be allowed to go on by herself at her own pace, but this was considered too dangerous. However, after the van had been brought to the last of countless halts with a boiling radiator, the CO told her to go ahead and suffer the consequences. With enormous relief, Chris and the family roared on ahead, reached the top of the escarpment with no difficulty and stopped under a tree for the convoy to catch them up. There was no dangerous enemy awaiting them there, only an old man with a flock of goats, who offered her some milk for the children.

Other memories of this journey included meeting an Italian prisoner of war, somewhere near Nanyuki, reading *The Lady in White*, and camping near a bombed Italian chapel with painted frescoes on the walls. The campsite at Yavello was the best remembered. The family were putting up the tent in the rain on a hillside overlooking the small town of Yavello, when a message came rippling through the camp. "Your husband has arrived, Mrs Sandford." The reunion had been made. After that they left the convoy and went on their own. Almost the last great memory of the journey was the distant sight of Addis Ababa, with black thunderclouds gathering over Entoto, perceived from a picnic site near Akaki. The journey had been accomplished, and they were once more in Ethiopia, where they were to stay for the rest of their lives.

15

THE YEARS OF RECONSTRUCTION 1941-1945

Reading through the files and letters that deal with this period in the lives of Chris and Dan is rather like looking at an old black and white film that is being projected too fast. One feels quite breathless at the hectic jumble of people and events as they rush past. The figures seem to move in a series of jerky encounters, each rapidly breaking up and yielding to an equally spasmodic successor. One thing is certain, life was not dull and Dan, with his insatiable appetite for tackling problems and trying to find solutions for them, had little time to sit back and relax.

By the end of 1941, the Anglo-Ethiopian agreement was being worked out in preparation for signing by the Emperor and the British Government in January 1942. The control of Ethiopia was threefold. There was the Emperor, anxious to regain his personal power, but knowing quite clearly that he had to rely on his ally for financial, advisory and military help in areas still harbouring Italian resistance. There was the Occupied Enemy Territory Administration under Sir Philip Mitchell, with Maurice Lush as his deputy. This organisation was there to keep law and order in a country from which the enemy had been expelled and to see that enemy civilians were cared for and helped to leave. The fact that they were not in enemy territory but in the country of an ally, did not make it any easier for them to operate. The third control was the British military force. They were still engaged in active warfare against pockets of Italian resistance, with the help of Ethiopian troops. In consequence many areas had to be under their jurisdiction. Furthermore, they bore the burden of much of the financing of the Ethiopian troops, and put certain unsettled areas out of bounds for Ethiopian Government control. Dan, as the Emperor's personal and military adviser, was the focal point for a great deal of the discussions and arguments, acrimonious and otherwise, that had to take place, before Ethiopia under her Emperor could emerge as a united and progressing country. It is interesting, at this moment, to remember the phases of Dan's life up to date. He was trained for the army, he had been an Administrative Officer in the Sudan, and he had been an adviser to a Governor at Maji. In this he was well equipped to understand precisely how all three controlling bodies approached their negotiations. Over and above all this his own views were sufficiently firm and well-informed for him to maintain a sound judgement.

Dan's role in the negotiations that led up to the signing of the Anglo-Ethiopian Agreement in January 1942, was a very arduous one. He was not only the mouthpiece of the Emperor but also, in many respects his adviser. At the same time the British side regarded him as a convenient auditor of things that none would have dared addressing to the Emperor himself. Charles Matthew, the legal adviser to the Ethiopian Government, Austin Matthew, the Anglican Chaplain who had arrived from Jerusalem with a large party of Ethiopian refugees and Dan, shared the same house, and the flies on the walls must have heard many a fiery battle of words being waged when negotiators, including Maurice Lush, came in to discuss matters. Dan spent three months in England at the end of 1941, negotiating the draft terms of the agreement and joining in meetings presided over by Sir John Anderson and attended by Anthony Eden. He returned to Addis Ababa in December 1941 and it was nearly another two months before the agreement was finally signed. It was with Sir Philip Mitchell and Maurice Lush that the final terms of the Treaty had to be worked out and agreed. There were times when the two brothers-in-law were in total disagreement and their tempers were often strained but, as Dan wrote in February 1942, 'in the end the signatures were affixed in an atmosphere of great friendliness all round and reasonable satisfaction on both sides. I think it is a sound document, taken as a whole and the two responsible parties, the Emperor and Sir Philip Mitchell deserve credit.'

Shortly after the signing of the Anglo-Ethiopian agreement, Dan took up the post of adviser to the Ministry of the Interior. This meant that he became involved in a large number of schemes to get governmental machinery working in a way that would not only make the Ethiopian people realise that the Emperor was determined to establish law and order, but also satisfy the British military and political personnel that Ethiopia could rule herself, once British help had been withdrawn. In another of his letters to Chris, he writes . . . 'one of the most delicate jobs I have is the choosing of the British personnel to stay on under the agreement . . . My chief reason for coming down here (Nairobi), is to get half a dozen men whom I have got my eye on.' In another letter he writes of getting things moving in the Departments of War, Communications and Commerce. Of all the British Advisers that came and went during the following ten years, perhaps the two that stood out most were Charles Matthew as Legal Adviser and Frank Stafford as Financial Adviser. However there were many others working for the OETA and for the military presence in the country who did a tremendous amount of sterling work before they left for other duties.

Maurice Lush was in the forefront of those who came to help Ethiopia get back on to an even keel, but he and Dan did not always see eye to eye and it says much for the two of them that, once business matters had been dealt with, all friction could be forgotten and real friendship continued. One of Dan's letters of 21 March 1942 says: 'Maurice came back from Harar on Friday . . . we had a sparring match on the 'phone . . . the fact is that I am a red rag to a bull to him and all who think like him. They think I am blind to the faults of the Ethiopians and am out to spoil any plans sponsored by the OETA . . . Of course the Ethiopian is as irritating as can be and little do they know of the number of times Charles and I face each other across the table, shaking our fists to heaven and screaming a hymn of hate against some futility and the obstructiveness of those we try to serve.' One of the most interesting facets of the British military and political presence in Ethiopia was the way in which the different provinces of Ethiopia were dealt with. Where there were pockets of Italian resistance or Italian fostered resistance, the British military presence was of major importance. Although the Emperor appointed a Governor, the British had the final word on what areas were completely under military control, and maintaining the delicate balance between these two authorities, depended entirely on the personal characteristics of the two. In other provinces, which bordered on to Kenya, the Sudan, or British Somaliland, the complications were a little different. The British officers were there to advise and direct the Ethiopian Governors, and see that British money was spent in the best way possible. There was also the eternal problem of borders, where one side was always certain that any marauding elements were from across the border and therefore blamed the ineptitude of the authority responsible for them. In most cases these matters were dealt with pretty efficiently, with British and Ethiopian officials co-operating together. In his position as adviser to the Ministry of the Interior, Dan was the central point to whom many of the reports were sent, so that he could sort out the problems and refer them to the right departments.

It may be of interest to look at two of the provinces and their different problems during this time of change. In Wollo Province in 1941 Major Kenyon-Slaney was SPO at Dessie, and very comprehensive and detailed exchanges of information were passed between him and Dan. There was considerable unrest in the province, where the Wajiral Gallas were opposed to the Emperor and had been given large quantities of arms by the Italians, in order to disrupt road communications over a large area. Action to subdue them had to be taken by the Ethiopian Army, not the British. However, everything had to be directed through the British presence. The village of Cobbo was the centre of the Galla insurrection. The agreed strategy was to weaken the rebels by attacking the village from the air, and later destroying it on the ground. But everything possible was done to limit the damage and unnecessary loss of life. Women and children were urged to evacuate the place and the rebels themselves allowed some time in which to hand in their weapons. The plan was eventually carried out by Ethiopian forces and was successful. At the same time as this type of military action was taking place, arrangements were being made for the transport of large quantities of grain to the north. Conditions in prisons, generally poor, was being improved, Italians were being repatriated, as were eight hundred Sudanese living near Dessie, the capital of the province. Another very able Britisher, called Hugh Foot Gaitskill, appeared on the scene in 1942. On 28 August, Dan wrote to him as he was about to pay a visit to Dessie, to suggest various things that needed to be carried out. The Governor of Wollo was the Crown Prince and his deputy was Col. Asfaw. Dan advised Foot Gaitskill to try to establish good relations with Col. Asfaw by giving the impression that he had come to help rather than to inspect. He should try to find out about the budget; whether the administrative machinery laid down for the province existed; whether the police force was operating properly; whether the prisons were working; whether instructions about the surveillance of enemy aliens were being carried out; what restrictions on movement were being enforced and what taxes were collected along the road; and miscellaneous other matters including Public Relief and Medical Services.

The second province to be looked at was that of Jimma, where many of the problems were the same as Wollo's. The reports sent in from the members of the British administration, however, had a certain racy quality which gave them a peculiar distinction. One of the points of dissension was vehicles. The Emperor, when on a visit to Jimma, had noticed a certain number of vehicles including two buses, that he urgently required. As a telegram from one British General to another said: 'The Emperor is under the mistaken impression that the British are deliberately starving him of transport . . . His African mentality will not understand that the proper course is to wait until they have been brought in and distributed by British military authorities here . . . Lush recommends that, although this procedure is irritating and untidy, he should be given the transport in the hope that this will end a cause of continual unwarranted friction.' The Emperor gained two buses and five cars! But, as one can imagine, the expressions and the words, rather than the deeds, were what hurt. One of the problems in Jimma province was Fitaurari Geressa, who had been Governor of Jimma until he was removed for malpractice; he had then organised his own band of rebels against the government and the British administrators. He presented a highly complicated problem, his misdemeanours including the abduction of some Italian from hospital and an attempt to remove several vehicles from Jimma. And yet, despite all this, he was rumoured – however improbably – to have joined forces with Ababa Aregai, most loyal of Patriots. One British report gave brief notes on the Ethiopian personalities with whom the British had to deal. Some were nominally allies, others were openly rebels but almost all were difficult to deal with.

In 1943 a man who ultimately became a close friend of the family, Major Sandy Curle, arrived in Jimma to take up his post as Adviser. He sent very regular reports in to Dan, almost all of them positive and constructive in their attitude to the problems. He was deeply concerned to see that trade, agriculture, roads and other facilities were developed as quickly as possible. Dan wrote to him several times to the following effect: 'I am finding your letters most useful. Try as far as possible to omit remarks that will cause resentment if I circulate them.' And again: 'Please, like a good fellow, refrain from the joy which it gives you of adding phrases and comments in your letters in such a form that I cannot circulate them.' – 'Apart from this his reports and letters were quite excellent.' Major Curle found that, as ever, the chief problem was a question of finance; the buying power of money was very low and the pay due to police, soldiers and prison officers was several months in arrears. Under persistent pressure generated by Curle's reports, the prisons were gradually improved, schools started and trading increased. In May 1944 Dan wrote to Curle to say that he was handing over to Dallas in the Ministry of the Interior, and added, 'It has been very pleasant working with you and I am sorry the official link is now snapped.' Their personal friendship nevertheless continued, because when Sandy

Curle took up the post of HMG's Consul in Addis Ababa he and his wife became very interested in the school Chris was to start, Mrs Cecil Curle being one of the first teachers to join the staff. They were both wonderful characters, flamboyant and dynamic and in future years the British Community remembered with affection, the sight of Sandy swinging from the rafters in the Ras Hotel, at a St. Andrew's night ball.

The early 1940s were a most exciting and absorbing time for Dan and all the other advisers, mainly British, to be in Ethiopia. There was a tremendous amount of work to be done in setting out the structure, mechanism, and financing of government departments. During 1941 Dan drafted some notes on the system of administration in Ethiopia, and these were discussed with other advisers, notably Charles Matthew and Frank Stafford. In April 1942 Dan produced a draft set of regulations for the 'Organisation of the Ministry of the Interior', and Stafford produced a similar one for the officials and staff of the Ministry of Finance in the Provinces. Three months later Dan was still waiting for the Emperor's Private Secretary to tell him what the Emperor's views were. In July 1942 Dan wrote a Memorandum on 'Improvements in the Machinery of Government'. It seems that this was mainly an effort to suggest ways of speeding up and implementing decision-making. In March 1943 he produced another draft, this time entitled 'Outline of Programme of the Ministry of Interior', and in May some notes were written on 'The Reform of the Ministry of the Interior'. In all these notes and memoranda there were three major elements that had to be recognised and dealt with: responsibility, time and money. Responsibility needed to be delegated, from the Emperor through his ministers and ministries, passing on to provincial governors, right down to the municipal secretariats. What was actually happening was that decision making and subsequent action were being held up, right at the top, in the Council of Ministers. Punctuality was essential when paying salaries and preparing budgets and all too often action was delayed because the information on which it could be based was not forthcoming. It was difficult to send money out to the provinces when contracts of salaries and questions of tax had not been resolved. Another factor in the urgency of all these matters seemed to be the visits of various dignitaries from Great Britain, coming to discuss matters of State. Over and over again Dan was obliged to suggest that the various drafts and decisions should be ready before the visit of such people as Lord Moyne and Duncan Sandys.

Once back in Addis Ababa, Chris settled down to the familiar routine of education, of entertaining visiting delegations and of providing house room and respite to the many expatriates engaged in various jobs.

Many of the old servants had turned up when Dan arrived back in 1941, but alas, not Nanny Tziggie. She was too ill to be there to greet him, but he did see her once before she died. Hapte Michael still reigned in the kitchen, Wolde Mariam was promoted from groom to house boy and Haile from the kitchen to be general factotum. When their parents were entertaining, Stephen and Philippa took note of the excellent dishes carried along the back passage to the dining-table. They also noticed that Wolde and Haile supported themselves during the exertions of serving the meal by making sure that all half-empty glasses were dry by the time they got back to the kitchen. This may have been the reason for Hapte Michael's drunken protests at being deprived of his share. Out in the driveway, the car boy, Ambassie, would be looking closely at all the visitors' cars. If he noticed that any of them had a particular gadget or piece of equipment not to be found on the Sandford's car, he would quietly detach it while the car owner was being dined inside. Spare parts were almost impossible to find at that time in Addis Ababa, and you drove your car until it fell to pieces round you. In his own view Ambassie was merely being imaginative and loyal to his master, but irate telephone calls would be received by the Sandfords the following day and return of the precious items demanded. On one occasion, as Dan was arriving back home, after having been in his office in the palace grounds, he turned a sharp corner and the bottom of his Arditta car just fell off. On another occasion Dan was teaching Philippa, aged eleven, to drive the car down the drive of the house and insisted that she went nearer the wall to improve her parking. Obeying his "go on, go on," she drove into the wall and knocked it down.

With Dan in his position of adviser, there were a great many social engagements which he and Chris had to attend and reciprocate. Chris had a special pink dress with a bolero and both had diamanté decoration on them. This dress lasted for years as one for special functions. It eventually ended up in the costume cupboard of the English School and went on adorning stage theatricals. Right through this period and for many years to come, Chris and Dan met an enormous number of extremely interesting people from all walks of life and with all manner of political, governmental and economic reasons for visiting Ethiopia or for staying there to work. The anecdotes about these personalities are many and often amusing. Wilfred Thesiger, adviser to the Crown Prince in Wollo, used to come into Addis Ababa and stay with the Sandfords and be coerced into attending social functions. He would get ready for a dinner party chanting the while, "What shall I put on Mama, to walk in the heavenly throng?" Col. Doll who was part of the peace treaty delegation led by Earl de la Warr, would come to the house to play the piano for relaxation. Sir Ronald Storrs, out on a three day visit, entertained the Sandfords by whistling hymns and classical music to his own piano accompaniment. One gentleman, who worked at the British Museum, spent the whole evening after dinner chasing a small green moth as it flitted round the room. The ceilings were so high that a step ladder had to be brought in and held by the ever useful Ambassie while this octogenarian lepidopterist clambered up with his net. Dan warned his two children that, should the Emperor ever have reason to telephone the house he would announce his presence by saying, 'C'est moi'. Dan would telephone the house and say 'C'est Moi' and the children never knew who it really was. He would also tell the story of an Ethiopian colleague being seen talking to the Emperor on the telephone, bowing continually as he spoke and being rather annoyed when laughed at by Dan.

The first time that the family went out to Mulu Farm after their return was in September 1942, just at the end of the rainy season. Philippa, who was then nine years old, recalls it vividly. 'We drove out of Addis Ababa along the road and were met by horses and carriers at Debeli's house, just before the Sibilo river. It was just before the feast of *Maskal*, but the river was still very flooded. We had acquired horses by then and the two I remember were the white mule, Georgina, which K.T. rode and Sultan, a big brown horse which was Dad's and the only one tall enough to be capable of riding across the river. So he made the crossing at least four times, bearing Mum, Dad, K.T. and me in turn. Stephen was deemed too small to manage him alone, so he was carried like a sack over someone's shoulder with the water lapping very close to his face. I remember being terrified, with one stalwart leading the horse and another clinging on to me and the stirrup leather, and probably shouting, "*Izosh, Izosh*". The river was rising and the last few got across just as grass came floating past, and it was now deemed to be too dangerous for anyone else to cross. It had taken a long time to get that far and we set off towards Mulu in the rain and mud. It was certainly dark as we got to the River Aleltu. K.T. fell off Georgina as she toppled into a hole but remounted and continued with her back bowed in a silent, stoical way. Stephen also fell off and his horse, Spotty, bolted. We arrived at Mulu to find a shell of a house and took refuge in the only room that did not leak, the room next to what ended up as Dad's office. I remember Mum feeding us on hot tea and brandy. I wish I could remember more of Mum and Dad's feelings, because it must have been an epic home-coming, but I do remember the excitement of it all. The next day was beautifully sunny and we put up the big tent inside the drawing-room. People started arriving and I remember Zoldi in particular. He had been chief gardener at Mulu ever since the early 1920s. Various articles started arriving too. Chairs left on the edge of the lawn, the leopard skin, torn and shaggy with its green surround, and finally the top of the round dining-room table, without its legs. The lawn still had indentations in it where the flower beds had been, and the rose bushes sported a few straggly flowers. That day or the next we went down to the pagan ceremony of the blessing of the river.'

The position of Mulu Farm was rather indeterminate at this time. At the time of the Emperor's coronation in 1932, the farm had been handed over to the Empress – the partnership came to an end and the Sandfords simply paid a rent. In 1935, when Dan had gone to Maji and Chris had taken the children to England before the Italian invasion, Mr Ossent, Dan's Swiss partner, had taken over the management of the farm. However, when the Italians had taken over, the Sandfords had agreed that the Ossents should make what they could of the farm during the occupation. Mr Ossent did not live out at Mulu, for safety reasons, but ran the town side of the farm business, thus becoming an absentee landlord. After the recovery of the country Dan was fully occupied with his work in Addis Ababa, and had no time for looking after Mulu. Now Chris returned and the house at the farm was refurbished and made usable. The time was then ripe for totally new negotiations. Many people privately thought that the farm should be a gift to Chris and Dan, but this was not apparently feasible and Dan himself never really expected it. While negotiations were going on to arrange a new lease, some Ethiopian friend told Dan that he had heard that Mr Ossent was in fact negotiating to secure the lease for himself. This caused some ill-feeling and Dan and his friends asked for a 'commizzione' to be set up to decide the issue. This was done and Dan was granted the lease. Until this conflict intervened the children of the two families had often played together and visited each others' houses but the Ossents put an end to this when the dispute started. Once Dan had been given the right to lease the farm, the Ossents left for Kenya and the produce from the farm came to the Sandford house and was sorted out there. The large slabs of butter were patted into smaller pieces and the strawberries were taken from their heavy cardboard cartons and put into smaller, lighter ones. The Sandfords acquired an old-fashioned tradesman's bicycle and Zerefu, the town trader, would go round with his butter and strawberries, selling to both shops and private people. From the Sandford's point of view, the farm was only a weekend and holiday farm at this time and was to stay so until 1949. This did not mean that they were at all casual about the farm business. On the contrary, lots of work was done to improve efficiency, especially in the output of strawberries, other fruit and vegetables, and flower gardens.

There was great excitement in the family in 1942 or 43 when Ealing Studios put out feelers about making a film on Mission 101. They came out to Addis Ababa and decided that the scenery round about the upper and lower farm would be ideal for making the film and for a short time there were great thoughts about how rich everyone would be made by the film rights, but, alas, nothing came of the plan except that the lorry the studios had bought to take timber and other effects out to Mulu, was given to the Sandfords. The lorry was nicknamed the Bussing Nag. From time to time the young in England would receive letters from their mother saying that the studios could not make up their minds whether to make Dan a young and handsome hero with some romantic connections with a beautiful dusky Ethiopian maiden or leave him as the stocky, bald, middle-aged colonel, with supposedly no romantic ideals at all. This was yet another wonderful idea for money-making that died before it could hope to materialise.

For the youngest two of the family Chris started the same sort of home education she had run before 1935. Philippa and Stephen had their school time-table and lessons in the house, and, as before, K.T. was there to help. But there was a difference. This time the house was in Addis Ababa, not Mulu, and right from the start there were other expatriate parents and Ethiopians who wished to have their children taught along with the two young Sandfords. K.T. taught maths and Latin and continued to be a martinet as regards time and quality of work. She would never, for example, let the children miss a minute of her lesson even when the fire engine arrived to top up the water tanks because water was short or had been cut off. The children delighted in playing with the leaky hoses and joining in the general mêlée, but not during K.T.'s lesson. Every evening, after homework had been done, a story was read to the two. Dan was sometimes able to take part; he would read Scott's novels and even some French, such as *Malplaquet, Le Mauvais Petit Chien*. When Dan was unavailable, K.T. would read something else and among her favourites were *Some Experiences of an Irish RM* or *The Casting Away of Mrs Lecks and Mrs Aleshine*.

They also became familiar with Shakespeare and the unwary visitor was often roped in to read a part.

Among the Ethiopian children who were helped at this time, there were five who deserve special mention. The first was Amaha Desta, the son of Princess Tenagne Worq, the Emperor's eldest daughter. He was an invalid but he used to come and be taught by both K.T. and Chris. Then there were 'The Four Boys' as they came to be known by the Sandford family, in both Ethiopia and England. They were Michael Imeru, son of Ras Imeru – a cousin of the Emperor, Amaha Aberra Kassa, grandson of Ras Kassa of Selahle, Zaudi Gebre Selassie and Endlecachew Makonnen, the son of Betwoded Makonnen who was married to a cousin of the Emperor. The four had their main education at the Haile Selassie Secondary School, where Amaha managed to get an incredible 110% for Amharic examination, but they certainly came to Chris for some tuition. Zaudi, who was always a little portly, used to arrive in a little Fiat, into which he could only just squeeze, and, as the car was not in prime condition, he frequently had to be pushed down the drive, in order to get it started. Later on in their careers, the four came to England in 1945 to continue their education, first at Malvern and Millfield and later at Oxford. They were still in regular contact with the Sandfords, because Tom, Dan's younger brother, became their guardian in England and they spent some holidays at the Sandford house, Brookside. There was a memorable Christmas holiday at Brookside, where charades were the order of the day and Zaudi, wrapped up in the green velvet dining-room tablecloth, made a very convincing nautch girl. The concluding event that Christmas was the quarter mile walk from the house to the bus-stop, with the four returning to school and Amaha's tightly packed case bursting its locks, spilling its contents all over the road and having to be repacked while an advance guard tried desperately to keep the bus waiting. All four, in their different spheres, made notable contributions to their country when they returned from Oxford, until the revolution in 1972. That tragic event killed one of them, imprisoned a second, and forced a third into exile.

Sunday evenings at the Sandfords became an institution

that was to last for many years. It was open house to anyone who wished, but Padre Austin Matthew always came. There were hymns with Chris at the piano and always ending with *Absent Friends* and *Now the Day is Over*. Then came the games, among which Shak, The Spirit Rests and Charades figured prominently. Chris also played the piano at the church on Sundays. Its original situation was near the Itegue Hotel, but it then moved to another building just off the Haile Selassie Street. Other memories of these four years are connected with various trips that the family made within Ethiopia itself. Some were brief, such as a trip to the Blue Nile with personnel from the British Embassy. During the climb up from the gorge, the lorry boiled and the water cap flew off. Steam spread everywhere, scalding those nearby. On another occasion there was a trip to Wolissu, during one night of which a hyena made off with a basket containing food, and dropped several things out of the basket as he made a large circle round the camp. One of the best remembered trips was one to Lalibela where there were over fifteen churches, all hewn out of the rock, standing below ground level. On the first night out, they were entertained by an old friend, Dejazmach Mengasha Aboyie, who allowed young Stephen to fire a machine-gun at the hillside opposite the camp. A few minutes later a local resident wandered down the path through the area at which he had been shooting, luckily still alive. The family went by lorry to Dessie where they were entertained by Wilfred Thesiger, Adviser to the Crown Prince. He was in a state of permanent shock at the amount of bread the Sandfords managed to consume, and was always having to send out for more. Their progress from Dessie by car to Waldia and then onto Lalibela by mule and caravan had the character of a royal visit. Dan had obtained official letters from the Crown Prince to all the local dignitaries, and at every camp there were gifts of *ingera*, *talla*, yoghurt and sheep. When they arrived at Lalibela they were shown all the churches by the priests and they had their camp moved from one site to another to enhance their view. Two incidents made their journey memorable. The family stopped by a river to join in the religious ceremony commemorating St. John the Baptist and the Epiphany, and Dan had a bell full of holy water poured all over him. Later on in the journey, Chris's and Dan's tent collapsed on the two of them during the night. Eight years later, when their second daughter, accompanied by two English teachers, did the same trip, with similar letters of introduction, she received the same generosity and courtesy which makes travelling in Ethiopia so rewarding.

Thus the period when Dan was adviser came to a close, but not as yet, his service to the Emperor and Ethiopia. 1945 was to open a decade of important events in the Sandfords' lives and bring about considerable changes and challenges.

16

1945-1956
FAMILY CHANGES, AND THE FOUNDING OF A SCHOOL

These years were to bring tremendous changes in the family as each of the Sandford children grew up, trained and got a job. It must have been very difficult for Chris and Dan to feel that they were really keeping in touch with their progeny, and giving them advice and support in all they were trying to do. At times they had to rely on help and suggestions from the several aunts and uncles who were in England. This did not always work out as well as might be expected, but it was characteristic of the family that of the six children, five came back to Ethiopia at some moment in their lives to work there. This was not because their parents held a domineering control over their lives, but because there were opportunities to be taken and work to be done, and because, in fact, life in Ethiopia offered them so much, especially the continued contact with their parents and the home they had made for the family in the twenties. A brief look at each member shows how much their background affected their futures. The eldest daughter, Christine, took up her medical training at the Royal Free Hospital in London in 1940. She had already met John Banting, whom she was to marry, while she was completing her training, and she and Eleanor, her sister, lived in a cramped attic in Taviton Street near Euston Station for two or three years towards the end of the war. Christine and John became engaged once he had returned from the Far East and he then went to Cambridge to read Engineering. Dan, in a letter to him mentioned that engineers were badly needed at that time in the Municipality in Addis Ababa and suggested that he might consider a post there, but this proposal was never followed up. Their wedding took place in 1947 at the church in Ewhurst, and Chris and Dan came back for the event, bringing with them Philippa and Stephen, both due to start school in England. All the remaining sisters were bridesmaids at this first wedding whose celebration was only temporarily jeopardised by the unwillingness of the dressmaker to believe that Philippa, aged thirteen, could be so much the tallest.

Eleanor finished her Froebel teachers training in 1943 and taught at Hampstead High School for Girls for four years, before spending a year at a small private school in Leatherhead, in order to be able to live at Brookside, where Chris's mother still lived and had broken a hip. She was then offered the chance to come and teach at Chris's school, and in the summer of 1948, she accompanied Philippa and Stephen out to Ethiopia to join the school staff. She was to stay there till 1976, first with her mother as her headmistress and later with her husband, Leslie Casbon, as her headmaster.

Dick, the eldest son, finished his schooling in 1942, at Shrewsbury, being head boy in his last year. He joined the army and was shipped out to India and then Burma. At the beginning of 1945 he was wounded during Japanese counter-attacks on a bridgehead over the Irawaddy River while trying without much success, to encourage some mules to cross. He spent some months in hospital in India and then returned to England.

Audrey, the fourth of the Sandford children, had a more chequered schooling and training than any of her brothers and sisters. In 1935, when she came back from Ethiopia at the beginning of the Italian invasion, she was first taught at home and then went to stay in Plymouth with Chris's brother, Cecil, and his family. Owing to wartime pressures her secondary schooling was split between the familiar Wycombe Abbey and Benenden, evacuated to Newquay. Later, denied the musical training which was her first preference, she took a diploma in Domestic Science, and, subsequently, a secretarial course. In the meantime she studied singing privately. She then accompanied Dan to Ethiopia in 1947, after her sister's wedding, and served him for a year as private secretary when he became Director General of the Municipality. In 1948, before returning to England, she became engaged to Bartie Knight, one of the wartime Friends Ambulance Unit in Ethiopia. They were married in 1949 and lived at Brookside for over a year while he completed a degree in English. The place was kept open for Philippa and Stephen, both at boarding school and Audrey, at least, had an opportunity to continue studying singing as she had always wanted.

Philippa went to Wycombe Abbey for her secondary education and then continued her training at Egerton College of Agriculture in Kenya, where she obtained a diploma in Agriculture. After Stephen finished his schooling at Shrewsbury, he spent a short period of time in Germany, on military service, and then went to Oxford with the idea of joining the Colonial Service. While they were living in England their older sisters were able to offer them homes and shelter, either at Brookside, until it was sold, or in their own houses. Christine, the eldest, was in medical practice in Rugby where her husband John was with BEC. Their home there and later in Worcestershire, was a haven, not only for brothers and sisters, but later for the next generation. Christine was the only one of the Sandfords' children who did not come out to Ethiopia to work there, but even she came and spent six months helping at the Princess Tshai Hospital while 'on holiday'.

Early in 1945 Dan wrote to the Emperor, saying that he did not feel fully occupied at the Palace, especially as he was 'a man of energy and experience' and that he felt that he would like his position to be on a contractual basis. He suggested that, as well as his present duties, he might do an advisory job, either to the Prime Minister or to the President of the Chamber of Deputies. Another suggestion that he made was that he and Chris might be attached to the Ministry of Education, he as Adviser in General and she to assist in particular with female education. A few months later, the Minister of the Pen, *Tsafe Tizaz*, Wolde Giorghis, approached Dan to ask if he would consider accepting an executive post. Dan replied that he would consider any attractive post which, for special reasons, the Government could not adequately fill with an Ethiopian. "Then," said the Minister, "I offer you the town of Addis Ababa." This was the post of Director General of the Addis Ababa Municipality. In June 1945, Dan's contract was signed as Director General of the Addis Ababa Municipality. He was to stay at the Municipality for three and a half years, and though he found the work absorbing and interesting, he also found being in an executive position a tremendous and rather frustrating strain. Of necessity he had his finger in every pie. For much of the time everything ran smoothly. Occasionally, however, the administration faltered and demanded extra attention. Sir Patrick Abercrombie, the well known British town planner, was asked out to Addis Ababa early in Dan's time of office. He prepared plans for the development of the town as a model city in all respects. Sir Patrick was accompanied by his daughter, Deb, who livened up Addis Ababa society. She made an instant hit with the British Military Mission in Ethiopia and 'Deb's Colonels' were much in evidence when she was around. She also shocked K.T. with the shortness of her skirts. Sir Patrick did not stay long but some efforts were made to make use of his plan. He felt that he had never received adequate remuneration for his work and, when he was asked to help find a well qualified and interested town planner from England, there were delays and changes of plans, with each side blaming the other for the breakdowns of negotiations. An English town planner never did materialise and Sir Patrick himself returned to Ethiopia only once. In September 1947 a Five Year Plan for Addis Ababa was drawn up, and Dan himself was responsible for much of the drafting.

The plan, together with estimated costs and proposals for fund raising, was divided into eight sections. These included town planning, water supplies coupled with the building of reservoirs, communications, road-building, sewage and rubbish disposal (in which respect nothing could beat the nocturnal hyenas for efficiency), health services, housing and finally various installations such as markets, lorry parks and municipal buildings. Dan's daughter, Audrey, helped with the typing of the five year plan as did their extremely co-operative and efficient translator, an Ethiopian called Shamsu. The topic of building reservoirs brings back memories of a revealing interview given many years later by the Ethiopian Director General of the Municipality. During a shortage of water in the town he was asked why such a thing had been allowed to happen by the municipal authorities. He replied with perfect sincerity that there was no shortage of water in Addis Ababa; there were merely more people living in the town.

One particularly urgent need that Dan felt in his time at the Municipality, was knowledgeable technicians to ensure the practical running of the various departments. Many of the most efficient of these were Italians, and employing the past enemy was always a slight problem. There was one very notable Italian, called Signor Branca, in charge of the water system, who was very courteous and urbane. None considered asking him to leave, because he was much too efficient and, in fact, quite irreplaceable. The head of WHO, a Greek named Dr Messinezy, was most helpful in matters of public health. He and his wife became good friends of the Sandfords, and Dan used to enjoy teasing the lady who was readily persuaded to believe absurd improbabilities. She helped Chris for some time in the school. Later their daughter went to Wycombe Abbey school. Another great character who appeared in the Municipality at this time was 'Ginger' Marshall. He was a strong-minded and hard-working Englishman who had worked with the fire brigade in Cairo. In Addis Ababa he was put in charge of the Municipality garage, where he had control of the fire engines, the hearses, the dust carts and anything else that was mechanical. As can be guessed from his name, he had red hair and a red moustache and a temper to match. He became a firm friend of the family, and used to come to the Sunday evenings at the house and play his accordion. One of the stories of Ginger Marshall was that he was asked to help move a lion from the Palace to other accommodation at *Sidist Kilo*. Resisting all cajolement, the lion refused to move into the cage that was to transport it to its new home. So Ginger decided to place a large mirror at the back of the new cage. As soon as the lion saw its reflection it leapt into the cage and smashed the mirror with its paw, but not before the door of the cage was shut quickly behind it.

In the summer of 1945 Chris and Dan tried to get back to England, mainly in order to see their eldest son, who had been wounded. However, with the war in Europe just ending, they and the two youngest children, Philippa and Stephen, having gone as far as Cairo, could find no transport to England. Money was running very short and eventually only Dan went on. As ever, since they were in Egypt, they made the most of their time there, with visits to the Pyramids and Sphinx, the museum, the City of the Dead, and Groppi's, a restaurant famous for its ice cream. Chris returned to Ethiopia with the children, and in order to make a little money she went to Harar and taught at a school there. K.T. Stephenson and the two children accompanied her.

The British Council had come to Ethiopia in 1944 and had started making a great contribution to education and educational facilities in several places in the country. At Harar, one of the cities chosen, a British Council Centre and a girls' school had been set up. Miss Margery Copeman, who ran the school, was on leave and Chris had offered to take her place, while at the same time K.T. agreed to run the British Council Centre.

In Harar the two children were taught at home, but Philippa unwillingly attended sewing and piano lessons at a convent. From them she derived no enjoyment at all. This stay in Harar must have lasted for about four or five months and meant that one Christmas had to be spent there by the family. The Christmas was memorable for two reasons; the first was the Christmas dinner, in the shape of a sucking-pig which made a gallant effort to avoid the pot on Christmas Eve by rushing down the road with Haile in hot pursuit. The second piece of excitement came on Christmas morning itself, when Philippa managed to set the tree alight when lighting the candles. In spite of these misadventures, the Sandford family Christmas was a happy one, despite Dan's absence in England.

Once back in Addis Ababa after their Harar adventure, Chris began to consider the question of starting a school far more seriously. Her own children would be going back to England for their secondary education in 1947 and it was already obvious how much need existed for schooling for expatriate children, whose fathers had jobs of sorts in Addis Ababa. There were schools for missionary children, a French Lycee and an Italian School. Educational facilities for Ethiopians had been badly neglected during the Italian occupation, and though the Emperor was putting all possible emphasis on the restoration of a sound system, there remained much to be done. The British Council was giving a great deal of aid, not only in running a centre where there were evening classes, a library and a cultural centre, but also in providing British teachers to run schools. The General Wingate School, a secondary school for boys, was funded entirely by the British Council, and in many other ways they gave assistance. In Addis Ababa itself and all over Ethiopia schools were being set up, and British teachers, among others, were coming in to help administer them. Members of the Friends Ambulance Unit, which had first come in 1942, stayed behind and took on many other types of work. Michael Vaizey became the doctor in charge of health at the Ministry of Education, Bartie Knight, was now teaching English at the Greek Community School. Ken Tipper was headmaster of another school and Harold Waller took on the running of an orphanage in Addis Ababa. Selby Clewer became architect to the Ministry of Education and frequently helped Dan with advice on town planning.

The Friends Ambulance Unit, first founded in the 1914-1918 War was reinstituted in 1939 to provide conscientious objectors with some organised activity that might give them the chance to be useful, without clashing with their principles. Ethiopia was the first country to be liberated from Axis domination and the FAU leaders were quick to realise that work in that country might provide a suitable opening. By early summer of 1941, it was agreed that a party of about forty men should be sent there to provide some sort of emergency medical service. This group trained at Livingstone College, near Epping Forest and while on their course had several outside speakers, one of whom was Chris Sandford. She told them what it was like to live in the country she knew so well. The contingent arrived in the summer of 1942 and was quickly put to work in Addis Ababa and in the surrounding areas. Most of them came in contact with the

Sandfords during the years and many of them became real friends of the family, especially those who stayed on after their initial period of service came to an end.

Bartie Knight had a fairly vivid recollection of his first personal encounter with Chris. 'I was sent to Hadama to run the improvised clinic and hospital to plug the gap left by the departed Italians. After I had been there two or three months, I had a totally unexpected and unprecedented visitor in a grey Ford car. She told me that she was driving down to Hawash in order to gather information about some bridge (in connection with the Ealing studio film that was going to be made about Dan). She asked me to accompany her. I was quite shocked, saying I could not miss my regular day's work, but she overrode my objections and I soon found myself a passenger in that Homeric vehicle. The road was poor, and we suffered what seemed an endless succession of punctures that taxed the skill and patience of Haile to the uttermost. The rubber solution was defective and the patches could be persuaded to stay in place only by getting the inner tubes pumped up rapidly inside the tyres. As I was a guest, free of responsibility, there was no occasion for me to get agitated, but it was my first experience of one of Chris Sandford's most notable characteristics, her ability to remain completely unruffled in trying circumstances.' Several of the FAU later brought their families to Ethiopia as did other expatriates who came out to do a worthwhile job. For the children of these families, there was a great need for schooling that would help them to spend three or four years away from their regular education and then be able to go back, without having fallen behind in their schoolwork. It was this consideration, perhaps more than anything else, that made Chris think seriously about starting up a school to fulfil these needs. Already several other children had joined hers in lessons at the Sandford home, but this was not adequate enough to cover the situation. Another personal matter had also arisen. The oldest son, Dick, having come out in 1946, to recuperate after being wounded and hospitalised, needed space and quiet in the house. The result was that Chris approached the British Council and discussed the need for a school with Henry Littler, the representative.

Henry was one of the great visionaries of that period of the British Council and he had some very clear and all-embracing ideas of what the British Council could do to help a country to value and enjoy what the Council offered. The Council was allotted a large compound quite close to the business part of the town and Henrv made the most of it. He lived on the compound and was readily available for anyone to consult. There was then a utilitarian building well equipped with classrooms and there were British Council staff as well as people like Chris and K.T., who would come in to help teach evening classes. The rest of the compound was fully utilised to show British culture at its best. There were some attractively laid out gardens and a good car park. There was a tennis court, on which all members of the Anglo-Ethiopian Club could play whenever they wished, and finally there was a club house. This could be used by any nationality, but was essentially the Anglo-Ethiopian Club. The Council Library was housed there supplied with the latest British newspapers. Tea, coffee, drinks and snacks were served and there was a continual programme of evening culture; records, live music, play readings, cards, talks and dances. Royalty, Ministers of State, Ambassadors, businessmen, teachers and students from every walk of life could come and join in. Some people became almost institutions there. Col. Banks, who was head of the team of British Police who were advisers to the Ethiopian Police Force, was a most regular member. He would come daily after working hours and be unavailable to talk to for at least half an hour, while he had a cup of tea and read the latest newspapers. Stephen Wright, who fitted eminently into the role of an erudite professor, was to be seen pouring over some book in the library before going to take evening classes. Henry himself would always be at any social event, seeing that the right people sat in the right chairs and making all feel exclusively welcome. Side by side with this most important social and cultural aspect, the British Council was generously supporting schools all over the country, by appointing British teachers to work in them, by supplying them with books and papers, and by acting as an examination centre for the British School and Higher Certificates. There was also the General Wingate School, previously mentioned, which was totally staffed by British teachers appointed by the British Council. It was one of the most regrettable mistakes ever made by the British Government, in their dealings with Ethiopia, to insist on closing the Council, in 1951, in pursuit of economy. The Emperor never really forgave them for this withdrawal. It happened that the British Council opened a new centre in Delhi at the precise time they closed in Ethiopia and it is said that when the British Council Representative attended an audience with His Majesty to inform him of the closure, the Emperor asked why the British should think that it was more important to open a centre in India than to retain their friendship with Ethiopia.

Be all this as it may, when Chris approached Henry Littler to request the use of the British Council rooms as a school premises during the daytime, she found him most willing and helpful. His one stipulation was that the school should be open to anyone who wished to come and could pay the fees, and that Ethiopians should be made particularly welcome. It was from this moment that the school became yet another enterprise in which the Sandfords became totally involved although this time Chris was the central figure with Dan a dedicated and loyal supporter. It was a gigantic step into the unknown and required both patience and faith. There was never a lack of children to be taught, but the required capital outlay on equipment, classrooms and staff could not possibly be covered in a casual way by fees charged. One of the first things that had to be positively accepted was that the school was a private venture and not part of the British Council, however much aid and encouragement the Council might want to give. For this reason there had to be some stable form of financial backing to cover initial costs. It was here that Chris and Dan had such good fortune in the kind of Britishers who were in Addis Ababa at that time. First of these was Mr Nadel, a Polish Jew by extraction, and a wealthy businessman. He helped the Sandfords approach all the business firms in Ethiopia that had British connections. Following the example of urgent persuasion they gained sufficient steady backing during those first, rather precarious years. It was not easy and feelings would sometimes run high if the business brains did not think that Chris was running affairs in a sufficiently organised way. Jeff Wetherell, attached to the firm of Mitchell Cotts, called the Sandfords 'a couple of useless babies in business', and was quite sure that matters were mismanaged, but he became a good friend of the family later on and his daughter attended the school for many years. Two more very good friends were Sandy and Cecil Curle. He was now British Consul in Addis Ababa and was greatly respected by all the community. He had great rapport with the British Arabs from Aden and with some of the Indian traders. He helped encourage British business ventures to give aid to the school, and every year for quite some time, he invited all the British Arab traders up to the Consulate for a large and gorgeous tea-party. Being strict Muslims, they could not be offered any alcoholic drink. Having got them all there, he would tackle the richest and request a substantial donation. The hat was then passed round and everyone was expected to be equally generous. They always enjoyed being asked to contribute in this way and the head of the Arab community served on the Board of Governors for the school for many years. Many of them sent their sons and even daughters to the school and there was always a good relationship between them and the school. Sandy's wife, Cecil, was an equally good friend. Their daughter, Christian, attended the school and Cecil taught almost full time. Christian Curle was a bridesmaid at Philippa's wedding in 1956. With her Embassy connections Cecil Curle was able to find several willing helpers for the school from the unoccupied wives of diplomats and business men. Also very helpful at the time was Ruth Davies, an American Missionary whom the Sandfords had known before the Italian occupation; and she and her children were staunch supporters of the school.

The English School, as it was called, grew rapidly and within two years had reached nearly one hundred pupils. There were boys and girls, from the age of three to School Certificate standard, and many, many nationalities. Classes were still small and very often two age ranges would be run together, to make the most economical use of both teachers and space. Aid came from the British Council, the Ethiopian

Ministry of Education, British business men and fees. Teachers' salaries were casual and small because none was employed on contract. However, Chris realised that the time had come, in 1947 or 1948, when it would be necessary to start engaging staff on contract from Britain, so that their interests were focused on the school only. The British Council offered to interview suitable people and Miss Ethel Bennett was appointed in London to the post of supervising the Preparatory Department. She was the first of a long line of teachers who came out from Britain to work in Ethiopia and found that the country had something special to offer. It was not the money, it was not the housing, it was not the chance to get on in their careers. The frustrations, the disappointments, the clashes of personality were all there, but somehow, there were very few people who came out to teach that did not find the life in Ethiopia an enjoyable and satisfying challenge.

By 1948 it was obvious that the school would have to find premises of its own. With numbers reaching one hundred and an ever increasing demand for places, Chris and Dan started looking around for properties to rent. Quite near their house was a large compound that had become the property of Ras Ababa Aregai. He was one of the patriot chiefs who had waged ceaseless guerilla war against the Italians during the occupation and had never been captured. When the Emperor returned to Ethiopia, Ras Ababa and some of his troops had occupied this large compound which had been used as a hotel for Italian troops to use when on leave. Before the Italian occupation the site had been the Ministry of Education and several of the older buildings had been built in the traditional materials of mud and wattle, with corrugated tin roofs. When the Italians converted it to a hotel, they added several more buildings of stone and plaster including outside bars and cafes. There were four squares of grass where one could sit out under the shade of trees and, at the back of the compound, there was a large area of grass where tents could be pitched. Once the pressures of war were over Ras Ababa had no more need of his patriot army and had built himself a much more suitable establishment high on the slopes of the Entoto Mountain. The compound was in a very good position, not too near the centre of town and quite close to the British, Belgian and Russian legations. The existing buildings were big enough to house the school as it then was, and there was plenty of room for expansion. They included enough space for playing fields to be laid out and a big hall which could serve as the school assembly hall. All that was needed was a sound financial foundation, adequately resourced, for the venture to be successful.

1948-1949 was a notable year in the lives of the Sandfords, in some ways a period in which their roles in public life were reversed. Dan retired from government life early in 1949 and spent the next few years doing everything he could to help ensure that Chris, as Headmistress and founder of the English School was able to run and expand the establishment, without being threatened by recurrent financial problems. The school was to be fee-paying and this was to be the major source of income, but, at the same time, there would have to be substantial assistance from outside in order to start on a firm footing. Both of them set about the business with their usual unruffled optimism and in September 1949, the English School opened on its new site with over one hundred children, a teaching staff of nine or ten, a labour force of about the same number, and a Board of Governors to oversee and help manage the finances.

Much of the heavy routine of getting the school on a sound financial foundation fell to Dan, but the reputation of the teaching qualities and the educational standards of the school were the responsibility of Chris. It was here that her special characteristics came into full bloom. Her warm-hearted zest for life, living and knowledge was very infectious and pupils, parents and teachers responded with affection and loyalty. She expected a high standard of work from herself and from those around her and never lost her sense of values. It was as much an acknowledgement of her capabilities and standards, as regard for Dan's hard work, that produced the financial backing of the school from so many varied sources. The British Council, for many years, not only gave financial aid but also helped in more practical ways. The Alexandria Schools Trust helped out with a yearly grant and periodic inspections. The Ethiopian Ministry of Education paid the rent for the first few years of the school's life. The Emperor gave a present of large double desks, which, though very cumbersome, were used for a very long time. Several British firms, including those run by the Aden Arabs previously mentioned, gave annual grants for several years. Among those who served on the Board of Governors were, the British Ambassador, the British Council representative, the head of the British Community, a representative from the Ministry of Education, and several representatives of British business firms, especially if they had children in the school. The Ethiopians on the Board were either parents or concerned with education. Board meetings were always lively affairs, with the Sandfords' incurable optimism on the one side counterbalanced by the financial pundits' cautious attitude to progress on the other, both subject to the conventional views of British and Ethiopian diplomats.

The Sandfords gave up the house they had lived in since 1942 and moved on to the school compound, together with their daughter Eleanor and K.T. They used a large central school room in the main block as their sitting and dining-room, but had their bedrooms across the compound in the stone built block where Ras Ababa had lived. Chris had one of the outside bars converted into her Headmistress's office, with flowers growing on the ledge of the old bar and glass put in above, so that she could look out over the garden squares and keep a close eye on what was going on. As soon as there was room to expand, the numbers grew and many different nationalities eagerly competed to get their children into the school. The curriculum was based on that of traditional schools in England tempered with memories of the PNEU system Chris had used for her own children in earlier years. The older pupils were entered for the Cambridge matriculation achieving fairly good results. But Chris never let tradition bind her and the immediate needs of Ethiopians were always a matter of careful thought. Quite early on in the development of the school, two needs became obvious. The first was for the education of older girls. During the Italian occupation education had played a very minor role and many of the young men of the nobility had left the country and achieved their education elsewhere. They were now coming back and several of them were finding jobs in government where they would meet with foreigners, but their brides-to-be had not had the same chance of education or of mixing with other cultures. Chris saw one immediate way of meeting this deficiency. She created a 'Brides Class' for young ladies of fifteen and sixteen. Here they learnt how to read English and to do such simple mathematics as was required by housekeeping and everyday shopping. In addition, they learnt some European cooking, the right way to set a table, the art of sending and answering invitations and a very wide general knowledge, so that talking to foreign diplomats would not prove to be too much of a burden. Their own culture and innate courtesy would take them far, but a little supplementary guidance would make their lives easier. For the first five or six years of the school's life the Brides Class proved to be very valuable and successful, under the main guidance of the wife of a Britisher who was helping train the Ethiopian Air Force in Bishoftu, Norma Nutman. After those first six years, Ethiopian girls had a better chance of normal education, and the need for the Brides Class receded. In its place was put something called 'Remove Class' and this gave a very general education, combined with concentrated English language, to adult ladies of various nationalities, many of whom had children in the school and needed to learn English to keep pace with their offspring.

The second need for Ethiopian children in particular, prompted the starting of a very small boarding section. This again was aimed at the Ethiopian aristocracy, where both parents were either busy with growing international business and diplomatic exchanges, or when the father who needed his wife with him, had been appointed to be governor of an outlying province where there was no proper education for their children. In these cases, Chris was begged to take in the children and look after them, for both their physical well-being and their educational needs. In those early days there were seldom more than a dozen children, boys and girls, between six and twelve years old. Those who could, would go home for the weekends while the few who were left needed to be looked after and entertained.

The boarding section of the school caused as many problems as it did pleasure and profit, and needed a fair amount of extra help and care. An Ethiopian matron was installed and this forged a link with the past, because Tsedale was the daughter of the Sandford children's nanny, Tziggie. She had some training as a nurse in a hospital and closely resembled her mother. She ruled the boarders in a firm but friendly way and later became a mainstay of the school's organisation, when she took over the duplicating machine and helped in the office. Wolde Mariam doubled up as major domo in the Sandford household and as the supervisor of boarders' meals. This earned him the name of '*Abba Mestet*' or 'Father of Giving' and he was held in great affection. Years later, when Chris died and several young men and women who had been among her boarders, came to condole with the family, hair-raising stories were told of the mischief that they had got up to and the terrible crimes they had committed as boarders. It seemed an appropriate way of remembering their Headmistress at her wake.

As the school grew, so it became more necessary to have teachers appointed on a contract basis, rather than relying on such as could be found by chance among the local community. K.T. still stayed as mathematics teacher in the secondary department and the older she grew, the more severe and unbending she became. One year she had a group of seven children in the pre-certificate class, among whom was Daphne Heyring, daughter of the Headmaster of the Wingate School. During the end of year examinations Daphne obtained 25% in her geometry exam. When, in fear and trembling, she told her father of the result, he was understandably angry, but he was interrupted by his daughter, who despairingly offered him a crumb of comfort by adding "but I was top of the class." Another local find was a Hungarian refugee called Madame de Fenicsz. She was an artist and was small, grey-haired and very active. She always wore a man's deerstalker hat and was an excellent teacher of art in the senior school. Through the British Council Chris appointed teachers contracted to live on the premises, in growing numbers, as soon as the school could afford them. Part of their contract required them to take turns in looking after the boarders at weekends, because, as time went on, Chris and Dan tried more and more to spend the weekends out at Mulu Farm.

No school run by Chris – and in Addis Ababa – could fail to have its progress marked by revealing incidents. One was of a Jewish family whose home was in Aden. Sometime early in the 1950s they had their house burned down around them and they had fled to Ethiopia with virtually nothing. They had come to Chris and begged her to find room in the school for their four children, who spoke hardly any English. The father even offered to buy enough desks for the children, if only they could be allowed floor space. Mr Shelemay had reputedly been a member of the Stern gang. The British Embassy were dubious about Chris accepting the children into the school but she maintained that it was the best way to make them pro-British. The four children stayed for many years at the school and all did very well. The eldest, Margaret, when being asked which School Certificate subjects she wished to take, was discussing Bible Knowledge and Chris suggested that, as she was Jewish, she could take the paper on the Old Testament only. Margaret was very indignant, feeling that she was missing something, and insisted on taking both Old and New Testament papers, gaining a very creditable mark in both.

There were two irrepressible Italian brothers in the school, Mario and Franco. They were good-looking, clever and athletic but did not take easily to behaving quietly in class. One day the eldest, Mario, was brought to Chris by an exhausted teacher for some serious misdemeanour, and, in exasperation, she ordered him to run round the circular flower garden in front of her office for the whole of the twenty minute break time, where he could use up his energies and be under her eagle gaze. He had run ten minutes of the time, when his brother Franco came to see her and somewhat anxiously told her that Mario had some defect to do with his heart and was not allowed to run for any length of time. The punishment had quickly to be brought to a close, before the lad suffered serious consequences. None knew whether Franco thought up the excuse on the spur of the moment, or whether it was the truth, but Mario grew up to become a doctor in later life.

One evening, when Chris and Dan were at a cocktail party at the British Embassy, a self-important gentleman came up to them and said, "I understand that there was a serious international incident at your school today. I hope that you have the matter safely in hand." Chris, utterly mystified, said that she was unaware of any such event, but would look into the matter. Upon investigation, she discovered that an Egyptian diplomat's son had been having an argument with an Ethiopian lad and had thrown something at him. The Ethiopian had ducked, and the missile had hit the Swedish Ambassador's son on the shoulder. None of the three lads had thought anything of this, but their parents had talked about it and it had come full circle to be talked of as an international incident. A multi-national school such as the one started by Chris in Ethiopia, can show up some of the happiest, but at the same time, saddest aspects of this century. In any classroom in the school, there would be about a dozen different nationalities, boy and girl, about a half of whom were Ethiopians living in their own country and the rest 'foreigners', all learning by using English, within the British system. There were no nationalistic or colour problems among the children themselves, such issues simply did not exist for them. They had their loves and their hates among their fellow pupils but they were related to bullying or being pretty or ugly, fat or thin, quiet or noisy, and it was only when the parents put ideas of racism or colour into their heads that any question of international discord raised its head. An example of this occurred many years later, when the Israeli-Egyptian war was on. An Israeli and an Arab boy were close friends in a class but the Israeli parents came to the teacher and asked that the boys should be separated. This was done the next day by organising a 'general post' in the classroom, without the issue being raised in front of the children. Two days later, however, both the boys came to the teacher and begged to be allowed to sit together again, as they 'could help each other in lessons'. Their request was, of course, granted.

In the seven years that Chris was Headmistress of the school in its own premises, a solid foundation was laid, that was to carry the school through quite troubled times and still maintain it on an even keel. Chris was not only Headmistress, but mother too, and with Dan insuring that the financial basis was sound, the school became what is best described as a family venture into education. Though it was officially called the English School, the local population knew it only as *Ye Sandiford Tamarebet*. The staff looked on her as not only their boss but also their mentor and someone to turn to when in trouble. The parents were often friends as well and they and their children would come out to Mulu or meet on other occasions. It was this co-operation and ease of communication that led to the school being much more than just an educational establishment. It became an active centre for all kinds of British, Ethiopian and International projects and efforts that did an enormous amount to fill expatriate lives with fun and interest.

17

LIFE IN ADDIS ABABA AND MULU FARM

Chris and Dan were a focal point in so much that went on in Addis during these years and Mulu Farm, once it was established that the Sandfords had the lease, also emerged as a haven of rest and interest. It was during these years also that their family grew up and came back to Ethiopia to work or visit or do both. A diary was kept by members of the family of the holiday period in the summer of 1948 and extracts from it show clearly how much the farm meant in terms of home to all of them. Audrey at the time was secretary to Dan at the Municipality, Eleanor was on the point of joining Chris in the school and Philippa and Stephen were back for a holiday from boarding schools in England:

'*1 August 1948.* We were all up fairly late after exhausting last minute preparations for the arrival of the family; the three tents had been pitched and furniture allocated. We were two minutes late for church, but as Mummy was playing the piano for it, they could not start without us. After church, we dashed back to the house and Dad drove off to the Sibilo (a river sixteen miles from the farm) to fetch the boxes of strawberries and butter. The rest of us tried to get rid of the swarms of black ants that had invaded the tents. At three o'clock we rushed to the airport, as EAL offices had told us that the plane was coming in, but it turned out to be the BOAC plane in which we had no interest. We returned to the house, swallowed a cup of tea and returned plus Daddy to the airport. As the plane door opened we saw an enormous red and white hat and the general exclamation was

k

"that must be Eleanor" and it was, and Philippa and Steve were close behind. We got back to an enormous tea . . . The Davies came in to welcome the new arrivals . . . We then had our hymns, all the favourites including *Hold the Fort*, *For All the Saints* and *Immortal, Invisible*. At eleven-thirty we took Padre home and retired, happy to be more or less united and sad to think that any should be left in England.

'*3 August.* After a somewhat restless night in the tents owing to a terrific thunderstorm, we assembled for breakfast and then Mummy, K.T. and Eleanor went to school, Daddy and Audrey to the office, and Philippa and Stephen went out riding to visit some of their more dubious acquaintances amongst the army or riff-raff of the town. In the evening we had Bartie Knight and David Buxton to dinner and then all went down to the Anglo-Ethiopian Club to the weekly record programme, on this occasion an all Brahms concert.

'*8 August.* Five of us went to early service and then back to breakfast. Then we all went to church and on to have elevenses with the Abels. Then we all went home and got ready for a picnic. Some walked up to the picnic spot as the car could not take us all. We just managed to have our lunch before the rain came. In the evening we were twenty-three to hymns and after supper we played charades. Audrey sang a bit and Mr Marshall, who runs the Municipal garage, having brought his accordion, played a few songs with Mum while the rest tried to sing to their accompaniment.

'*9 August.* Audrey and Philippa went into town for last minute shopping before going out to Mulu, and then to the garage to collect the Ford car . . . Everything was loaded into it and we set off. Mum (driving) and K.T. in the front and Eleanor, Stephen and Philippa in the back with the chauffeur. Daddy, Audrey and David Buxton were following an hour later in the Jeep station wagon. The Ford got up Entoto after boiling once and Philippa and Stephen and the chauffeur had to walk about a third of the way up. Once at the top, it refused to start for a long time but finally we got it going and reached KM thirty-four without another stop . . . When the others arrived we all mounted our respective animals and set off to the Sibilo River. There we discovered that the bridge was under water in the middle so we took off our boots and socks and waded across it. On the other side we waited for our mounts to swim across; some of the horses were rather good swimmers but the poor pack donkeys came across almost submerged. We got to Mulu to have a lovely tea at seven and supper at ten-fifteen.

'*11 August.* Daddy and Audrey had to go back to Addis Ababa as office work called. Harold Waller came up from the Muger where he and his wife have been staying. It was very wet all afternoon and David and Eleanor did a lot of carpentry, making a meat safe.

'*12 August.* Stephen and Eleanor went out shooting early . . . Philippa and Eleanor had an hour's learning how to write Amharic with David . . . Mummy, Eleanor, Philippa and Stephen rode round the farm looking at crops . . . Stephen and Philippa cleared the lawn of hay . . . K.T. and Philippa went down the garden to tie lettuces for an hour. Eleanor has been making a music stand out of bamboo.

'*15 August.* Harold and Margaret Waller came up from the Muger and we went for a swim, followed by a picnic lunch at the Boumfeta Waterfall . . . In the evening we had hymns, making quite a good choir with our augmented numbers. We performed an operetta to the elder members of the family; it was proclaimed a great success.

'*18 August.* We did our various allocated jobs in the morning. Eleanor has taken on the pruning, Bartie and Audrey the making of wash-stands and the erecting of supports for the raspberry canes, Philippa worked in the stable and Stephen on any odd job there was going. Bartie and Audrey announced their engagement, but only for the family ear and were toasted in Madeira.

'*19 August.* Today was the feast of *Buhe* and the servants presented us with dozens of loaves of brown *Buhe* bread.

'*20 August.* We had almost exhausted the haunts on the farm, but the one remaining was visited for lunch and a swim . . . The Grotto . . . It was looking rather lovely with a lot of water coming over the little waterfall into the pool. We rode home just in time to avoid a thunder-storm.

'*24 August.* It was rather a wet morning, so we did our chores and had lunch at home. At three-thirty we started to walk to Dadi Mulle's wood for tea. When we got there

Stephen went off to hunt guinea-fowl and medakwa. Presently we heard shot after shot ringing through the wood, some of which whistled unpleasantly close overhead . . . Eventually Stephen came, bearing a hare and a partridge.

'*27 August.* Down the Muger, Steve and Harold left camp at six-thirty to go shooting. Margaret and Philippa got lunch ready to take down to Gulle to eat. They met Harold and Stephen at Marco. They had only managed to get one guinea-fowl. They had lunch and looked for a place to swim but couldn't find one. Up at Mulu the rest of the party went to see the Bole River which was very full.

'*28 August.* Stephen and Philippa came up from the Muger to breakfast. We then all rode to market where we made some purchases, such as sugar cane. We then rode to Gabriel, a church, visiting a milk station on the way. From Gabriel you can get the most beautiful view. Lunch met us on the way home.

'*30 August.* The family went down to the Muger. K.T. and the Davies family and the Vaizeys stayed up at Mulu.

'*31 August.* Stephen went shooting but was unsuccessful. The rest of us went down to the plantations . . . We met Stephen at Biddu and then all went to Gulle for lunch. We bathed in the river and then started back. A brief thunder-storm overtook us on the way back . . . After supper a party of cattle herders came and serenaded us for about an hour.

'*1 September.* Daddy and Mummy left early to go up to Mulu and the rest of us all set off to go to the Bole Waterfall. We got there after having hacked our way through the under-growth and clambered across landslides. When we were there we got drenched with the spray. Half way back we tried to swim in a stream and then had lunch. When we got back to camp we found the Davies family arriving . . . After a cup of tea we set off up the mountain to Mulu. Most of us did it very slowly as we'd already been a long way . . . It was a very good way of spending Granny's birthday.

'*4 September.* In the morning Philippa and Stephen went shooting and managed to get a partridge. We saw Dr Vaizey down the Muger and then all went to watch the plough being tried out. At twelve-thirty we went down for a swim and on to The Pimple for lunch. At five o'clock we went to The Big

Tree for tea but it began to rain so we came back to finish.

'5 *September.* Stephen and Philippa went out shooting and got a medakwa, which was a good end to their hunting. After breakfast we inspected all the cattle and pigs. Eleanor, Audrey, Philippa and Stephen all chose two oxen each and named them. Then we went down to swim and on to the Monkey Place for lunch. It started to rain so we finished under a bush . . . After tea K.T. read to us and then we had hymns at eight-thirty. We sang one for Aunt Ethel, because it was her birthday.

What a wonderful holiday.'

Another facet of life in Addis Ababa, with which Chris and Dan were fully concerned, was the well-being of the Anglican Church. In pre-Italian times the church had been established in a house with a large room near the central Itegue Hotel and had been ministered to by the Rev. Austen Matthew, who was a great friend of the family. During the Italian occupation Padre Matthew had been in Jerusalem, helping with Ethiopian refugees and he had come back in 1941. During the forties he had used a building nearer the Ras Makonnen bridge, on the main road into Addis Ababa from the east, but it was very small and cramped, with little parking for cars. Once the Sandfords had rented the English School premises, it was decided that the school hall could also serve as the church on Sundays. It was large enough to house the growing congregation and was much more convenient for access. There was plenty of room for the congregation to park their cars and it was considerably nearer to the British Legation than premises right in town. Austen Matthew found a small house quite near to the school gates and was conveniently close to the Sandfords to be a regular participant in Sunday evening hymns and supper. On one particular occasion, the presence of the church in the school hall was of great benefit to the Sandfords. When their second daughter, Eleanor, married Leslie Casbon, who was teaching at the General Wingate School at the time, the church ceremony and the wedding party were held at one and the same place, with the guests moving informally from the service to sit on chairs set out under the trees in front of the Sandford's sitting-room. The school kitchen was used to prepare the feast and school chairs and tables served a useful purpose. This wedding was the first of the Sandford weddings to be held in Ethiopia and was a wonderful example of how much impact Chris and Dan had made on both Ethiopian and foreign residents in the country. Wedding presents included five heavy gold bands from the Emperor, part of which was used for making the wedding rings; a carpet from the Crown Prince and family, a portable typewriter from the Emperor's second son, Prince Makonnen; three cows from the labourers on Mulu Farm, a picture of the valley between the school and the British Embassy, painted by the Ambassador, Dan Lascelles, most of the Ethiopian food by the school servants, a clock from the British community, a carpet from the Board of Governors of the school and a tiny silver bowl in the shape of a rose from a pupil in Eleanor's class. The parents of Endelcachew Makonnen, one of the 'Ethiopian boys' mentioned previously, came to the wedding and since they were expecting to be guests of honour, sat down in the chairs awaiting the groom and best man and had to be asked very politely to move elsewhere. Fred Abel lent his rather nice looking car for the bridal couple to be driven through the streets of Addis Ababa and up to the top of the Entoto Mountain, where a much shabbier car was waiting to drive onto the camp chosen for the first night of the honeymoon. From all walks of life and from all communities, the Sandfords' friends came forward to help make the wedding day a success.

It was during the early fifties that the British community as well as other users of the Church decided that the time had come to build a church and chaplain's house. As two of the oldest residents, Chris and Dan took a great part in the discussions and the preparation of plans to bring this project to fruition. Many money-raising events were organised and all possible sources were tapped. From the Emperor and members of the royal family came gifts and money and by 1954 the St Matthew's Anglican Church was built on the road leading out of town towards the British Embassy. Shortly afterwards the chaplain's house was also finished. Austen Matthew retired in 1954 and continued to live in his house near the English School until he died, in 1969. He was greatly loved by his congregation, especially by the Sandford family, and he was also held in great affection by his Ethiopian friends and by the Ethiopian Coptic Church. For many years he helped in the translation of the Bible into Amharic, instead of the ancient Church language of Gee'z and was very highly regarded for his deep knowledge of Hebrew and Amharic, although when he spoke the latter to them, ordinary people could not understand him. It was always rather embarrassing to be asked to act as interpreter between him and a pedlar on his doorstep.

In the early 1950s Ethiopia, as a committed member of the United Nations, sent a contingent of troops to fight in the Korean War. This created an interesting sideline in the Sandford activities, because of a policy decision that some of the officers needed a crash course in English. Not very far away from the school were the barracks of the Imperial Bodyguard, a picked force for defending the Emperor. Dan discussed their requirements with their commanding officer and it was agreed that about one hundred of the officers should attend evening classes at the school for two or three nights a week to learn English in as many varied ways as possible. Dan himself took classes in tactics and modern warfare, Chris taught geography and social studies, K.T. taught grammar and composition, and Eleanor taught English literature. This kept most of the teaching within the family, although Norma Nutman also helped out, as did various other people from time to time. The students varied tremendously; there were some young dare-devils of lieutenants who thought it all rather fun and were eager to get on, and there were some rather staid colonels, who, though brave enough, did not really want to embark upon war yet again in a very far country, but who were loyal and determined to do their best. Towards the end of the course students of one class were encouraged to give a public show of The Pyramus and Thisbe scene from *A Midsummer Night's Dream* to their fellow officers and an invited audience, including the then British Ambassador. It was most successful, the slightly portly colonel who played the part of Wall being notably comical, and was generally appreciated. The British Ambassador earned the bad mark of the day, however, with his solitary comment that the teachers had been unable to teach their students how to pronounce 'th' correctly. Examinations were held at the end of the course and those who passed well were sent to Korea. As an indication that this was not a universally desired objective, one officer returned later and remarked, slightly ruefully, that if he had not done so well in the examinations, he might have avoided being sent to Korea. But it was an interesting interlude and gave enjoyment to both Sandfords and the officers quite apart from earning the school some welcome extra income.

When the British Council started cutting down the number of its staff and activities in Ethiopia, many of the social and cultural functions that it had carried out were taken over by the Sandfords within the school. Most of the British Council's library was given to the school, with the proviso that others could use it. Musical evenings continued to be held in the Sandfords' sitting-room in the school. Harry Shore, a Cairene Englishman who worked in the Post Office used to run these evenings until some alleged faulty handling of a new issue of stamps obliged him to leave the country. Scottish and country dancing were a regular feature, with Chris playing thc piano, if no records were available. Amateur dramatics started to play an important part in the British community and Chris, with her passion for Gilbert and Sullivan, started off a long line of comic operas which were to become a familiar feature of entertainment in Addis Ababa over the next twenty-five years. One of the first was performed in the Adowa Cinema in Addis Ababa. For two nights this involved using an extremely narrow stage on which the scenery, already constructed, had to be erected. There were no dressing rooms and very little space for performers to wait behind scenes. This meant that the entire cast collected in the house of the Ashleys, who ran the British and Foreign Bible Society, in order to dress. They then walked in full costume across the piazza in the centre of the capital and on into the cinema. The orchestra, with Chris at the piano, was mainly made up of Armenian friends belonging or attached to the family Nalbandian. They were gifted musicians, but had seldom, if ever, seen a comic opera before and the conductor frequently had to recall them to their playing and discourage them from watching the scene going on. The double bass player, in particular, interspersed the notes he was playing with deep chuckles of laughter as he suddenly understood the very English humour of *HMS Pinafore*. Drama and music were not the only problems on this occasion. Two of the sailors, a Canadian and an Irishman had rather too much to drink on the last night of the production and Chris and the family were concerned to see that they behaved with decorum in the Bible Society's premises and did not disrupt the show too much. All went well till the closing curtain when the two men, not being content with the back row, joined the soloists in the front line. This was luckily a minor offence and in no way took away the pleasure that was given by the show.

After Dan retired from the Municipality, there were conflicting demands on his energies. He gave Chris the fullest support in the running of the school, by doing the accounts and seeing to the maintenance of the buildings and the compound. But, in addition, he gave much of his mind to the re-establishing of Mulu Farm as a profitable concern. He would dash out to the farm every Wednesday to check on the day-to-day running. This entailed a pre-breakfast departure in one of the ancient vehicles, and a two-hour drive to the farm. Breakfast on arrival and then a tour round the farm on horseback to see that all was well, to discuss plans with Tesfai, the foreman, and to pay the wages and make other disbursements. The car would then be loaded up with produce in the afternoon and he would drive back to Addis Ababa to arrive for supper. The farm produce was brought in on other days by carrier, as in previous times, and boxes containing strawberries, butter and cheese would arrive in Addis Ababa at about six in the evening. In the height of the fruit season there would be nine to twelve carriers employed at any one time. The produce was then repacked and taken for sale round Addis Ababa in an old-fashioned butcher's bike and by Guraghies with the sales boys going with them. The proud rider of the butcher's bike was a man called Zerefu, who was chief promoter of sales and absolutely honest but not very highly educated or imaginative. Concluding the day's accounts with him demanded of Dan a monumental reserve of both patience and deduction. Roars of fury broke out if either broke down.

Friday was always a red-letter day . . . departure to Mulu for the weekend after school. In those early days of the school Chris never had lessons in the afternoon and work ended at one o'clock. This was a great boon for those seeking to escape for the weekend on a Friday. A wide range of things had to be collected from all over Addis Ababa, and the familiar cry "We'll pick it up on the way" sounded several times. The car would be loaded with everything imaginable, from Chris's school books for correcting to poles for a building, sacks of cement and empty boxes for fruit. Then came departure, by now probably well-advanced into the late afternoon, followed by a tour round Addis Ababa to collect everything and cram it into an already impossibly-filled car and then off with Chris at the wheel. Up the Entoto Mountains, with the car frequently boiling, out along the Selulta Plains on the gravelled road and then off on to the grass track that was remade every year by farm workers, with causeways that had to be built up across the rivers after each rains. Chris always carried a supply of sweets which she flung to the local children as they risked life and limb in dangerous pursuit of the passing car. K.T. would have a bagful of bones that she had saved during the week to throw to the mongrel curs that would come out from the houses as the car passed. If it was wet, the car would often get stuck and the driver would demand to be pushed with the repeated order of *giffa, giffa.* Then everyone else leapt out and the local passers-by were persuaded to come and join in the effort. Once Mulu was reached, the weekend was spent going round the different projects, with Dan concentrating on the arable and cattle side and Chris on the flowers, fruit and vegetables. It was, nevertheless, a combined effort. Chris would correct books in the evening and Dan would work on the farm accounts with Tesfai. Sunday morning would see the foreman from the Muger Valley coming up the mountain to report. Often there would be a walk to see the forestry behind the house or the fruit and vegetables below the house. Then lunch and the journey back to Addis Ababa in time for dinner, which remained a meal at which all were freely welcome until they retired to live in Mulu.

So the fifteen years since the return of the Emperor drew to a close and in 1956 Chris and Dan 'retired' to Mulu. This did not mean retirement in the usual sense but merely a change of purpose in what they did with their lives. During those fifteen years they had met and exchanged ideas with hundreds of people of world renown; royalty, heads of state, political and diplomatic leaders, doctors, scientists and intellectuals from all over the world. They always stood out, among the British community, as two people with a great love for Ethiopia and the will and the energy to work hard for the betterment of conditions there, in any area whatsoever. The Ethiopians themselves held them in the greatest affection and respect, so that the children and grandchildren of notables were always anxious and ready to come to the school. The Emperor's grandson and several of his great grandchildren were pupils there and this was a measure of the degree of trust that was accorded to Chris and Dan.

One other significant factor may be mentioned here. The Sandfords had six children, and their adult lives and connection with Ethiopia should be briefly looked at. Christine, the eldest, spent thirteen years as a child and then six months as a doctor in Ethiopia. She was already married when the parents re-established themselves in Ethiopia so could only manage a short spell working in the country. The second child, Eleanor, spent thirteen years of childhood and then twenty-eight years of teaching in Ethiopia. The eldest son, Dick, spent eleven years of childhood and fourteen years working with FAO in Ethiopia and is still frequently in the country, working for non-governmental organisations on relief and rehabilitation. Audrey spent eight years of childhood and then two years working for Dan as his personal secretary in the Municipality. Philippa had seven years of childhood and twenty years of farming with her husband at Mulu Farm, until the farm was confiscated by the Communist Government. The youngest, Stephen, had five and a half years of childhood there and, up to date, has spent sixteen years working for the World Bank and ILCA, while his wife first taught at the school and then became Headmistress. Four out of the six have spent most of their adult careers working in Ethiopia. What was it that made them go back? Was it the presence of their parents and the example of their happiness and their energy, and their faith in results? Was it the undeniable call of Ethiopia and her people and their attitude to life? These are difficult questions to answer, but Jim Marshall's song, 'Once you have drunk of the waters of Ethiopia, you will return to imbibe them again,' seems to be very true for the Sandfords.

18

BACK HOME TO MULU FARM – 1956

In 1956, when Dan was seventy-two and Chris was sixty-one, they were free to concentrate on farming once again and added to it many other new interests and projects. They both continued to keep a very close eye on the running of the school, under the headmastership of their son-in-law, Leslie Casbon, and were unfailingly supportive of all schemes and improvements that took place. Dan continued to take a real interest in the setting up of agricultural shows and other projects of the same kind. Out at Mulu, with the help of World Neighbours, they started up a scheme for Community Development which was to be most successful. They still came into Addis Ababa for a day or so every week and kept up with the visits of foreign dignitaries of every kind. In spite of all these distractions, their main aim was to restore Mulu Farm not only to its original glory but to improve upon it. From 1948 to 1958, while Mulu was being slowly rebuilt, their youngest daughter Philippa, their son Dick and his wife, Anne, all helped in the work by spending time there and inaugurating new ideas and reviving long-standing plans. Finally, in 1958, Philippa and her husband, Michael Langdon, came from Kenya where they had been working in the Department of Agriculture and agreed to manage the farm, although both Dan and Chris continued to be vitally interested and very involved in it. It says much for the characters of Dan and Chris that their two sons-in-law were able to run the farm and school successfully, remaining in constant contact, and at the same time have the greatest affection and admiration for their seniors. The reverse was happily and equally true.

It is appropriate to include at this moment some recollections of Chris and Dan noted by their son-in-law Michael Langdon. 'My first introduction to Dad and Mum was when I was on "local leave" from the Kenyan Agricultural Department in 1955. Just across the road from the airport, on an open piece of ground, tremendous activity was apparently in preparation for one of the very earliest agricultural shows. After receiving a quick nod of introduction, I was put to work sorting out various plant exhibits. I was immediately struck by Dad's great enthusiasm for whatever he was doing. Almost invariably this would be something for the benefit of the Ethiopians. By this time Philippa and I presumed we were engaged, but this was obviously very much in the balance as far as Mum was concerned, because a book that she and Dad gave me as I left again for Kenya had written on the flyleaf, "To Michael, hoping he will come and visit us again."

'One day about the same year, Mum was half way through a lesson in her capacity as Headmistress of the English School, when she suddenly became aware of an appalling smell. She decided that the drains really must have their annual overhaul, but was brought up short, as she left the classroom, by a heap of something on the steps. This had been tenderly laid there by Dad, to show her the product of his very first attempt at making silage at Mulu . . . My mother, who came out to Addis Ababa for our wedding, stayed on a few days with Chris and Dan. On her first trip to the farm, the old Chevrolet truck, habitually overladen, didn't quite make it to the top of Entoto and shuddered to a halt. "Maud," said Chris, as if she had every intention of stopping just there, "we thought you might care to get out and see the view from here." My mother, in all innocence, thinking this would really be a nuisance to everyone, declined the offer initially, but then the truck began to run backwards and so "Perhaps I will," she said, stepping very quickly down from the truck.

'Dad and Mum, married for over fifty years, were such a devoted couple that they were an example to everyone. Mum ran the domestic and social side of their lives and was a very matriarchal and no-nonsense sort of personality, but there was never any doubt as to who wore the pants in the family. This would be portrayed to perfection every time Mum's plans in Dad's view were too outrageous, when he would quietly say, "No, I don't think we will do that, Chris." Without protest or discussion, Mum would drop the idea like a hot coal.

'One night when Dad was doing the last rounds at the English School, before electricity was completely installed, armed with a large torch, he opened each store room door and swept the torchlight quickly round the room before going on to the next. In one of these stores there were up-ended oil barrels in which grain had been stored. For some reason or other he kept his torch shining for just too long on one barrel in the corner. A thief, hiding there, could bear the suspense no longer and slowly rose out of the barrel, blinking in the torchlight. When asked what on earth he thought he was doing, he said he was just looking for a box of matches.

'Mum was well known for her large sun hats which were made locally at Mulu and could be bought for less than a dollar. You knew it was her driving towards you because of the large brimmed hat, though very little of her face could ever be seen. Once a New Zealand nurse, who worked at the Community Centre at Mulu, borrowed the car to drive into Addis Ababa and also borrowed Mum's hat. Driving through a red light traffic signal she was immediately flagged down by a policeman, who walked round the car, saw Mum's hat, albeit with someone else under it, and said, "Ah, Mrs Sandford," and waved her on. Mum always liked to *hear* the engine of the car when she was driving; as she got older and engines got quieter, she needed to accelerate more and more to get the necessary volume, slightly depressing the clutch the while to reduce forward speed. Once arriving at the farm in Dick's Land-rover, which she had borrowed, she said, "Oh Michael, just have a look at the Land-rover, will you, there's a strange smell!" – There was too, the clutch was on fire! When Chris's driving licence was withheld, as it was arbitrarily decided that she was too old to drive any more, she was extremely indignant. The fact that the licensing authority was quite right, was beside the point. At the very next civic reception that Dad and Mum were invited to, Mum button-holed the Mayor and explained the position to him very carefully. He undertook to help her, providing she promised only to drive to and from the farm. Mum thoroughly enjoyed the social life, but both she and Dad had very definite ideas about visitors they did and did not want to entertain at Mulu. Whole nations were written off as unsuitable. Mum often threatened to write a book entitled 'Ambassadors I have known'. Certainly they had known a great many, both in Addis Ababa and at the farm. Dad was inclined to be very impatient with any pomp and self-importance. He also had a healthy loathing for simpering and gushing females. This was portrayed to perfection by the revolted expression on his face when, as he climbed out of his car at an Embassy reception, the Ambassador's wife swept down the steps to the car, screeching "Darling" . . .'

During the years when Dan and Chris were weekend farmers, an impressive amount of progress was made on the farm and much experimenting carried out. Their eldest son, Dick, came out in 1949 with his newly wedded wife, Anne. They came out by boat to Massawa and then made a perilous journey down by road, first to Asmara and then south to Addis Ababa. As an introduction to Ethiopia, it was hardly the most glamorous of methods of arriving or travelling, and even when they actually reached Addis Ababa there was another slight contretemps. Eleanor drove the car down to meet them at the bus stop in town. The family house was on the road from the north and she had kept watch at the end of the drive, so that she could follow the bus to its final stop and be there as they disembarked. This was a good idea, except for one thing. She parked the car on a slope a little behind the bus and ran along to greet them. Suddenly she heard a roar of fury and turning round saw that the car had not held on the brakes and had rolled into the back of a small taxi. As a result a great deal of argument and finally some handing over of cash had to be endured, before the exhausted passengers could be taken away home. Anne had taken a course in cheese making while in England and while the couple were looking after Mulu Farm for a year, she was able to experiment in the making of cheese. She tried out at least five varieties, among them Cheddar, Pont L'Eveque and Wensleydale, but the two most successful were the Cheddar and a soft white cheese that looked like a cream cheese but was made of milk. The milk for this came not only from the Zebu herd on the farm, but also from six outlying milk stations to which the local cow owners could bring their milk. Some of this was separated and the cream alone sent to the farm to make butter, but some came as it was. As had been the pre-war practice, they were paid by the month for what was produced. Sometimes they were paid cash and sometimes with grain that had been grown on the farm and stored for that purpose. The grains they liked best were *teff*, barley and wheat, and this method of payment was used during the rainy season when grain prices in the local market were high. A wonderful cheese press was constructed of tree trunks on a lever principle but it was not always easy to get the weight evenly distributed and some of the cheeses would develop a list to one side. Part of the hillside was dug out near where the milk house stood and the cheese press was tucked into the rock, where it could keep cool.

Fruit was still an important part of the farm produce and several experiments continued to be made. The Jaffa oranges that had been planted in the lower farm had all sprouted below the graft in the intervening years and so had become bitter, but they made excellent marmalade that was sold in large quantities. Jam from the strawberries and plums was only made when there was a glut of fruit. Avocados were also started on the lower farm and some peaches were tried out there, as well as on the upper farm. New plum varieties were tried out, but none approached the standard of the Methleys planted in the early days. The Emperor loved these plums and once said that he had tasted plums all over the world but none as good as the ones from Mulu. The plum season started in January and each year at plum time a basket would be sent up to the palace with plums, strawberries and peaches, labelled *first fruits*. A thank you letter from Tafara Werq, the Emperor's Private Secretary, always came back and thereafter, until the end of the season, the palace car would appear two or three times a week to buy more. The first fruit offering went on right up until the time that the Emperor was made prisoner. Other farming experiments continued. Beehives were bought in Kenya and some were given out to the local farmers, with queen bee excluders in them to give purer honey. Another experiment was flax. This was grown and then retted in a large pit near the canal. There it soaked until sufficiently rotted and then the stalks were dried and pulled through a bed of nails to extract the fibre. Unfortunately Dan found no buyers for it. Pyrethrum was also grown and Dan hoped to make great strides in this commodity, but this project never expanded, although it was very useful on the farm and a good pesticide against the strawberry green beetle. A patch was grown on each strawberry plantation and the headman of the garden had to sun-dry the flowers and grind them with a pestle and mortar. Other experiments included the afforestation of the east side of the Bomfata valley, behind the house. Pines, cyprus and wattle were all tried. The wattle was tried for use in the tanning industry, but the trees never grew well, probably because of the many illegal cattle that used the valley for grazing.

In 1957 Dan and Chris suggested to their daughter Philippa and her husband Michael Langdon that they should come from Kenya and run the farm. Mike had been working for the Kenya Agricultural Department and Philippa had completed her training in agriculture at Egerton Agricultural College in Kenya. In June 1958 they came up by car, with their dog and son penned in among all their belongings. If the farm was to support two families it was obvious that it would have to be developed to the limit of the resources available. For many years the farm had not been laid out in fields, except for the strawberry plantations and orchards. Much of the ploughable land had been let out to farm staff and other local farmers on a quarter crop rental basis, and many of the labourers had their houses, with their cattle byres and patches of eucalyptus trees, right on the farm. This had to be changed. Dick and Philippa had already surveyed the farm and had assessed where the field boundaries should be. During the first two years of their management, Mike carried out a vast amount of land clearing, putting up fencing, digging irrigation canals and rehousing farm staff. About two hundred acres of the farm were laid out into twenty or thirty acre fields. A new tractor and other farm implements were bought and the idea of putting out some of the work to contract was put into effect. All the fence holes were dug by contract by one strong man who found that he could earn three times the normal daily rate. Every line of poles had to be straight so that any holes out of line would have to be dug again. The gang of farm staff, following up with poles and wire and urged on by Mike, could never catch him. Dan and Chris were very enthusiastic and encouraging, and gave these innovations their full support. They also continued to be very much involved with the running of the farm. Dan continued to sign the cheques and, until Mike's Amharic improved, there were regular evening meetings with Dan, Mike and the foreman, Tesfai, to discuss the next day's work. Chris continued to develop the plant side of the farm. She reached over one hundred varieties of roses and many shrubs as well. She arranged that visitors could come to the farm and walk down from the lawn along a shrubbery path past the spring, then along a narrow canal past bedding plants and roses and finally up the hill to the car park and past the mass of fuchsias. On their way they could choose what plants they wanted to buy. She was ably assisted by Sanbata, her knowledgeable gardener who knew every rose by name and could recognise not only the flowers, but the leaves of a plant. He collected seeds for re-planting and planted the cuttings for the roses. Chris did the planning for a great many gardens in Addis Ababa, including those belonging to Embassies, businesses and private houses. On one occasion the First Secretary of the Russian Embassy came out to order plants, closely watched and monitored by his driver, who was obviously a KGB man with final authority over him.

Perhaps the greatest innovation of all was the importing of red poll cattle from Kenya on to the farm. First of all the necessary farm buildings had to be constructed to receive them. These were put up with the aid of an Arab carpenter with a British passport and a reference from son-in-law Leslie Casbon which said, 'The bearer is a good, plain carpenter under constant supervision'. In May 1960, the first twenty-one calves came up from Kenya on a Dakota freight carrier. Mike had spent some time in Kenya choosing them and was with them in the plane. He had agreed that the calves should be hog-tied and tranquillised and laid out on large mattresses in the plane. The plane was late leaving the airport and the pilot had said that if they did not leave at once they would be landing in the dark on a strip without landing lights. The journey was not totally successful. The tranquillisers only worked half an hour before they were due to land and as a result the calves spent three hours threshing about on the floor of the plane and lying on each other's heads. Mike arrived somewhat bruised and battered and two calves died en route. It was the first plane load of imported cattle that the airline had ever handled, so there was considerable interest shown by the airline staff, many of whom had not gone home but awaited the arrival of the aircraft. The calves had to be carried out of the plane, still half doped, on to a large lorry and then straight out to the farm, arriving at about midnight, where most of the farm staff were still around to help and very excited to see the foreign cattle. Two years later, another lot of calves were brought up from Kenya, but this time they were not tranquillised and merely halter-tied to a rail. However on this occasion Mike was surprised to see a steward rush up to a calf standing near a window in the plane and put his hands over the calf's eyes. On being questioned he said, "I thought she might be nervous during take-off."

Dan and Chris were very proud of the imported cattle and took a great interest in their management and feeding. A visit to the cattle sheds and the inspection of silage were high on the agenda for visitors to the farm. Later on the red polls were crossed with the local cattle and many of the local farmers were encouraged to buy the half-breeds.

One of the major schemes that Dan and Chris took over, once they had 'retired' to Mulu, was that of Community Development. World Neighbours is a non-governmental American organisation and their programmes are mainly self-help projects at the village or community levels in the fields of agriculture, public health, animal husbandry, village industries and in education for both children and adults. Mr Merlin Bishop was an American who ran the YMCA in Addis Ababa and became involved in World Neighbours. Together with Chris and Dan, he decided that Mulu would be a good place to start a development project. Though, not surprisingly, the project had to survive several setbacks, it was a most successful effort. It was envisaged by World Neighbours that Chris and Dan would be the administrators for the first five years during which money would be provided by World Neighbours, but that after that time the various Ethiopian Ministries would take over and be responsible for their particular sections. The local people would help by providing the labour and much of the building materials needed. Dan used to get fairly impatient with the slowness of the local community to bring the materials such as timber and thatching grass, and would often provide what was needed off the farm, rather than delay the progress of building. When the first grant from World Neighbours was made in January 1957, it was decided that the building of a school was the major requirement and a large hall was built to be partitioned off into three rooms for Grade I pupils according to their ages, with a separate classroom for those who could already read. The school was opened in December, with a staff of the local priest, one Government teacher and about eighty pupils. Over the next few years a Grade was added each year, together with new classrooms and new teachers. In 1958 a building was put up for a Health Centre, consisting of a treatment room, a laboratory, a waiting room and a lecture room. UNICEF and WHO gave most of the equipment while World Neighbours provided furniture and an ambulance. At the start of the Health Clinic, Mrs Pollock, an American nurse who had been working with the American Presbyterian Mission, came out for a year to help. She not only worked in the Mulu Health Centre but also used the ambulance to visit all the surrounding villages on their market days and to go to nearby towns such as Chancho and Sululta. She used to get into her bath fully clothed when she returned from one of her market visits, to ensure that the fleas went down the drain and not into the house. In October 1960 two New Zealand nurses came and continued the work.

They were great favourites with the locals and with the Sandfords and were extremely efficient at their job. In the beginning, when language was a problem, they were frequently disconcerted by the translation of reported symptoms, such as the familiar complaint that a patient was 'burning inside'.

During the early years, Dan and Chris persuaded World Neighbours to pay the fares and allowances for two VSO lads to come out and help in the community. They had to turn their hands to anything; helping with physical activity in the school, with the organisation of the schoolchildren's allotments, with ambulance driving and house building. One of these lads, Ian Snell, eventually married Beverley, one of the New Zealand nurses. Besides the school and the Health Centre, the Ministry of Agriculture had two extension workers at the Community Centre and they were there to provide a simple veterinary service for the cattle, advise on the school gardens and poultry keeping, and give talks at local markets on management of pastures and water resources. In the last three years of the scheme the two VSOs from Rolls Royce were replaced by three other energetic young men. With Mulu Community as the centre, other projects were developed in five or six other places, all within a distance of twenty-five miles or so, and all supervised by an Ethiopian Community Development Officer.

As one can imagine, none of this materialised uneventfully. Dan and Chris spent many long hours seeing Government officialdom in Addis Ababa, gently spurring the local people to providing the workforce and the building material, planning and seeing to the construction of buildings, watching over the VSOs and making sure that their time was really well-spent, and above all encouraging everyone into emulation of their own boundless enthusiasm and energy. With Chris's particular interest in education and health and Dan's in farming skills and overall planning, the Community Development kept them extremely busy doing what they both liked to do – helping Ethiopia along the road of progress. The Emperor was interested in the project and came out to visit the site once and stayed to lunch with the Sandfords. On that occasion he presented a shield for athletics at the school, which was a very good way of keeping enthusiasm for physical education going. At the end of five or six years, World Neighbours ended its commitment to the project which was taken over by the government. Naturally, some of the developments continued successfully and others less so. Both Chris and Dan continued to take an active interest and were there to advise and give help when asked but they were no longer the driving energy behind everything. Government officials tended to find that Mulu was a little off the beaten track and wanted to move the administrative side of the project to Selulta and this, of course, was resisted by the Sandfords. Nevertheless, it is impressive to look at what was accomplished during those first five years. There was schooling up to 6th Grade with particular attention paid to farming, gardening, poultry, handicrafts such as carpentry, leatherwork, sewing, and hat making. Physical education was encouraged so that children might participate in inter-schools athletic meetings; Scout meetings, adult literacy classes and training for assistant midwives and dressers were also held. On the health side, market places were visited regularly and patients vaccinated. Mother and child clinics were started as well as pre-natal clinics. Vitamins, soap and milk were given to mothers and children. A club was started, with films shown and a reading room. Cards, table tennis, darts and dominoes were all provided. The centre was provided with piped water, pumped up from the nearest spring, and electricity from its own generator.

Quite apart from the real interest this project stirred in the Sandfords, it also brought them into contact with a great many organisations that gave assistance. Having given up living in Addis Ababa they might have been expected to lose contact; in fact the reverse happened. Organisations such as WHO, UNICEF, UNSAID came out for business and stayed for pleasure and the Sandfords' circle of friends and acquaintances never diminished. The people working for Water Resources exemplified this. They were given permission to use a site just above the stable as a refuelling station for their helicopters. Petrol was stored there in barrels and they would normally land on top of the hill above the house. Once a helicopter landed on the lawn and blew some of the thatch off the roof, so this was not encouraged. On one occasion they took Chris and Dan down to their house at Kusai in the valley below and then brought them back a few days later. On this occasion a worker in the valley was given a lift too and this infuriated the foreman, Aderra, who was not there at the time. However, he was reconciled to this slight by being allowed a trip in the helicopter on another occasion. Chris also had a flight with them right up to the Boli Waterfall, which must have been an exciting ride.

Their weekly routine during these years shows how much energy and interest Dan and Chris expended on different projects. Breakfast was usually at about nine and after it the day's work would start. Chris would busy herself with household matters and then go out to the gardens where the roses and other plants grew. There she would deal with orders for plants or discuss what seeds should be bedded out. Dan, with shirt sleeves rolled up and a sleeveless pullover, a brown battered trilby hat and worn corduroy trousers would walk over, staff in hand, to the Community Centre to see to the day's plan of action and generally stir Haile and his band of workmen into greater action on whichever building they happened to be working. Lunch at two was followed by a siesta. Much of the letter writing and the reading of the latest books was done then. Both of them went out again at about four, very often in the car, to look round the farm and observe any of the new ideas that Mike and Philippa were putting into action. 'Tea' was at six in the evening and then they both got down to office work. This might consist of making up records, fruit records or the Community Centre's accounts. Dinner at nine was followed by bridge whenever possible. While K.T. was alive, she made up a threesome, which was barely tolerable, but if they could capture the help of Mike or Philippa or anyone else who happened to be staying, then there could be a foursome. Bed always followed a hot bath at around two in the morning.

On market days they visited the various sub-centres of the community project, because one could be sure of finding the local land-owners and governors there. Dan and Chris would habitually exhort all of them to get down to work and build

The Sandfords, with their two youngest, Philippa and Stephen.
With them are Padre Matthew and Miss Stephenson, 1943.

Chris and Dan on the ponies they bought for their silver wedding anniversary: Silver Wedding and Silver Eagle.

A view across the farm from the hill behind the house.

A rubber dinghy used to cross the Sibilo River during the rainy season in order to reach the farm.

The Emperor Haile Selassie meeting members of the Board of Governors of the English School, 1954.

The pupils, the staff and the Board of Governors of the English School, 1954.

The Infant Class of the English School, having a lesson in the garden, 1954.

The family on the steps of the British Embassy after Chris had received the CBE in 1966. With them are the British Ambassador and his wife, Sir John and Lady Russell.

The Community Centre at Mulu Farm.
This was started in 1957.

The pupils of the school at the Community Centre.

The Emperor Haile Selassie visiting the Community Centre.

The ambulance, provided by World Neighbours
for the Community Centre.

The christening party for Eleanor Margaret Casbon, the only granddaughter to be born at Mulu Farm. Zoldie, the gardener, is holding her. 1955.

The front lawn of Mulu Farm.

The yellow climbing roses at Mulu Farm.

At home: Dan and Chris.

their own schools. Once the medical Land-rover had been given to the project there was a convoy of two vehicles. While the clinics were being held, Dan and Chris would be talking to the teachers and officials whom they met. On Wednesday afternoons they used to go into Addis Ababa for two nights. On Thursday they attended the mid-week Holy Communion service at St. Matthews, and the rest of the day was spent in a round of the various ministries, extracting from them things needed for the Community Centre, drugs for the clinic, books for the schools and vaccines for the veterinary work. Dan never ceased to act as perpetual prodder of officialdom. He felt his role to be that of a *this is what you should be doing man*. It was hard work and the various ministers' hearts must have sunk as he came to visit them, for this always forced them into some sort of action. On Thursday night the couple would have dinner with Leslie and Eleanor or with Dick and Anne. Chris would still be asked to play at rehearsals of any Gilbert and Sullivan opera going on. On Friday they returned to Mulu in the afternoon, and Saturday was recovery day. Then came Sunday, which was the great day for visitors. There are countless stories about the adventures and misadventures of guests at Mulu, whether they were there for the day or for longer, and they form rich memories for those who were there. David Hamilton, a teacher from the Wingate School, and his mother came out for a weekend and Chris had forgotten that she had invited them. So they were kept at bay with tea and scones till after seven o'clock in the evening, while Philippa rushed round helping to get their rooms ready. Another gentleman, coming to stay for the night, mentioned during the conversation over tea that he was allergic to bees and the doctor had told him that the next time he was stung could be fatal. Chris had been refining honey in his bedroom earlier in the day and when this happened, bees normally swarmed in to enjoy the honey. She had to send Dick in to crawl all over the floor of this room to make sure that there were no comatose bees left nestling in the reed mats. On another occasion, a Frenchman out to visit a project nearby refused to have his soup plate changed, saying that the French used the same plate for the next course, and then turned it upside down for the pudding. He finished off his meal by wiping everything up with a piece of bread and finally eating that.

Besides people who came to stay with the Sandfords as guests in their house, there were also many others who came as parts of organised groups. The school in Addis Ababa was the source of several school camps organised by the whole family during the rainy season. They were encouraged as another source of income for the farm and also to help parents who were stuck in Addis Ababa during the rains and had not made any real plans for children on holiday. These camps would last for ten days or so and the children would be introduced to riding and swimming and trips round the two farms. The great problem of these camps, apart from the feeding of the hungry hordes, was to make sure that they had enough dry clothes to wear the next day, as the children invariably got caught in the daily storm and were soaked to the skin. A whole room in the back quarters of the house was kept for this purpose and charcoal braziers were kept alight day and night. On one occasion, Eleanor, riding out from Addis Ababa with a few of the prospective camp members, was introduced by a young lad of thirteen to the American system of dating. He had not been in Addis Ababa for long and he explained that he had already made a list of all the females he had come in contact with and she was suitably impressed to learn that her name was fourth on the list. Other groups that came out were Scouts from different schools in Addis Ababa. They would camp below the house and outside the wire fencing, but near enough to use the spring of drinking water. Dan particularly was always interested to meet these young people, talk to them and listen to what they had to say. The Sandfords and the Langdons would take the groups round various parts of the farm and explain what was being done and why.

Chris's and Dan's children and grandchildren were constant visitors at Mulu Farm, which was, indeed, their second home. With Eleanor, Dick, Philippa and later Stephen working in Ethiopia, their parents' home was a focal point at which all of them met. The grandchildren also felt that they were part of a closely knit family. During holiday time there was always the opportunity to be with the grandparents at Mulu or at

Kusai in the valley, with expeditions to the Boli Waterfall, or the Cave, or the Monkey Place or swimming in the Bomfeta or chasing partridge, guinea fowl or ducks with a 2.2 rifle. Weekends during school time were also readily feasible, especially when a road was put through right to the end of the farm promontory for the new *telferique* which brought limestone up from the Boli Valley. The school that Chris had founded also played its part in the family plans, because the dreaded sending away of children to school in England could be put off until they reached their teens. Christine and Audrey, the other two members of the Sandfords' family also brought their families out for holidays from time to time. Christine came out twice with John and their three boys. Later on the two younger boys, David and Tim, both came out, between school ending and university starting to spend a year teaching and helping on the farm. Audrey and Bartie were working, first in Dar-es-Salaam, later in Egypt and Lebanon, and on two or three occasions Audrey and some members of the family came up for a visit and joined in all the family ploys. Chris and Dan had twenty-three grandchildren and all of them, at one time or another, visited Mulu Farm and stayed with their grandparents. On the reciprocal side, their far-flung family gave Chris and Dan some wonderful opportunities to go and stay with them in England, Tanzania and Lebanon. The daytime activities for the grandchildren may have been bound up in their parents' participation, but the evenings were made very special to them all by Grandpa's stories of *Jane Elizabeth and the Little Green Men* and Granny's efforts at the piano with singing games such as *See the Bunny Sleeping*, *Here We Go Looby Loo* and as they grew older, *Sir Roger de Coverley* and *Gathering Peascods*.

It was not only their close family that came to visit Chris and Dan. They also had the great joy of having other relatives to stay. Chris's mother, the indomitable Florence Lush came out twice to stay. She had already been in 1929 but she came again in 1952 and 1955. She was a much travelled lady by that time, because, after the house in Ewhurst was sold she went to stay with her eldest son, Cecil, and also visited her youngest son, Maurice, as he moved round the Mediterranean.

She stayed with Diana and Maurice at Geneva, Rome and Tripoli and was not at all daunted by further travel. She had a redoubtable companion called Miss Osborne or Ossie for short, who revelled in new experiences but whose lack of caution rendered her prone to accidents. There was one occasion when Granny, as she was universally called, and Ossie were left to have supper on their own, and were offered paw paw for the first time. When asked how they liked this new fruit they replied, "Not much, it was so hard and dry." They had eaten the pips and not the flesh. Granny, like her daughter, was imperturbable. This was shown up once when she was in the front seat of the old grey car, being driven out to Mulu by Chris. In the back, together with the usual large amount of goods and bodies, were K.T. and daughter-in-law Anne and her baby, Susan. Dan was coming out later, having seen Dick off at the airport. Chris got the car half-way up the road over the Entoto Mountain, when the gears refused to work, the brakes failed and the car started to go backwards down the hill. Haile leapt out of the back, picked up a stone and chased after the car hoping to get the opportunity to stop it by jamming the stone behind the wheel, but without success. Chris managed to steer the car all the way down the straight part of the hill, but knew that she would never make the corner at the bottom. So she decided to steer for the ditch at the side and came to rest rather sharply by hitting the edge of a culvert. All the passengers in the back were shot out of the open rear of the car and received cuts and bruises. Most serious of all K.T. broke her arm. The only people unhurt were Granny and Haile. All the injured were taken off to hospital by some means or other while Granny was left in the front seat of the car, watched over by Haile. Dan was telephoned at the airport and he and Philippa came to the rescue. They found Grannie entirely oblivious of the usual huge crowd of onlookers and sightseers and she asked Dan to thank those kind people for being so nice to her. She was also heard to say, "How stupid of K.T. to be so careless," when informed of the accident. On the second time she came out in 1955, she was present at Mulu when her great-grandchild was born there. It was a great occasion, because it was the only time that a member of the family was actually born at Mulu. All the necessary professionals were there. Christine, a doctor, was visiting, an English midwife friend was staying and large numbers of family were all around in support. The christening of baby Eleanor Margaret was held at Mulu, ten days after her birth and a very good photograph of four generations was taken; Granny Lush, her daughter, Chris, her granddaughter, Eleanor and her great-granddaughter Eleanor Margaret, with about ninety years' difference in age from the oldest to the youngest.

Both of Dan's sisters visited Ethiopia during the fifties and stayed for a short time. Betty's visit in 1950 is remembered by those who met her at the airport for the fact that her determination to exceed her normal weight allowance caused her to carry off the plane a raincoat whose sleeves had been rendered rigid by having another coat stuffed into them. Another vivid memory of her is when she had to cross a very flooded Boli River on a trip to visit the bump at Mulu and, not being exactly used to horses, had to cling to Dama's mane for dear life to avoid being swept off. That particular summer Philippa and Stephen were out on holiday and they were due to return to England with Betty but had to send telegrams to their respective schools notifying them of their delayed return. These read 'Cut off by floods'.

In 1954 the younger of Dan's two sisters, Ethel, also paid a visit and stayed for a few months. She was taken to see the sights and again her visit was highlighted by several strange events. She was taken to visit Jimma and the area round about by some of her nieces and nephews. The whole group was booked into what they thought was going to be a rather high class hotel in Jimma itself. When they arrived, they found that no rooms had been prepared although the Italian manager was most apologetic. He ejected some personal friends from enough rooms to house the party, but the only member to be decently accommodated was Ethel. One family slept on mattresses on the floor of the room from which a toilet had been removed although the drainhole had not been filled in. The food was inordinately priced and to crown everything the brakes on the vehicle failed on the journey back to Addis Ababa and it was only by Leslie

Casbon's cautious driving, using low gears and a depressed clutch, that the party reached home safely without Ethel being aware that anything was wrong.

Emma Awdry was also a beloved guest at Mulu. She had been out in the early 1920s when her son, Vere, worked at the farm and she also came out in 1958 and 1963. On the latter occasion her grandson, Robin Oldridge, was out at the farm, following in the footsteps of his uncle and working at whatever he was asked to do. Emma was as imperturbable as Chris and enjoyed her stay, both in Addis Ababa and at the farm. She became very deaf and in later years had to be careful about what she ate but, in spite of all her difficulties, she took a really informed interest in all that was going on, appreciating and enjoying the hustle and bustle, and the different dramas that ensued. She kept a diary during much of the time that she was there, and it shows very clearly what an alert interest she took. Diana Oldridge, Emma's daughter and Robin's mother, managed to come out for a short visit after both Chris and Dan had been trying to persuade her for over forty years. Diana and Maurice Lush also came out twice during this period. Once in 1959 and again in 1974 after Dan's death. It was familiar ground for Maurice and he had many friends to look up and old memories to revive.

Two other friends of Chris's should be mentioned specially. One was Phil Downes. She and Chris had been friends at Girton College, Cambridge, and both had become teachers. After Phil had retired, she came out to Addis Ababa to visit the family and also to do some work with the blind. She had a wonderful personality and was calm and efficient and yet had a great sense of humour. She enjoyed every minute of the life at Mulu and made a cheerful and interested member of any camping trip that Chris and Dan used to take. The other friend was G.M. Ward, or Gym Ward, as she used to be called. She first met Chris when they were teaching together in Beverley in 1936 where she had been the PE teacher. She came out for several visits after she had retired and was always made very welcome at Mulu. She had a more prickly temperament than Phil and often used to annoy the younger generation by being too protective towards Chris and being outspoken about how she felt they should behave. For all that, she was good company, and Dan used to tease her unmercifully when she was inclined to be dogmatic. She also enjoyed the camping trips and was especially helpful on a trip that Chris took after Dan's death, when she drove to Massawa and then went by boat to the Gulf of Aqaba where Audrey met them and drove them to Beirut. Gym Ward went on by air, but Chris stayed and eventually drove across Europe with Audrey and some of her family.

Both Chris and Dan had the gift of making friends and keeping them, but in the latter part of their lives it was to Chris in particular that so many came for advice and comfort. They were both imperturbable and ever-optimistic and those in trouble or grief were always made to feel welcome and free to talk. Dan's advice was usually more astringent than that of Chris, and he was not always patient with pessimists, but both were always ready to listen and help where they could.

19

THE LATTER YEARS OF SO-CALLED RELAXATION

One of the greatest joys that Dan and Chris had, after they left public life, was to be able to go camping. If they could have companionship in the form of visitors from England who could be persuaded to go with them or members of the family, so much the better. Otherwise they would decide on a reason for a trip, pack the car and then be off. With their sublime faith that the Almighty would keep a benign eye on them, they almost always managed to get to where they wanted and in one piece, but through the years there had to be several rescue operations mounted when the car broke down or the weather proved too bad.

Dan, with his never fading interest in new projects, especially in agriculture, was very keen to go and see forestry projects in the province of Arrussi and cotton growing at Arba Minch. They also did more than one journey northwards across the Blue Nile and into Gojjam, which was Dan's special area in Mission 101 times. They travelled down to the Red Sea at Assab, through Danakil country and over the hot, dry plains that lie below sea level. They travelled south towards the Kenyan border and into Borana country and they went east to see the walled town of Harar. When they were not accompanied by friends or relatives, then the one car was loaded to capacity. They usually had two servants with them, Aberra, the general factotum and perhaps Isheti, the cook, or just another young lad to do the fetching and carrying. They had a suitcase of clothes, a very heavy old army bell tent, mosquito nets, a box of food, a box of cooking and eating utensils, a two hundred litre tin barrel cut in half longways to make a bath, several other tins containing petrol, paraffin, oil and water, heavy old camp-beds with mattresses and bedding, a satchel of books to read, a couple of petromax lamps and a shabby old radio on which to listen to the BBC news. Chris would don her shady straw hat, made on the farm, and settle down behind the wheel of the car, with Dan beside her, completely trustful that she would drive perfectly safely. The two servants would squeeze into the next row of seats, with last minute extras stuffed all round them and the rest of the luggage would be in the back or on the top of the car. The springs would be dangerously flat and the tyres would almost certainly need some repairs before they had gone too far along the gravel roads that they travelled on. They would stop for morning coffee along the road and have that from a thermos, already prepared and then later stop for a picnic lunch. If lunch could be taken in a place where there was something of progress to be observed – that was a gain. After lunch they would take a nap under a tree and then get in the car and move on. If the journey was to take several days, they would start looking for a camping site around four in the afternoon where both water and wood were available. As soon as the site was chosen, the camp chairs were found and set out in the shade. Then after wood had been collected and water drawn, the all-important tea was prepared. Once Chris and Dan were thus ensconced, with or without guests, the work of putting up the camp was started by Aberra and his mate. The tent had to be pitched, the beds made, large tins of water had to be heated for the bath and supper had to be prepared. If they were travelling in countryside where the name of 'Sandiford' was known, then the local chief or *ballabat* would often come with a gift of some eggs or chickens and some bottles of *talla* or *tej*. Then news and views would be exchanged. Once darkness came the petromax lights were prepared and the night calls of hyena, jackal or owl permeated the night. After supper all food articles would be put in the front of the car for safety, the utensils covered by a large tarpaulin and left by the fire, the half-barrel bath moved into the verandah of the tent and made steady by having some stones put on either side of it and then filled with hot water for a bath and some cold beside it if necessary. Chris and Dan then retired to the tent for their baths, followed by some reading in bed and the two servants made their beds in the back of the car. Reasonably early the next day a cup of tea was brought to the tent and breakfast eaten, followed by packing up and preparing for the day. Sometimes, if it was more convenient to use a hotel for one of the nights away, they accepted this alternative, but the tent was much more comfortable than the smallish hotels usually found away in the country. When they passed through a sizeable town they stocked up with bread, oil, macaroni and petrol, and perhaps some fruit and eggs but for the most part they carried butter, jam and marmalade from the farm, sufficient for their needs. A game of bridge, if there was company, or scrabble if they were alone, and the evenings passed as they did at home. If there was any serious mechanical fault or the supply of tyres had run out, one of the servants either went into the nearest town on a local bus or passing truck, or even back to Mulu to ask for help to be sent. When they got to their destination and asked to be shown round whatever it was they had come to see, they were always greeted with respect and affection and their genuine interest was felt to be very encouraging. Their trips were not necessarily long ones; sometimes they were only for a weekend down to the Rift Valley lakes, where their children used to like to take their families. Sometimes they went to the Awash Valley reserve and camped beside the river, with the hippos regularly coming out of the water to eat the lush vegetation, always very curious about the odd humans who invaded their territory.

As well as camping inside Ethiopia, Chris and Dan also made several very successful trips abroad. Audrey and Bartie Knight were in Dar-es-Salaam, where Bartie was Principal of a Teachers' Training College and they visited the family three times, in 1953, 1957 and 1959. On the last occasion they went down with Emma Awdry, who had been staying at Mulu, by air to Nairobi and then finished the journey by sea from Mombassa. While in Kenya they visited 'Tree Tops' in the Kenya game reserve, where animals can be watched from a high platform above the salt-licks. Dan took especial pleasure on this occasion, in spitting on to the backs of elephants as they passed below him. Chris visited England in 1961 to see her mother just before she died and in 1973, after Dan's death, she travelled by car to Massawa with Gym Ward and then across the Red Sea to Aqaba, where Audrey collected her and drove her to Beirut and eventually across Europe to England.

One of the highlights of the 1960s was the State visit of the Queen and Prince Philip to Ethiopia and in a letter to Emma Awdry, Chris vividly describes the whole event:

'I thought you would be interested to hear of the Queen's visit, which did not, alas, include Mulu. She had to go and see the Mitchell Cotts plantation in Tendaho – cotton, and very hot and dusty – but they have put a lot of British money into it as well as Ethiopian. Anyway, we all had a very good time. We and all the children went to see her triumphal arrival from the airport, and sitting on the stone terraces in front of Africa House (made at intervals rather wet by exuberant fountains) we could have thrown an apple (not a tomato!) into the stage coach as she drove past us and in at the Palace gates. We had a great scuffle to get home among all the thousands of cars in time for the State Banquet in the old Menelik Palace only one and a half hours later, but just got there in time to be shown into the big reception room which was quite empty until the Corps Diplomatique was ushered in. As we have Embassies from all European countries, most African States, USA and South America, and a few from Asia (but not so far China), this is a wonderful sight as the Africans and Asians wear their national costumes, and very glorious they are, from Nigeria, Ghana, Tanzania especially, though the Arabs from Yemen and Saudi Arabia look fine too. When we were all lined up in came the two crowned heads! The Queen looking quite lovely in a shimmering green dress with her orders worn across it and the most glorious diamond tiara, necklace and earrings, that sparkled with her every slight movement. On a velvet cushion on a small table guarded by a *Page* – an elderly Buckingham Palace retainer in velvet coat and knee breeches – lay the Field Marshall's baton which the Queen then presented to the Emperor with a few words. Discreet clapping from the guests and we then all walked out onto the balcony to see the most superb fireworks, (luckily the family could see these too, as it was a lovely night and they were visible from all over the town). Then clutching our place cards we went down a long flight of steps into the enormous banqueting hall which was all done up for the visit of the Heads of African States last year. We were lucky to be in excellent seats *above the salt* so could both see and hear the Queen and Emperor and their after-dinner speeches. They conversed with great friendliness all through the banquet. The Queen and Emperor came up the hall when we were all seated and a little herd of photographers were then driven up, allowed three photographs and driven away again. We did not move from our seats till they were allowed up once more after the speeches and then the Queen and Emperor passed down again and we all went home!

'The next day Dan and I were invited to a private lunch party at the Crown Prince's house of the Ethiopian Ministers and their wives, the British Ambassador and ourselves, which I thought a very nice compliment to Dan. It was rather a hurried affair as the Queen, after a long morning of engagements, was very late, but it gave an opportunity for the Emperor to have a talk with Dan when he expressed great pleasure at the Queen's visit and said how charming and vivacious she was and how he was enjoying talking to her. We had to do a quick change and be up at the British Embassy for Leslie to receive his MBE from the Queen. All the family above seven years were admitted and, as we left, were presented. Eleanor, Dan and myself, Philippa and Mike, Nicola, Eleanor Margaret, Fiona and Piers. You can imagine their surprise and joy. "She said hello to me," said Piers. Then came a garden party in the legation paddock, given by the Commonwealth Ambassadors and all the British Commonwealth Communities were present under their flags. I suppose the Queen and the Duke must have spoken to more than one hundred people each. They were wonderful. The next day they flew off to visit the cotton plantation and in the evening the Queen entertained the Emperor and his family at the British Embassy and Dan and I were invited to the reception afterwards – mostly Corps Diplomatique, though I was delighted that they invited old Padre (so was he) and one or two others like ourselves.

'Finally came Thursday when, after a show on the polo ground, they went on a riding picnic with the Emperor – and were one hour late for the visit to the English School. We had a lovely show for her of our six hundred and fifty children in thirty-two national groups – and many in national costume – and then the rain came and we had to take them into our old Assembly Hall just as she arrived. She was quite charming, talked to Leslie and Eleanor and the heads of our Senior, Junior and Preparatory departments, and then faced a cheering crowd of children, jumping up on a bench so that they could see her better – and then gave them two days holiday! That night she was made a "Freeman of Addis Ababa" at the new enormous Civic Hall and we had another tremendous banquet. By this time she had seen enough of Dan and myself to give us a friendly recognition as she passed up the hall. It all ended up with a display of Ethiopian dancing and she left next morning while we all returned to work – hundreds of strawberries, plums and peaches. Unfortunately Dan has also had a very bad attack of gout, very painful and incapacitating, but I am glad to say it is passing.'

The Queen's visit was in February 1965 and a year later, on 5 May 1966, it was the twenty-fifth anniversary of the Emperor's return to Ethiopia. This was to be an occasion of great rejoicing for the whole country, and in his inimitable way the Emperor set out to acknowledge his gratitude to the British Army for their help in the fight for Ethiopia's freedom. All the members of 101 Mission were invited and other representatives of those who had fought in the Gojjam Campaign. Chris's letter to her daughter, Christine, gives a clear idea of how the invited British Officers felt overwhelmed by the Emperor's generosity and courtesy:

'Just to give you some idea of the happenings of the last week which as we said would prove a very hectic one, though it has been very pleasant too and Dad has weathered it very well and enjoyed it all very much . . . After much excitement over dress proper to the various occasions – morning coat and tails, and dinner jacket and white waistcoat, and tie and grey waistcoat, and top hat for Dan (most of them twenty or thirty years old and in need of considerable cleaning, brushing and altering!), and a silver lace overdress to my eleven-year-old evening dress very cunningly constructed by Philippa (I thought the black and white one I got in 1961 rather gloomy for such a festive occasion as a Silver Jubilee), we came into Addis Ababa last Tuesday evening, so as to have a day before the great show on 5 May. That same evening all the members of Mission 101 who had arrived that day, as well as Orde Wingate's son and many others who had fought in the Gojjam Campaign turned up to see Dad between five-thirty and seven-thirty so we had a great gathering here all talking of twenty-five years ago and all, of course, twenty-five years older, so a bit hard to pick out. However, everybody was very happy to be here. Present as well was the Deputy Head of British Defence Staff and his young ADC – so they made a very happy party.

'The next day we were bidden to the Embassy for me to get my "gong" in order to be able to wear it at the banquet the next evening. [This was the OBE.] We were regaled with champagne but the lunch party had to be postponed till the Friday as the Mission 101 people and others had not been presented to the Emperor and so could not come to the Embassy. However, Wilfred Thesiger and Chapman Andrews managed to wriggle in as well as the friends from here and the family whom I was allowed to invite – Eleanor and Leslie, Little Eleanor and Fiona, Philippa and Mike, Piers and Christopher and, of course, the old Padre. So we were quite a party. It's a nice gong – the same cross but this time in blue enamel on a gold backing and lying on, rather than pendant from, the pink and grey ribbon. It looked nice on my silver dress. The next day – 5 May which is the anniversary of both Italian and Ethiopian entries – five years apart – we were bidden to be at the Thanksgiving Service at the church just above the Tafari Makonnen School at eight-thirty. It was, of course, packed with diplomats (including the Italian Ambassador), but one side was reserved for the British soldiers who had been invited and Dan and I sat at the front of that. The service took about an hour and was very impressive and well done and then we streamed out after the

Emperor for the Review of the troops. He did a tour down to the Arat Kilo memorial and back past The English School to the polo ground where he inspected troops and we proceeded slowly to the grandstand that had been erected just below the Ministry of Finance and opposite the garden of the lions. We had extremely good seats, but the review started at eleven and we did not get home till three-fifteen, no food meanwhile. There was a long speech from General Marid, the Minister of Defence, who was once Dad's secretary in Cairo, and then one from the Emperor with a very nice reference to the British soldiers who had helped in the liberation and a nice mention of Dad by name . . . Well we were not finished, but lay down a bit to recover and then arrayed ourselves for the banquet at eight o'clock. I am glad to say that Leslie and Eleanor were invited, but we could only secure invitations to the next evening's banquet at the Crown Prince's palace for Philippa and Mike. It was, of course, a gorgeous show and we were at the head of the long table stretching down from alongside the Imperial table, so saw everything except the film of the campaign in Gojjam in which Dad appeared, as this was at the far end of the hall from our seats at table. However, Eleanor and Leslie saw it well and Dad was greeted with a good clap. I cannot tell you how well the invited British officers were treated by HIM. They were all met at the airport by a car and chauffeur for each of them. Their hotel bills including all drinks were paid for by the Ethiopian Government and they were all received and presented with silver cigarette cases before they left. They were so overwhelmed that some of them were not far from tears at having been remembered after twenty-five years.

'The review was tremendous. First the *old contemptibles* who had fought in the first campaign against the Italians in 1935 – in their old uniforms and odd clothes – there were some women patriots among them; and then the whole of the modern army – a very impressive show – infantry, artillery, tanks and armoured cars, in enormous numbers, both from the regular army and the Imperial Guard, and finally the cavalry in all their glory of bright uniforms and pennants flying. I doubt whether any state of Africa could put up anything like it, and they were all extremely smart and well disciplined and wonderfully equipped. It was a terrific tour de force. We did not go to the Athletic Show at the stadium the next day, but Wilfred said it was excellent, and we had a wonderful evening party of about fifteen hundred people at the Crown Prince's palace.'

Almost immediately after all these celebrations, Dan went down with a severe attack of pneumonia, which caused no little anxiety, but thanks to prompt treatment and modern drugs, he recovered quite quickly. Chris's letter of 25 May speaks of his recovery and the desire to get back to Mulu and a normal routine. She speaks of going up to the Private Secretary's office, and receiving the gifts of the Emperor to all invited for the Anniversary celebrations, 'a very nice gold embossed cigarette case for Dad and a wonderful heavy gold bracelet with twisted elephant hairs and filigree gold for me.' She goes on to say, 'Meanwhile, loaded with all the presents from Dad's lady friends; whisky, brandy, bovril, horlicks, chocolates, etc., we shall proceed to build him up again. We are very much hoping for a visit from Audrey with Olivia in a fortnight's time and that will be the best tonic of all.' Dan adds his remarks at the end of the letter saying, 'It's good to be throwing off my pneumonia and be getting back to Mulu. Mum, as you will know, has been indefatigable and most efficient in looking after me, and no man could have had a more loving wife to care for him! And the family's good wishes have supported me and I am lucky and a happy man.'

It was from this time on that there was to be a gradual slowing down of Dan's physically active participation in life in general. He had recurring attacks of gout which were extremely painful and enervating. In 1967, he had what was probably a slight stroke which did not affect his movements or speech but which left him unconscious for several hours. Chris also suffered ever increasing pain from an arthritic knee and this cut down the amount of time that she could spend either walking or standing. Neither of them allowed these signs of increasing age to upset them or radically to alter their normal active lives, but always attentive of each other, they chose less energetic ways to go about their affairs. They would view the different farm projects from the car, instead of striding about on foot; they would let their guests wander among the roses and other plants, looked after by Philippa and Mike or Sanbatta, and then discuss them sitting on the lawn. However, Chris still went about laying out Addis Ababa gardens with unabated vigour, and during the 1960s she created the gardens of the Austrian, Indonesian, Indian, Australian and Yugoslavian Embassies. When working on the latter, she was amused and amazed to find a real *iron curtain* at the Embassy's front wall that was raised and lowered at the touch of a switch.

The next big event that is worth recording was Chris's and Dan's Golden Wedding on 14 November 1968, fifty years of a wonderfully happy marriage where love and trust, optimism and real partnership were a shining example to all around them. Their joint family letter, written a week later shows not only how much they enjoyed themselves but also how much their family and friends appreciated them.

Dan: 'We have had the most wonderfully happy Golden Wedding celebrations and we want to send a message to all of you who have been in our thoughts and who have had us in your thoughts, that we know that we have deep causes for thankfulness for our fifty years of great happiness and we feel that each one and all of you have contributed to our happiness by your constant love and countless kindnesses to us. Thank you! Thank you! Our young chaplain, Philip Cousins, walked out from Addis Ababa on the Tuesday, we began the day on Wednesday 14 November with a Holy Communion service at which Philippa and Mike were present with us and the children sang two hymns – one verse of *Now Thank We All Our God* and *Praise Him, Praise Him*. Then from four o'clock to all hours of the night we were at home (tea, cocktails and dinner) to over seventy family and friends (adults and children). We received many messages including eighteen telegrams and letters from all over the world and a lot of very kind presents including over twenty bottles of champagne, two wedding cakes, furniture, and from dear sister Ethel the cementing of our back passages. Since then we have spent two nights at Ambo with the families and a large party of friends, and attended a supper party at the Embassy to say good-bye to the Goulstons who are returning to Australia . . . And we've had numbers of visitors out here most days. So we've been happily busy; letter writing and so forth. C.S. doing most of it.

'On Wednesday we are invited to the Embassy again for lunch to meet the English School Board who are giving us a magnificent present of furniture. It is all rather overwhelming. Padre Matthew came out to our *at home* and I am glad to say stood up to it very well. We gave him lunch at a hotel in Addis Ababa in recognition of his many services to us all – a room full of parishioners; he made a speech and survived with no overtiring. (Over to C.S.)'

Chris: 'I don't think that you will get any Christmas cards this year as I shall still be immersed if not submerged in writing thank you letters for all our letters, cards (twenty), telegrams (eighteen), and presents. We have a back corridor down which you can roller-skate to the bathrooms, a suite of furniture, sofa and three armchairs into which you sink down and do no more work for the rest of the day, plastic and aluminium armchairs in the garden under an enormous umbrella (given by the Imeru family), a crystal goblet to hold lilies, watsonia and spekelia (from the Desta family of princesses and Skinder), a lovely white morocco bound Bible (from Amaha), a beautiful tea set in eggshell blue (from our Australian and New Zealand friends), Hamlins, Fitzgeralds and Goulstons, candlesticks and milk and sugar bowls in brass and beaten steel, enough eau-de-cologne to have a bath in, a golden plastic bowl, beautiful floral curtains (Boussac) in the sitting-room and books galore. I chose a complete set of Hardy from Dad that will keep me happy for months and replaces one that Phyl gave me fifty years ago. (Over to D.A.S.) ' **Dan**: 'And finally there was the very kind and useful gift from the family of the reconditioning of the car which is now looking and running as new. Amropa garage made a very good job of it and we thank you all very much indeed. Your (Audrey and Bartie) telegram came in on the day and gave us an added kick to our great happiness and we immediately looked up your Proverbs reference in Amaha's Bible and appreciated its aptness . . . (Over to C.S.)' **Chris**: 'The car is my greatest delight – gives me mobility which my legs are beginning to deny me – one arthritic knee is a great curse – and Dad loves his evening strolls about the farm which is now accessible in almost all cases to the car – and then, as I hope, tomorrow we do a little jaunt off to see some new development, this time to Assella, beyond Nazareth, where Poulson the Dane who visited Bartie the other day has his forestry plantation . . . '

One of the visitors who came out to Ethiopia in time for the Golden Wedding celebrations was Diana Oldridge, Dan's cousin and daughter of Emma Awdry. The Sandfords had been inviting her out for the past forty years, but this was the first visit she had ever paid. Her brother, Vere, had worked on the farm as had her son, Robin, and her mother had also paid regular visits over the years, so it was an added delight to the Sandfords to have her helping them to celebrate their special occasion. When writing of them both some time later, Diana quoted a passage out of T.S. Elliot's play *An Elder Statesman* which embodies much that the Golden Wedding celebrations were really about:

'But there's no vocabulary
For love within a family, love that's lived in
But not looked at, love within the light of which
All else is seen, the love within which
All other love finds speech –
. . . This love is silent.'

The 1960s saw the passing on of several of Chris and Dan's families and friends but in every case the memories left were of lives well lived and much to be thankful for. Chris's mother, Dan's eldest sister, Betty, and Emma Awdry all died in England and all had been loved and welcomed guests at Mulu over the years. K.T. Stephenson died in Addis Ababa while Chris was away in England. She had been part of the family for forty years and had done her stoical utmost to produce high academic skills in six Sandford offspring. Suffice it to say that owing to her and Chris's teaching the six of them had gained either scholarships or bursaries to schools in England. Her love of teaching was never in doubt and her help with the start of the English School was inestimable, though staff, parents and pupils alike would despair at times of ever winning a word of praise from her. She did not really think it was a good thing to encourage self-esteem among the young. Despite this stern exterior she was unfailingly generous to the whole family in all sorts of ways and became an integral part of the whole.

There was one other person who became part of the Sandford family and, as did Chris and Dan, ended his days in Addis Ababa. This was Padre Austen Matthew, who came to Addis Ababa in 1928 to be chaplain. Coming from Nyasaland, where he had been a missionary, he set up a small Anglican church in the centre of Addis Ababa. As has been mentioned before, he used to walk out to Mulu once a month, before the war, to give the Sandfords Holy Communion and when the Italians had invaded in 1936 he went to Jerusalem. He stayed there for the next seven years giving help and encouragement to the many Ethiopian exiles there and returned to Addis Ababa in 1942, first to be chaplain once more and then to retire. When Dan was in Addis Ababa in 1942, before Chris returned, he shared a house with the Padre and earlier on, when Dan was in Maji in 1935, it had been the Padre that had kept in regular touch with him and told him the latest news of the war and the Emperor's affairs. Once everyone was back in Addis Ababa and a regular routine had been established, the Padre was to be seen every Sunday night at the Sandfords' house joining in with hymns and the other events of the day. When he retired from the chaplaincy, he lived in a little house quite near the school gates, and after Chris and Dan left the school to live in Mulu, he still used to come to Sunday evenings, now hosted by Eleanor and Leslie. His life's great work was to help with the translation of the Bible into Amharic. Chris wrote of his death in the following words:

'You will be saddened to hear of the death of dear old Padre, some of you may have seen it in the papers. Dad and I had been in to see him last week on our way down to Langano where Dad and I had been lent a house for two or three nights while Eleanor and family plus Janet and Andrew camped. He seemed as he has been all these last few months, still more frail and a bit bothered with a cough, but was quite his old self, telling me not to shout because he wasn't deaf, and we said we would call again when we came back on Friday. But Miss Benson, who lives in our flat, went round just before we came back, and returned with a very bad report of his being in bed and very weak, so we held a family conference and Eleanor and Leslie said they would take him up to their house for the weekend. However, a doctor friend who was there, said he ought to be in hospital, so they took him down by ambulance to the Fil-Wuha hospital and he died there at six o'clock on Saturday morning. We all went in from here on Sunday morning and after a very beautiful service in church, he was buried out in the War Graves Cemetery in Gulele. Dad and I did not go out to the cemetery but came back here the same afternoon; but all the rest of the family and a great many of the British community were out there in gently falling rain. The Ethiopians were also in evidence. Present at the funeral were army generals representing the Emperor, the Vice Abuna Theophilus, with one or two priests and others from the RC, Greek and Armenian Churches, the three princesses of the Desta family, Michael Imeru and Tamrat Igizu, Governor of Gondar. So one felt they really paid tribute to all that he had done for them, especially during their exile in Jerusalem when he had looked after so many of them, very often out of his own pocket. He has been for so many years a member of the family that it seems strange that he is in his little house no more; but it was a quick and happy ending to a long life of service and we never had to subject him to being under nursing care and bedridden, which he would have hated.' . . . One of his co-translators, Belatta Merza Hassan, had come to visit him the night he went to hospital and followed him there and, unknown to the family, had spent the whole night in vigil by his bedside.

Before the 1960s drew to a close, there were two other events in the Sandfords' lives that are worthy of remembering. One was the arrival of their youngest son, Stephen, and his family to spend some years there, working for the World Bank. This was a great joy to Chris and Dan and meant that all six of their family had returned in the course of time to Ethiopia and had worked there as adults, some for only a short time and others for a good deal longer. It also added another angle of interest in discussing projects for improving life in Ethiopia. Pippa, Stephen's wife, was an added bonus to the staff of the English School and more grandchildren were there to grow up, as the older ones left for schooling in England.

Visitors continued to flock to Mulu and one of the groups included members of the Blue Nile Expedition, under the leadership of Chris Bonnington. This expedition was to make an exploratory trip down the Blue Nile by boat from just below Lake Tana until it joined the White Nile at Khartoum. Chris and Dan were thrilled that the expedition named one of the boats *The Sandford* and later sent back to the farm the tarpaulin that had covered the boat with the name painted on it. Several members of the family including Philippa went to the bridge over the Nile gorge to watch the launching of the boats and helped christen *The Sandford* with a bottle of local champagne. The expedition was successful in reaching Khartoum, but not without facing considerable danger and incurring some sad casualties.

20

THE 1970s AND THE CLOSING OF THE CURTAINS

The Sandfords' lives continued to be busy and full of interest, even though physical disability made them both less active on their feet. With four of their offspring all working in Ethiopia and bringing new visitors to Mulu, there was never a dearth of new faces for them to see and new ideas for them to listen to and comment on. The ever-growing farm, never ceasing to experiment with the introduction of cattle and ideas on artificial insemination was a tremendous joy to both Chris and Dan. The steady increase in the number of strawberries produced and the new efforts to capture an export market were matters in which they took a deep interest. At one time over fifty-thousand baskets were being picked a month and Mike had managed to get quite a fair quantity accepted in Djibouti, freighted by air, when he received an urgent telegram asking him to reduce deliveries for a while, as Djibouti residents had been eating too many too quickly and were suffering from *estomac malade*. There was no lessening of the orders Chris received for roses and shrubs and for setting out gardens in or around Addis Ababa. In one of his letters home, Dan wrote: 'One of you said to us the other day that we had been described as people who "keep Ethiopia ticking over"; well we haven't the cheek to subscribe to that description, but we certainly see a lot of people from all walks of life – UNO, British Services, Ethiopian, Government, business and what not, and of course, the family with their various jobs and chores: Mum and Leslie in all happenings in education, Dick and Mike in livestock and agriculture and now Stephen in banking. We ought to keep ourselves well-informed and I waddle along in their wake trying to remember a few of the things I am told.'

Sir Dennis Wright, when speaking at the memorial service for Dan in London, spoke of this hive of activity at Mulu. 'My wife and I, on a short return visit to Ethiopia in 1968 after an absence of six years, had invited ourselves for lunch – our visit would have been incomplete without the Sandfords and Mulu – and were delighted to find, as I recorded that night in my diary, Dan and Chris living in the same blissful untidiness. I can think of no more appropriate word than "blissful" to describe the atmosphere that Dan and Chris had created at Mulu. Those of you who have visited them there will know what I mean. They were the most striking example I know of matrimonial harmony and happiness which was reflected in all that went on at Mulu – in the comings and goings of their six children and their wives and husbands and twenty-three grandchildren; in the constant and always welcome stream of visitors, for many of whom a visit to Mulu had the significance of a pilgrimage: in Dan's and Chris's happy relationship with the surrounding Galla peasants: in the activities of the Community Centre which absorbed so much of Dan's interest in recent years.'

Another great source of interest to them was the decision to buy the site of the English School and the acquisition of the means to effect this. Chris naturally had a permanent place on the Board of Governors and was always deeply concerned with the improvement and enlargement of the school. When the school first used their present site, the rent for it was paid for by the Ethiopian Ministry of Education. This gradually faded out because the Board realised that the Ministry had enough problems on its hands without that expenditure. Some of the Ethiopian parents who had been educated in England themselves were nostalgically desirous to make the school into a replica of an English public school and so put forward suggestions for acquiring a property outside Addis Ababa, but this would have entirely destroyed the multi-national flavour of the school and was firmly opposed by the Board. The Emperor offered to give some land, but that was also too far out to be useful, and it was finally decided to buy the present site. To do that the school had to become an Ethiopian Association; this was accomplished and then the drive to raise the necessary money began. Every scheme possible was considered, every possible patron asked to belong, and among the most tireless workers and planners were the Sandfords. Their old friend, Henry Littler, who had run the British Council so excellently in the 1940s, was asked out for a year to get schemes going and to be fund manager. He and Chris between them were able to go and talk to all the nobility and royalty and seek aid. Plays, concerts, Gilbert and Sullivan operas, children's productions like *Noye's Fludde* and *Oliver* were all performed. Cricket matches, gymkhanas and carnival days were put on. The Emperor came to one carnival day and really enjoyed himself, going round the stalls and shooting at a target. A great draw at the carnivals was the international lunches that were set out in the school hall. Twenty or more of the nationalities represented in the school produced food typical of their own countries and people could pass along the buffet tables and choose from them all. The English table produced roast beef and Yorkshire puddings, cold ham and salad, followed by strawberries and cream. The fund raising campaign took three or four years but the whole amount was finally found by January 1974. The school became the property of the English School Association for a month. By March 1974 the revolution started taking over and the property was handed back to the nation.

Dan died on 22 January 1972. 'His last day was the normal happy one at Mulu with the Grisdale family spending the day followed by a game of bezique when Dan beat me soundly at eleven. Then at six he just stopped breathing.' So Chris was to describe his end. Dick, Stephen and Eleanor and their families were all at their camping site on the Rift Valley Lake of Langano, celebrating Eleanor's fiftieth birthday, and with great kindness the British Ambassador sent down a chauffeur in an Embassy car to tell them the news. This meant a three hour journey, with the news having to be first brought in from Mulu, also by car. On the Sunday morning, the next day, before the coffin was brought in to Addis Ababa, the country-side came out in force, shooting off their guns, while the ladies sat round in sympathetic silence. Then some of his old friends among the workmen bore his coffin to the car and all drove into Addis Ababa to St. Matthew's Church for the service, with a bus load of people coming in from the farm. Once Chris reached Addis Ababa she received a message from the Emperor. He was on a state visit to Lagos and news of Dan's death had been sent to him there. He requested that the burial should be delayed for a few hours to give him time to get back from abroad and be at the War Cemetery. He also asked that Dan should be given a full military funeral. The church was packed for the service and many more stood outside. People of all walks of life and of many nationalities were there, ranging from some of the princesses to workmen from the farm. Chris played the funeral march while the coffin was taken to the hearse outside and then Chris waited in the school until some sixth sense told her it was time to drive out to the War Graves Cemetery. She arrived there just before the Emperor. Six Ethiopian Army officers bore the coffin to the grave and Ethiopian Army buglers played the Last Post. Thus Dan was buried with full military honours. The Emperor then came and spoke to Chris and her family, as did many other friends from all over the world. Of Dan's many friends, Wilfred Thesiger was out in Addis Ababa at the time and was a very welcome addition to the family. Christine and her husband John flew out from England to be with Chris and though they did not manage to get out in time for the funeral, they were there for the recognised time of mourning in Ethiopia. Christine wrote a description of this period of mourning which portrays the great sense of togetherness that Ethiopians show in times of loss or trouble: 'It is the custom in Ethiopia for there to be a period of time when people come to the house of one who has died, to tell of his life and works, to express their sorrow and sympathy and to give support and hope to the relatives. These periods used to last a long time – the greater the person the longer the duration – but the Emperor had decreed that three days were long enough and suitable for all walks of life. The three days were spent in Addis Ababa – and this was expected by the people out at Mulu – many of whom had managed to get to the funeral anyway, but we and they wanted a day when they could come themselves, so this was planned for Wednesday 25 January. We spent the early part of the morning in preparation as the house servants had told us to expect some hundreds of horsemen and other mourners. It was, in fact, well planned beforehand and actually the servants in many ways took charge, told us how many to expect, and more or less what it would be appropriate to provide in the way of food and drink, and where different ranks should sit.

'As it was a fast day no meat or cheese or eggs could be eaten, so we put strawberry jam on rolls and provided parched corn, and *tala* (beer) and sweet tea. A tent was erected below the lawn and benches and chairs placed in the big office room at the end of the house. Outside on the verandah we put a table of flowers, a large portrait of Dad and his medals and ribbons on a white cloth, and on the next verandah chairs for the family. Meanwhile an open tent was pitched at the top end of the paddock and furnished with chairs. We could see groups of people and horses gathering all the morning over on the far side of the farm by the road, with an occasional blowing of horns. About midday we were told that all was now ready. Mum drove down in Stephen's car and the rest of us quietly walked down to the tent. Mum, Philippa and I sat on the chairs with Gym and Jane Leete near us; Stephen, John and Mike stood behind Dick, who, as the eldest son, stood nearer the front. As we arrived, the first lot of horsemen galloped into the bottom of the paddock led by Mamo, a local chieftain and witch-doctor with an orange feathery cape over his shoulders and hanging down in front; his horse was gaily caparisoned and he carried shield and spear and was accompanied by four or five other horsemen similary equipped with shield, spear and horses and followed by about twelve men bedecked with a motley collection of firearms. They galloped about at the lower end and were then joined by another chieftain on horseback with his retinue of horsemen and gun carriers, then another, and finally one chief riding with only one horseman but with four led horses, caparisoned round the neck, but with the rest of their bodies totally draped with silken covers which fitted over the saddle pummels and hung down in lovely soft blues and pinks to the horses' hooves. Each cover was bound in scarlet and had scarlet crosses on the sides. Horsemen and riders, followers and led horses circled at the bottom of the paddock. Then gradually they moved upwards, getting nearer and nearer to the tent, while the men gesticulated with spears and rifles and each chieftain shouted "Sand-i-ford," "Sand-i-ford," and then declaimed in Gallyna. The retinues joined in with cries and as the last of the horse parties came in, suddenly a host of people streamed in through the bottom hedges, silently and swiftly, and took up positions in two long packed lines at the bottom end of the paddock and up on the right hand side, making two sides of a square. Most of the women were grouped in the right angle, nearly all wearing white although some were in black. Most of them had brightly coloured head scarves, with a preponderance of scarlet, so that the whole scene, in the brilliant sunshine under a blue sky dotted with fat white clouds and with the Ethiopian red, green and yellow flag, was a mass of moving colour.' When the display and the eulogies were over, everyone went up to the house for the feast. People were fed in relays and their thirst was quenched with *talla*. By the end of a seemingly never-ending afternoon, even the helpers had had quite enough to drink.

Sir Dennis Wright, in his address at Dan's memorial service in London 5 May, quoted from Hugh Boustead's book *The Wind of Morning* when he said, 'He [Sandford] was a remarkable man . . . the ideal leader of the enterprise [Mission 101]: his astonishingly sanguine temperament – he had the faith of a Gordon in the success of any of his undertakings – gave him great strength.' When the horsemen at the Mulu wake spoke their eulogies, they said, 'Our father and friend who gave us schools and clinics and made us roads.' Chris in a letter to Diana Oldridge said, 'I can't be too sad because his life came to an end so serenely and naturally . . . so easy a passage to that far country where I shall rejoin him in time, as I have done before. I dread the loneliness, but one can fill even that with all the happy memories of our long partnership . . . It is one's memories that bring one happiness and they are so centred round our dear and lovely home that they come crowding in to bring solace and release.'

Shortly after Dan's death, Chris went north on a camping trip with Christine and John to visit some of the places where Dan had been during the Mission 101 campaign. It was then that she made the firm decision to get a book written about Dan. She was particularly anxious to write about the Mission 101 and Dan's efforts to restore Ethiopia back to the Emperor, though she was soon persuaded that other parts of his life would be of equal interest. During the last three years of her life, she spent a great deal of time and energy on collecting and compiling papers and letters to help with the writing. She did not feel that she could write the book herself, but she was anxious and willing to do the necessary research. Dan had many papers out at Mulu about the campaign and about his work as Adviser to the Ministry of the Interior and later as Director General of the Municipality. Her brother Maurice spent some time and effort getting out papers from the Foreign Office and the Ministry of Defence and sending her relevant passages. In 1973 James Grant, the grandson of Winifred and Fred Grant of First World War days, came out to spend some time at Mulu and help annotate those files. He did a supremely efficient job and much of the information in this book comes from those notes. Chris also attempted to master the art of recording her notes and words on tape. This was not always fully efficient, but she never gave up trying. Sir Christopher Cox, an old friend from past days, recommended John Barrett to Chris as a possible biographer. She had met him before when he had been visiting Ethiopia and she felt that she could work with him. He would be free to use the notes that she and James Grant had collected as the skeleton of his book. He came to Ethiopia in 1974 and made several trips into various parts of the country, with and without Chris, and met and spoke with Ethiopians who had been with Dan in the campaign or had worked with him in the various ministries. The book was written but not completed before Chris died. The ultimate impetus to get it published seemed then to be lacking.

Once Christine and John had returned to England after Dan's funeral, Chris flew to Beirut and spent time with

Audrey and Bartie and their family. Bartie was headmaster of the Quaker-run school at Brummana, which had students of many nationalities from both the Middle East and beyond. It was a different environment for a short time, but even there, in the best Sandford traditions, Gilbert and Sullivan operas were being performed with the music in Audrey's hands and the acting in Bartie's. Some of the senior students took charge of Chris in her wheelchair and pushed her vigorously over the tarmac to where the opera was being performed, with Chris hanging on for dear life.

Once back in Ethiopia she settled down to a busy routine, both at Mulu and in Addis Ababa. There was play-teaching with Vicci, the youngest of the Langdon family, in the morning, and the task of brushing her long curls. This was interspersed with writing up lactation charts, amounts of strawberries picked and the constant orders for roses and other plants. In the afternoon she quite often had guests to be driven around the farm. She went into Addis Ababa, usually once a week, and kept in touch with the progress of the school, the setting of gardens and the collecting of material for the book on Dan. Early in 1973 Chris began toying with the idea of visiting England, not by air, but by going on land and sea to Beirut and then joining Audrey on her annual overland trip by car through Europe. Diana Oldridge had invited her to come to the wedding of her son, Robin, who had worked on the farm for a year, but she wrote saying she could not get there in time and then went on to talk about her plan. 'It's still only a nebulous idea that I am toying with because I would rather like to see you all again before I am eighty and I want to make plans for someone to write either an account of the Patriot Campaign and Dan's share in it, or a biography of him. For either there would be much work to do in England and out here. I have been busy collecting his papers and other information from Ethiopian sources. I should also enjoy the trip across Europe that Audrey makes so successfully each year and I don't propose to come to England without one of my Ethiopian servants who can look after me and prevent my being an incubus to my friends and relations. I am selfish enough to feel that I shouldn't enjoy it without the devoted personal care they give me in fetching and carrying and washing my clothes, and making my bed – in fact all the luxuries of Africa that I wouldn't accept from anyone else, however much they loved me.'

By early May, plans were made, and Chris, together with Gym Ward, set off on her epic trip. Alas, she had not been able to get a visa for Ishete to accompany her, but the rest worked out well. In a letter written to Diana Oldridge on the 14 May, she says: 'Here we are, at Debra Markos, Gym Ward and I – on the first day of our journey . . . It will take us five days to reach Asmara and another few hours to run down to Massawa where we hope to find our German boat waiting to convey us to Aqaba – a trip of another five days with a two day wait in Jeddah, where luckily we have friends who will, I hope, let us pass the day in their air-conditioned homes instead of sweltering in the dock area. At Aqaba just east of the Sinai peninsula, we hope to find Audrey waiting for us and she will drive us first to see Petra, and then on to her home in Brummana. There Gym will fly on home after a few days (always hoping that Beirut airport is functioning) and I shall wait a couple of weeks and then I hope she will drive me home to Cowes, and I shall see England for the first time in twelve years. I hope I shall like it . . . ' They camped on the way and Chris drove for much of the journey, though she also had Igirsa, the farm driver with her, to take the car back to Addis Ababa. They duly arrived at Aqaba where they were met by Audrey and youngest daughter, Olivia, and then went on to Brummana via Petra and Damascus. At the border between Syria and Lebanon they encountered their first obstacle when Audrey was told she had not got the necessary permission to return to Lebanon. This meant a tiresome delay while she went back to Damascus to get it, while her passengers sat patiently waiting for several hours. After a few days rest, Gym Ward flew back to England and Chris stayed till June, when the family were ready to do the trip over Europe. This was in a Renault 16 with Audrey driving and Chris and two grand-daughters, Erica and Olivia, as passengers. Chris's tent and her relaxator chair were on the roof rack and all other luggage packed inside. They went by boat from Beirut to Athens and then by road. Chris took all the long driving days, nights in strange hotels, frustrating borders, in her stride – sitting all day long in her big black hat, composed and unflappable. They had a contretemps on the Swiss-French border with some rather drunk French customs officers who were questioning Audrey's right to a full British passport. Chris leant forward and with great dignity said, 'Mais c'est ma fille' which thoroughly deflated the said gentlemen who then allowed them to pass through.

Chris stayed in England until October. During that time, she spent some weeks with her brother, Maurice, in London, looking up and checking more papers and letters to do with the book and then went to stay with Christine and John in Worcestershire. She went to the Three Choirs Festival with Diana Oldridge and enjoyed herself enormously. The trip back over Europe with Audrey did not go quite to plan as a letter from Chris to Diana explained. It was dated 10 October and was written from Mulu. 'Just to tell you what happened to hurry me home a fortnight early – but so glad to be home, for my roses and the whole garden are ablaze with blossom and golden maskal out everywhere, which I should have missed if all had gone well. We had a splendid run all through Europe:

'*Sunday, 30 September.* La Havre – Nancy – wet but warm and we found a motel for the night.

'*Monday, 1 October.* Nancy to near Munich – crossed Alsace via Strasbourg and over the Rhine to Stuttgart – thought Germany rather dull – grey but no rain.

'*Tuesday, 2 October.* Left Munich to travel via Linz and the eastern Austrian Tyrol. Perfectly gorgeous mountains with a light sprinkle of snow even on the road but brilliant sunshine. Stayed in a motel near Villach.

'*Wednesday and Thursday, 3 and 4 October.* Right through Yugoslavia, dull in the middle and camped at Varda on the Greek border, sleeping in quite comfortable motels.

'*Friday, 5 October.* A heavenly day all down through Greece to Thermopylae where we found a strange hotel beyond Lamia.

'*Saturday, 6 October.* A trip off the straight road to Delphi, quite marvellous, ending in Athens where we were told our boat hadn't come in and there was war between

Israel, Egypt and Syria.

'*Sunday, 7 October.* Went off with lunch to Marathon, getting back in time to board our boat which then said nothing could induce them to go to Beirut – so we were left on the quay. We found a neat little Greek hotel in Eleusis and sat down to consider the position. Decided that I had better fly from Athens to Addis Ababa Tuesday night, and Audrey wait for a Greek boat that would take her and Olivia and car to Cyprus. I arrived Addis Ababa Wednesday 10 October; I hope she got safely home – perhaps by air to Beirut and the car would follow as best it could . . .'

It was a wonderful trip for Chris and a real opportunity to meet friends and relatives in England.

Maurice and Diana Lush paid a visit to Chris early in 1974, which she enjoyed very much though she found it a little tiring. While they were there, she had a spate of visitors and mentions Bishop Allison, David Buxton, Sir Christopher Cox and Ruth Davies. She was working very hard on the book about Dan, and Maurice was very anxious to help her make real progress. Dan's younger sister, Ethel, died early in the year, as did Gym Ward, who had been her companion on the trip back to England. Also during the early part of 1974, Chris made two camping trips, one with the Casbons to the west and one with Dick into Borana country.

It was also at this time that the rumblings of revolution began to be heard clearly. For well over a year there had been troubles in the schools and university, and dissatisfaction with government was being freely expressed. In her letters, Chris mentioned these in passing, though, of course, she was always cautious about expressing herself in writing at times when tempers were rising. In a letter written in June, she said, 'Our "polite revolution" grumbles slowly on, with little outbursts of temper, but three of my four original boys, who were the origin of the English School, are slogging away at reform of the constitution, as well as of the general administration – Endelcachew as Prime Minister, Michael Imeru as Economic assistant in the Prime Minister's Office and Zaudi Gebre Selassie as Foreign Minister.' Endelcachew had a daughter at the school and was also on the Board of Governors. He asked Chris if she would consider having the English

School renamed the English Sandford School, in memory of Dan, and this was very much appreciated by her. The detaining of so many of the older generation, including the Emperor and his family, was a sorrowful burden for her to bear and she was harrowed, as were many others, by the real difficulty of getting any information about friends. She wrote: 'These are searching times – heartsick for the old, with our long associations and close ties of friendship and loyalty – but frightening for the young who have taken up the job of fighting their own national character, and a wide open question mark for the future. As ever, faith and courage are the vital needs. Our daily life is little interrupted – a tiresome curfew that curtails family evening visits but it is as easy as ever to pass freely about the country . . . I have just had about thirty guests out for Rose Sunday today and I'm hoping to go in on Thursday, visit some of the princesses with our first strawberries, hoping a few will find their way through to Grandpa, who very much appreciated fruit.'

On 1 December, after the massacre at the end of November, Chris wrote: 'As you can imagine, we are living under a black cloud of horror since last weekend's happenings – panic and madness, I think, when they thought that they were being duped by their chairman, and there is nothing to be done but pray for them and their victims. I should say it was not premeditated, and everyone is shocked and stunned and as bewildered as ever. Philippa and I have spent the day at the houses of mourning of our murdered friends. Ras Mesfin's, the Duke of Harar's house where we were refused admission to the detained princesses (though I got in there the other day with strawberries), but were told to come back again at three o'clock when we were again refused; up to the Kassa eyrie where three of the family, Asrate, Amdi and Haile Kassa were all killed; to Endelcachew's house whom we mourn most deeply – one of the best men and my pupil – an aristocrat of the first water; and finally Tamrat Igazu, ex-Governor General of Gondar and Martha Imeru's husband. I told the last two that Philip Cousins was coming out to Mulu to hold a private memorial service for our particular friends, and they pathetically said, "Can we come?" but I doubt their getting here by 10 o'clock. Their husbands died without benefit of clergy and their church offers none to them – and our padre can hardly hold a public service in Addis Ababa . . . As in the coup (1960) they fell into the pit of their own imaginations and misgivings . . . They suddenly suspect their leader, Andom, of playing them false, and in a panic that they were being duped, killed their captives so that they could feel that they had accomplished something of what they set out to do – cut out the dead wood . . . Meanwhile Mulu Farm is gathering the harvest in, so far unimpeded, and the scheme for sending out the students of the university and the two top school grades, as instructors of the peasantry still waits its launching, and the Sandford School is helping to prepare its own thirty pupils for the venture. "One way of getting them out of the town," comments my gardener, Sanbatta. It's late; I've had a long and rather grisly day and I've really nothing to point the way to the future.'

The last five months of Chris's life were especially difficult ones for her. However, her loyalties to old friends remained firm and she was a constant source of comfort to those Ethiopians who had lost dear ones and who feared, not only for their own and their families' lives, but were bewildered and uncertain of the path which their country was taking. There were the young Ethiopian students who had been sent out into the countryside to help particularly with a literacy campaign, but also were meant to explain the new ideas to the local farmers. It hardly bears thinking about that one of the pupils sent out from the Sandford school to teach the peasantry near Dessie was the eldest daughter of Endelcachew the Prime Minister who had been murdered in the November massacre.

Then there was the position of the farm. It was a private venture and was running well and yet the profits were going into private pockets. With Communism prevailing this was not really to be commended and yet it was obvious that the farm, by employing a great deal of local labour, was of help to the community. In addition to that, it had been Dan and Chris who had set the Community Centre in motion and had worked hard to get it going successfully. On the surface, much remained as it was. The farm continued to flourish, the school continued to work and have a long waiting list for entry and the family went about the country continuing to work at projects or just to travel for holidays. But underneath there was an ever-growing pulse of uneasy mistrust and questioning. It was suggested to Mike that the farm was taking too big a share of the waters of the Aleltu River for irrigation and that the farmers on the other side of the river should have a greater share. The fact that they did not really want it was a minor consideration. The forestry up the valley of the Bomfeta River was often damaged by people letting their cattle graze through the trees and the local peasants were encouraged to feel that as this was not land under the plough, they had as much right to it as the owners of the farm. There was never any question of any danger to the life and property of Chris and her family; she was far too much loved and respected for that. But both at the farm and at the school there were these 'sessions' that were insisted upon by the government, where alleged victims had to come and say how they had been maltreated, scorned or exploited by their superiors. The old servants who had been with the family for years went to the sessions, listened and sometimes spoke but for the most part kept their counsel and were silent.

Chris maintained her outward serenity and calm during all this. She continued her work on the book and maintained her interest in the roses and other shrubs. She could not get down the garden so easily but she never failed to get on with the orders for plants. Early in April she came to the annual sports day at the school and thoroughly enjoyed taking a keen interest in all that went on. Then she went back to Mulu and there, after some days of great pain, which the doctors could not really understand, she died on St. George's Day, 23 April. Philippa, who was never far away, had arranged that Sanbatta, the gardener, should be weeding outside the front door, ready to call her at any moment. She was with her mother as Chris passed away. Dick wrote to Christine and John: 'Mum had a good sense of timing and, consciously or not, went off at the right time. She was not enjoying either her arthritis or the local changes. As you know, she had a very bad go of pain. Personally I do not think it was anything to do with her arthritis. She was quite different, telling us of pains all over her. All her doctor friends went out but I don't think they really knew what was getting at her. Anyway, it was only for a short time and then she appeared much better and her old self. I saw her on Saturday, as usual, after coming up from the valley and, although there was a little indirectness in her speech, she was cheerful and making plans to come into Addis Ababa. One of her doctor friends, Rae Martin, convalescing from hepatitis, was staying with her. On the Wednesday after her collapse, she died very peacefully. She had a good send off. As with Dad, the locals carried her to the road in local style. She had told us when Dad died that she didn't want a lot of wailing women at the cemetery when she was buried, 'women at the church, men at the cemetery'. We failed completely. Hundreds turned up at both; both sexes! You can imagine it. No wailing but very few dry eyes from either sex.

'On the Sunday we had the usual *Lakso* at Mulu. Food and drink for all. They all said, "She wasn't just your mother; she was mother to us all; she never distinguished between king and peasant, rich or poor." Many said, "You must keep the house in good repair. It was her home and will be her monument." . . . I doubt if any of us realised how much love she generated. Some of the letters have been really touching.'

The three days of mourning were also held at the school, and hundreds of people came to condole with the family. The feeling that it was a good time for her to go was there among many of the Ethiopians, who knew how hard the changes and the loss of friends had been for her. Three sisters of a high-up family, who had lost their father in the massacre, came to condole. They spent over an hour there, not in silence, as was the old custom, but telling Eleanor, with great glee, of all the terrible tricks they had been up to when they had been boarders at the school under Chris. It had obviously been a time that they had enjoyed and the boarding house had been like home, with Chris the matriarchal figure to be loved and respected at the same time.

The letters that were received by all the family from all over the world showed how much love Chris had engendered among so many people of so many nationalities. Her brother, Maurice, was, at the time of her death, in hospital undergoing an operation for a hip replacement. The brother and sister had been very close to each other, sharing many of the same interests, especially music. He had letters from the then Archbishop of Canterbury and HRH Princess Alice, who, as Duchess of Gloucester, had visited the school. One other letter was unusual and strangely touching. It was from Ethiopian Airlines office in London and said, 'Together with her late husband, Mrs Sandford followed in the tradition of great British expatriates, who in the past did so much to forge bonds of true friendship with other countries. By displaying everything that is best in the British character they were responsible for a great deal of the goodwill that exists between our two countries at present. A number of us are proud to have known Mrs Sandford and are conscious of the fact that by her death we have witnessed the passing of an era.'

Chris's memorial service was held at Tanglewood, Bewdley, where Christine and John lived. The house was packed and Philip Cousins took the service. Audrey played the piano for the hymns and several of the grandchildren helped with the readings. There was no doubt in anyone's mind that Chris, as Granny, Mother and Friend was in the top rankings.

Wilfred Thesiger, who wrote Chris's obituary for *The Times*, when speaking of Mulu Farm said, 'Here, through the years, the Sandfords kept open house, welcoming and entertaining everyone who turned up, and in later years their visitors were many. No intelligent person could visit them and not come away the wiser, for their knowledge of the country was profound and their opinions, though often at variance with current ones, always well-considered. It was a fascinating experience to be their guest, even if it meant sitting up until two or three in the morning, talking or playing bridge . . . When Dan Sandford died in 1972 a marriage that had lasted fifty-four years and appeared never to have been marred by dispute, came to an end. All six children were married, two sons and two daughters were working in Ethiopia, and the grandchildren numbered twenty-three. For all of them Mulu Farm was the centre of family life. Here Christine Sandford ended her days and although partially crippled by arthritis, she remained alert and active to the end. Many Ethiopians of every class and many people of other races, not least her own, must have felt a deep sense of loss when she died, for she was dearly loved by her friends, having a great gift for friendship. Some feel that her death, following on that of her husband and coinciding with the revolution marks the end of an era in Ethiopia.'

Three months after Chris died, Philippa and Mike were woken one morning early by their faithful groom Galata, to say that he had heard that they were to be ejected from Mulu Farm that day. It hardly gave them time to pack some suit-cases and pick up their youngest daughter before the authorities came to tell them to leave for Addis Ababa. Philippa, with her three youngest children left Ethiopia at once, because the summer holidays for the two boys at school in England were due to start and it was inconceivable to let them return to Ethiopia with no home at Mulu in which to spend the holidays. Mike followed on later, having tried in vain to get the hand-over of the farm put onto a more credible and natural basis. The question that was in everyone's mind was whether it would have happened if Chris had been alive, but there was also deep thankfulness that she had not had to witness that traumatic ending. Philippa, in a letter to her sister Christine in June, said, 'I still find it hard to believe that we shan't see Mum again. We miss her terribly. She was such a strong moral support and it was easier to face the uncertainties with her indomitable courage cheering us on. And no bridge! I've taken to patience instead! I don't really mean to moan. It's good to think of her and Dad together and I feel them cheering us on anyway . . . I refuse to think of our family's era in Ethiopia coming to an end. We do know it may happen but we don't wait for it and are carrying on as usual, planning the new strawberries and building a new milking bail . . . I do think that life may be very difficult for a while but at the moment the indications are that we may be all right if we can stick it out. The main thing is that our staff and neighbours seem to be very pro us, despite those students who are out on the *Development campaign through co-operation* doing their occasional best to stir things up. We remain friendly with them on our side. I just think they think it's 'the thing' to do . . . I do realise it is extremely foolish to be too complacent, equally there is a limit to the amount you can worry and until we know what's what, it is difficult to plan for anything other than our daily life. After all it would be quite wrong to think that Ethiopia did not need a change. She did very much in all sorts of ways and one can only pray that the best for Ethiopia will happen. If the best includes us staying, then marvellous, but if not, then I hope we won't be bitter about it.'

Both Dan and Chris would have agreed with all the sentiments expressed in that letter, the hope, faith, charity, humour and optimism and, above all, the loving desire that all would be well for Ethiopia.

The curtain closes on the lives of the incurable optimists, but in the memories of their friends and family, the pageant and scenery that lie behind the curtains are still richly painted in glowing colours of love and life and laughter.

GLOSSARY OF THE MOST COMMONLY USED ETHIOPIAN WORDS

Abba mestet Father of giving.

Afar A mainly nomadic group of people, also referred to as **Danakil**, living in the arid depression between the highlands and the Red Sea.

Amhara A very general term referring to the people of Cushite descent, living in the north and central part of Ethiopia.

Amharic The language of the Amharas, now the language of government for the whole of Ethiopia.

Azazh Military Commander: also used for Chiefs of a district.

Balabat A local man of standing and repute.

Belatta Councillor. Title of Senior Official.

Betwoded A very senior title meaning 'beloved' or 'revered'.

Buhe A feast in August, when children are given small loaves of leavened bread. It celebrates the Transfiguration.

Buret A cattle byre, made of thorn bush.

Cosso Hadenia adyssinica: a large tree with orange flowers, whose fruit is used as medicine for internal disorders, especially tapeworm.

Danakil A nomadic group of people living in the depression between the highlands and the Red Sea.

Dejazmach 'Commander of the Door': senior court official or general.

Doro Chicken.

Fikre Mariam A name meaning 'Love of Mary'.

Fitaurari 'Commander of the Spearhead': a military/honorary title.

Fouqara A traditional display of spear-waving and singing to show off martial prowess in front of the Emperor or a notable dignitary.

Gabar A system whereby a tenant paid taxes by working for a specified number of days on making roads, cutting wood, tilling the ground, etc.

Galla A very general term referring to the people of Cushite descent living in the central and southern part of Ethiopia.

Gallyna A general term referring to the language spoken by the Gallas.

Gasha A measurement of land consisting of about 40 hectares.

Gee'z The classical language of Ethiopia: Ethiopic.

Gharry A two-wheeled horse-drawn vehicle, introduced by the Italians and used as taxis.

Ghurage A small tribe of physically strong people living to the south-west of Addis Ababa who specialised in gardening and forestry.

Giffa An order, meaning 'push'.

Gombo A large, round, bottle-like earthenware vessel, used to carry or store liquids.

Habesh A colloquial term from past history meaning 'Ethiopian'.

Injera A large, flat pancake made of millet or maize flour: it is the staple food of the highland Ethiopian.

Izosh An exclamation meaning 'do not be afraid'.

Jan Meda 'The field of the Emperor'. A very large enclosed grassy arena where parades, festivals and horse-racing was held.

Jib Uccat A strawberry and cream fool; the actual meaning of the words is hyena's diarrhoea.

Joro Ear.

Lakso 'Weeping': the period of mourning after the

	death of a person, when friends come to condole.
Lij	'Child': a courtesy title for members of the nobility.
Maskal	A cross. The name of the feast of the Finding of the true Cross, which is held at the end of September. The name of the golden flowers that appear all over the highlands at the end of the rainy season.
Medakwa	The Common Duiker: a small antelope.
Minch Abbai	The spring from which the river Nile starts.
Neguse Negist	King of Kings: the title of Emperor.
Oromo	A word that is now more popularly used to refer to the Galla people.
Ras	The most senior title: comparable to Duke.
Sambaleet	Species of hyperrhenia: a tall, strong grass used for thatching.
Talla	Indigenous beer, made from barley.
Tanqua	A boat made from papyrus reeds tied together.
Tamarebet	School. Ye Sandiford Tamarebet means The Sandford School.
Teff	A small, grass-like millet grain, used for making injera.
Tej	Ethiopian honey-mead.
Tid	A small tribe, living near Maji.
Tishana	A small tribe, living near Maji.
Tsafe Tizaz	'Scribe of Orders': secretary, Minister of the Pen.

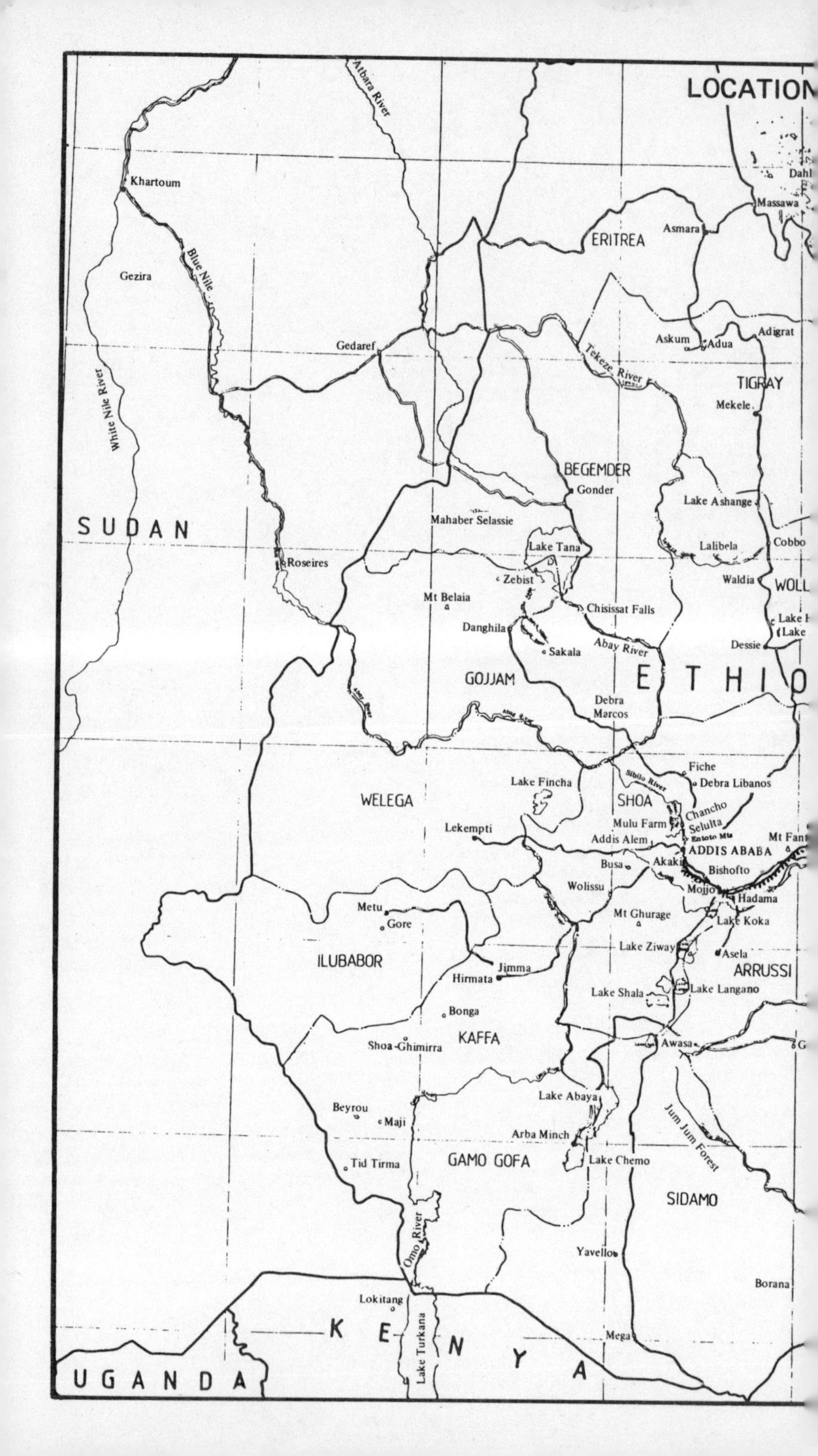
LOCATION
Atbara River
Khartoum
Blue Nile
Gezira
White Nile River
SUDAN
Roseires
Gedaref
ERITREA
Asmara
Massawa
Askum
Adua
Adigrat
Tekeze River
TIGRAY
Mekele
BEGEMDER
Gonder
Lake Ashange
Mahaber Selassie
Lake Tana
Lalibela
Cobbo
Zebist
Waldia
Mt Belaia
Chisissat Falls
Danghila
Sakala
Abay River
Dessie
GOJJAM
Debra
Marcos
Lake Fincha
Fiche
Debra Libanos
Sibilo River
WELEGA
SHOA
Chancho
Mulu Farm
Selulta
Entoto Mts
Lekempti
Addis Alem
ADDIS ABABA
Busa
Akaki
Bishofto
Wolissu
Mojjo
Hadama
Metu
Gore
Mt Ghurage
Lake Koka
Lake Ziway
Asela
ILUBABOR
Jimma
Hirmata
ARRUSSI
Lake Shala
Lake Langano
Bonga
Awasa
Shoa-Ghimirra
KAFFA
Lake Abaya
Beyrou
Maji
Arba Minch
Jum Jum Forest
Tid Tirma
GAMO GOFA
Lake Chemo
SIDAMO
Omo River
Yavello
Borana
Lokitang
Lake Turkana
KENYA
Mega
UGANDA